G000149781
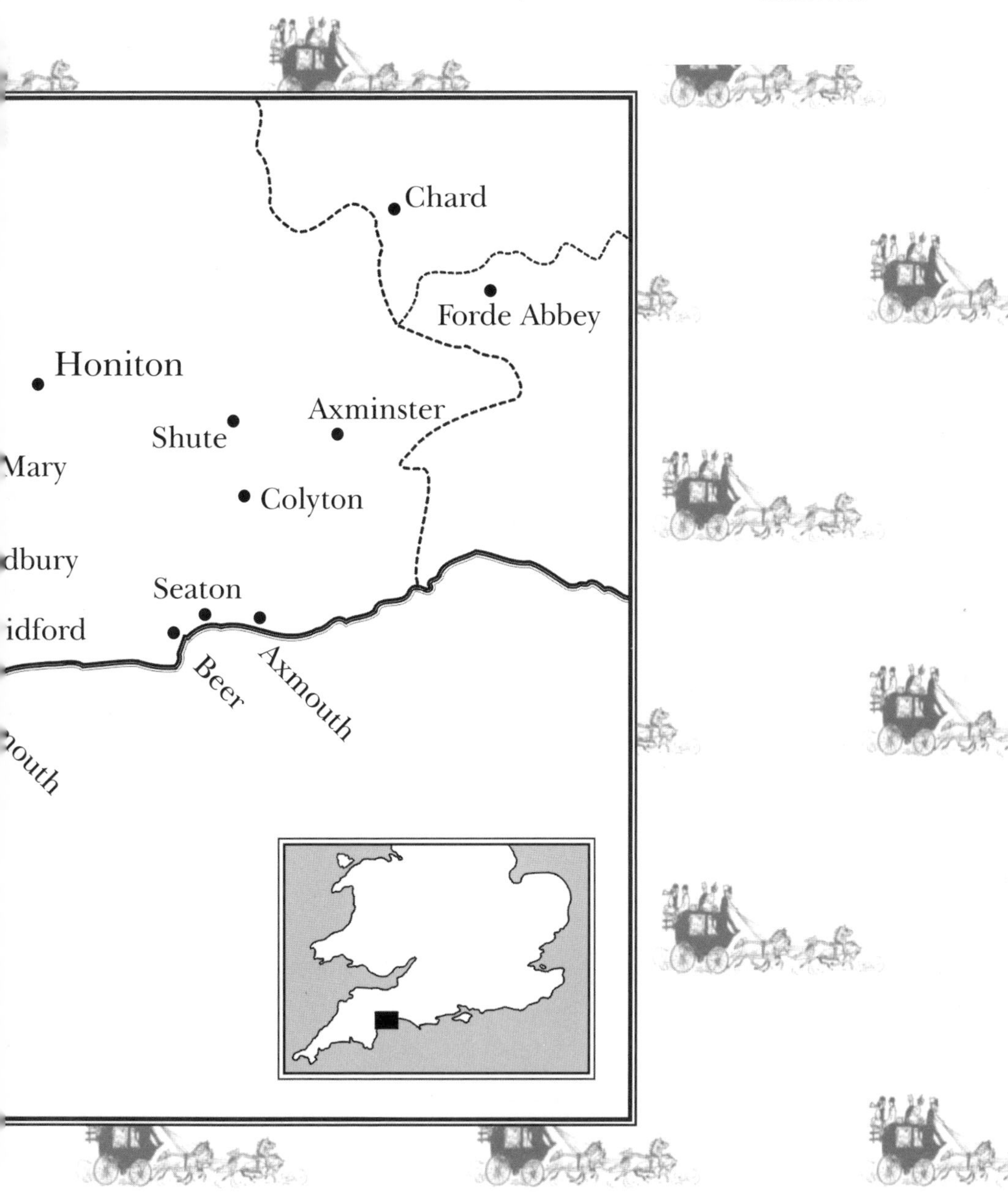
Chard
Forde Abbey
Honiton
Axminster
Shute
Colyton
Seaton
Beer
Axmouth

East Devon
The Travellers' Tales

Christmas 2003.

EAST DEVON

THE TRAVELLERS' TALES

Edited by
Todd Gray

THE MINT PRESS

First published in Great Britain by The Mint Press, 2000

ISBN 1-903356-02-4

British Library Cataloguing-in-Publication Data
A CIP record for this title is available from the British Library

The Mint Press
18 The Mint
Exeter, Devon
England, EX4 3BL

Designed and typeset in New Baskerville 10.5/12.6 by Mike Dobson, Quince Typesetting

Cover design by Delphine Jones

Main cover illustration, Knowle, Sidmouth, 1823.
Title page, Bicton House, 1849
Both courtesy of Westcountry Studies Library.

Sciurus carolinensis circumforaneus by Tim Wormleighton

Printed and bound in Great Britain by Short Run Press Ltd, Exeter.

For Eileen & Elaine

'A RECIPE TO MAKE A TOUR'

Take of good humour as much as you have by you, to this add a like quantity of a determination to please and be pleased, throw in a few bank notes by way of cement. Jolt these together in a coach & my life don't they do wonders.

Sarah England, mid-nineteenth century
(Devon Record Office, 337b/4/3a)

Contents

Acknowledgements

I would like to thank Paul Brough, Susan Conniff, Angela Hill, Ian Maxted, Eve McClare, Richard Morgan, A.J. Massingberd Mundy, Sir John Quicke, Tony Rouse, Margery Rowe and Christopher Wicket for their help with this volume. I am also grateful to the British Library, Cardiff County Council Library Service, Devon Record Office, Dorset Archives Service, East Sussex Record Office, Glamorgan Record Office, Isle of Wight Record Office, Plymouth & West Devon Record Office, Westcountry Studies Library and Wiltshire Record Office for assistance with publishing archival material. The extract from *English Spring* by Charles Brooks, © Harcourt Publishers, 1932, reproduced by kind permission of Harcourt Publishers. I would also like to thank the Westcountry Studies Library for permission to publish illustrations and my production team, Dr Mike Dobson, Delphine Jones and Hilary Tolley, for their much appreciated help and patience.

INTRODUCTION

East Devon has been a popular travel destination for many hundreds of years. It has always benefited through its transports links as the main thoroughfare to Exeter and as the gateway to the rest of Devon and Cornwall. This became all the more significant as Devon's roads became more travelled with the rise of the naval base at Plymouth, particularly during the Napoleonic war. Many visitors had little choice but to come through East Devon in order to reach destinations in South Devon, Dartmoor and Cornwall. In the late eighteenth and early nineteenth centuries East Devon also benefited from the rise in recreational interest at the seaside. Visitors from throughout the country, then as now, were attracted to the resorts of Dawlish, Teignmouth and Torbay as well as to East Devon's own watering places of Exmouth, Budleigh Salterton, Sidmouth and Seaton.[1] East Devon became a destination in itself. The subsequent accounts written by these travellers offer unique and often very different types of information: their descriptions provide unusual insights into the character of East Devon places and people. Moreover, they are intriguing as records of what aspects interested the outsider, like Stanley Baron who enthused about the red earth of Devon as he crossed the county border in 1933, and saw something different to what was familiar back home. Not all the comments were complimentary but each informs the reader who is interested in travel and in the history of East Devon.

THE TRAVEL ACCOUNTS

In this volume there are forty-five travel accounts written by forty-one individuals. They are all as varied as those who composed them. Eleven of the writers were from London, including both the first and

1. For the history of Devon's seaside resorts see John F. Travis, *The Rise of the Devon Seaside Resorts, 1750–1900* (Exeter, 1993).

last: the earliest is the well-known traveller John Leland in the early sixteenth century and the last visitor was Stanley Baron, a newspaper journalist, who travelled in the 1930s. The majority came from southern England, two of them from as far east as Norfolk, but there are also three Americans and one Italian. Few of the visitors are as well-known as Daniel Defoe and the majority are either largely unheard of or, in four instances, anonymous. Some wrote to inform readers or for their own purposes and the styles of writing are markedly different. A great number earned a living from writing and no less than eight of the writers were clerics. Nearly all were wealthy, or at least affluent enough to travel with at least one servant.

These forty-one travellers are not necessarily representative of the millions of visitors to East Devon over the last five centuries, after all only five of the writers were women. Few visitors leave behind them written records of their impressions; one such traveller was the poet John Keats who passed through Honiton in May 1818, composed a letter to a friend and neglected to mention the town or any other place he saw in East Devon.[2] Countless other accounts were written but have not survived. The writers in this volume, with one partial exception,[3] share a common attribute: not only was each a stranger to East Devon but they recorded their experiences firsthand and these accounts have managed to survive.

There are many other reports of visits which have not been included, generally involving famous people, of tours for which there are not firsthand accounts. One notable example is the visit by the Royal Family to the West Country in 1789. Other individuals wrote accounts of this tour including of the stop at Honiton of which it was noted that 'as their Majesties approached Honiton, they were surprised and delighted with the appearance of near 400 girls, neatly dressed with white ribbons, headed by the young ladies of the boarding-school in white. A sight so *nouvelle* drew tears of sympathy from the eyes of her Majesty and the Princesses. From Honiton the Royal Party proceeded to Sir George Yonge's at *Eastcot*, where they dined, and drank coffee and from thence drove to Exeter'. This was printed in *The Gentleman's Magazine*[4] as was an even shorter account

2. Hyder Edward Rollins (ed.), *The Letters of John Keats, 1814–1821* (Cambridge, 1958), 283.
3. See below, the tour by John Evans who included an account of Sidmouth by the Reverend Harris.
4. 1789, part 2, 1142.

of the visit to Axminster which noted 'At Axminster the Royal Party stopped to see the carpet manufactory, and were shown the whole process. The Queen gave orders for several pieces, and a handsome sum was left to be distributed among the work-people'. A comparison of this report with another account is interesting: a news report appeared in *The Sherborne Mercury* shortly afterwards and this was subsequently copied by an unidentified reader into his, or her, commonplace book.[5]

> Axminster, Devon September 5th 1789
>
> On Thursday the 13th of August 1789 this place was honoured with a visit from our Gracious Sovereign, the Queen, their Royal Highnesses the Princess Royal, Princess Augustus and Princess Elizabeth, attended by the Ladies Courton and Waldgraves, Lord Courton, Colonel Digby and Gwynne, &c &c
>
> When their Majesties arrived at the Turnpike Gate, they were met by Sir John Pole (of Shute House) and the principal gentlemen of the town with white rods, cockades &c, and a band of music, who escorted them to the George Inn. His Majesty having been previously informed of a curious Manufactory of Carpets that is carried on in this town, graciously signified his intention of visiting it, & immediately walked to the Manufactory, attended as above.
>
> When they arrived at the Front Gate, they were met by the proprietors (Messrs Whitty & Son) who conducted the Royal Visitors to the Work Shop, the avenues to which were covered with a variety of rich beautiful carpets, & the work shop, which their majesties entered, was likewise carpeted, and decorated with several elegant pieces of the manufacture, so that it made an agreeable appearance.
>
> There were twenty young women who worked the shop selected, who were all neatly dressed in clean white gowns, aprons and handkerchiefs, and a purple ribbon round their waist with 'Long Live the King' in Gold Letters. Those were ranged in two rows, ten on each side, without side several looms, for their

5. Devon Record Office, Z19/15/20, p.45.

> Majesties & Princesses to walk between them. A band of music was placed behind a curtain, on each side the stairs, and some good singers on the other side, as soon as their Majesties and the Princesses were all in the room, the workers paid their respects by a low curtsy and as they were rising, on a signal, the Music struck up 'God Save the King'. The men and women accompanying it, with their voices, which was truly melodious. When they had sung the [con]gratulations, the women made another low curtsy and were all instantly in their work. Their Majesties were highly pleased.

This report is based on a letter from the carpet factory owner to the editor of *The Sherborne Mercury*. Some years later he copied out the original letter in which he had written:

> As their Majesty's with the three Princesses were pleased to honour this town on Thursday last with a visit to the carpet manufactory I would beg leave through your paper to give account of the transactions of that day to the public.
>
> On Tuesday evening last we were informed from Weymouth that their Majesties intended on the Thursday following to honour the manufactory with a visit and that it would be agreeable to them to walk through the town from the George Inn if it could be done without their being much uncomoded by the crowd. On this information as much preparation was made for the receiving and accommodating the Royal visitors as the shortness of time would permit. The streets were all properly cleared and decorated with arches, garlands &c, and a way railed in from the George to the manufactory to keep off the crowd which was immense. At the Manufactory all the avenues from the street to the shop were covered with a variety of rich beautiful carpets, & the work shop, which their Majesties entered, was likewise carpeted, and decorated with several elegant pieces of the manufacture, so that it made an agreeable appearance. There were twenty young women who work'd the shop selected, who were all neatly dressed in clean white gowns,

> aprons and handkerchiefs, and a purple ribbon round their waist with 'Long Live the King' in Gold Letters.
>
> When their Majesties arrived at the Turnpike Gate, they were met by the gentlemen of the town with white rods, cockades &c, and a band of music, who escorted them to the George where they alighted and immediately walked away for the manufactory, attended as before. When they arrived at the Front Gate, they were met by the proprietors who conducted the Royal Visitors to the Work Shop where the workers were ranged in two rows, ten on each side, without side several looms, for their Majesties & Princesses to walk between them. A band of music was placed behind a curtain, on each side the stairs, and some good men singers on the other side, as soon as their Majesties and the Princesses were all in the room, the workers paid their respects by a low curtsy and as they were rising, on a signal, the Music struck up 'God Save the King'. The men and women accompanying it, with their voices, which were truly melodious. When they had sung the congratulations, the women made another low curtsy and were all instantly in their work. Their Majesties were highly pleased with this mode of reception and the Queen and Princesses joined in the chorus. They then attended to the workers and asked many questions concerning the principle and processes of the manu-facture and seemed thoroughly pleased with every part. They then walked back again to the George amidst the acclamation of a vast multitude. Their Majesties condescension was to be greatly admired, to take such a walk in order to gratify the curiosity of surrounding thousands, and they behave with as great a degree of affability as was consistent with their dignity and exalted station in life. Their Majesties, Princesses and Royal Suite then took their departure for Honiton amidst the joyful and loud Huzzas of the admiring and well-satisfied populace.[6]

The original letter shows how the editor reduced the letter for publication in *The Sherborne Mercury* and the historian's difficulties

6. Devon Record Office, Z19/20/2, pp.987-8.

of trying to ascertain the actual events of the Royal visit. But the travel accounts which form the main body of the book are not like these two reports. Instead, they are first-hand accounts in which personal observations of the travellers are made and as interesting as the letter is, it would be more informative to have the personal views of the Royal family of these events and of Axminster.

Other accounts have not been included because of the form in which they were written: for instance, some travellers made only very brief notes of their experiences such as Edmund Spoure who wrote in 1694 'From thence [Axminster] we came to Honiton, a large handsome town, famous for vast quantities of fine bone lace that is made there'[7] and an anonymous visitor only wrote of East Devon that Cullompton was 'a pretty neat town, seeming to consist chiefly of one wide and straggling street'.[8] Likewise William Schellinks, a Dutchman who was in the West Country in the 1660s, merely wrote 'We came through several villages to Honiton, 15 miles, and stayed there at the Golden Lion; this is a market town and much lace is being made there. On the 22nd we rode in the morning to Axminster, 8 miles, and from the hills saw Portland.'[9] Likewise, Thomas Pennant, a known traveller, left a disappointingly short account of his entire tour of Devon in 1787:

> Saturday the 7th [July] got to Teignmouth came through Exeter, a fine old city. Monday the 9th went to Sidmouth & Exmouth, neither place so pleasant as Teignmouth, which delightful spot we left the 23rd of July, lay at Exeter and dined at Honiton on Thursday, in our road from Teignmouth went to see Lord Lisburne's [estate which has] a good house [Mamhead] and the grounds about most beautiful, commanding a fine view of Exmouth, Powderham Castle and an extensive prospect of the sea. Lay at Axminster.[10]

Their writings were probably written just for their own purposes and intended as an *aide-memoire*.

7. Todd Gray, 'A visit by Edmund Spoure through Devon in 1694', *Devon & Cornwall Notes & Queries* (Spring, 1995, XXXVII–Part VII), 217.
8. Anonymous, *Journal of a tour performed in the summer of 1807* (1809), 26.
9. Maurice Exwood and H.L. Lehman (eds), *The Journal of William Schellinks' Travels in England, 1661–1663* (Camden Society, 1993, 5th series, 1), 129.
10. Clwyd Record Office [Hawarden], D/NA/850.

Some other writers have not been included because their tours are available in print, such as the lengthy travels of the Reverend John Swete in the 1790s which have just been published,[11] and there are other tours which remain unpublished but which will hopefully form part of a second volume on East Devon travellers.

The length of each account is greatly influenced by the writer's main purpose in travelling and in recording his or her experiences. The majority of them were what are now commonly, but pejoratively, called tourists. Many accounts are actually entitled 'Tours'. Nearly all were travelling from east to west on one of the old roads to Exeter, either from Cullompton where they came from Taunton and Bristol or via Honiton and Axminster from which they would have come on the coastal route from Dorchester or on the main London road. Nearly every writer visited Honiton.

Thirteen of the accounts are drawn from manuscripts and nearly every one of these has not been published before. Some individuals chose to write in personal journals or diaries for private purposes, but even then it must be questioned, what writer does not wonder whether their writings will some day be read by future generations? Some manuscript accounts would have had a wide readership. Travel accounts were, long before the holiday video, passed around to friends to impress them by showing the curious experiences enjoyed in places far removed from home.

In order to understand any travel description, it is essential to consider the writer's purpose in recounting their experiences. Many of the accounts included in this book were intended from the start to be books although a significant number of the writers modestly claimed in their prefaces that they merely succumbed to the pressure of their insistent friends and published their experiences. One writer, John Evans who composed *The Juvenile Tourist*, asserted that his book was only written to educate the young. Many writers needed to either entertain or inform their readers because of the pressure to sell books and the descriptions may dwell on amusing or interesting aspects of their travels instead of the ordinary or mundane.

The accounts often reveal nearly as much about the traveller as the places visited. A good picture of Mrs Parry Price or of the Reverend Butcher, for instance, can be drawn through their observations of places and other people. Their experiences are often very

11. Todd Gray (ed.), *Travels in Georgian Devon: the illustrated travel journals of the Reverend John Swete, 1789–1800* (Tiverton, 1998), II.

revealing, and unique, of people and places in East Devon. Mrs Price's account of Honiton, in particular, is very informative.

Finding suitable travelling companions could be just as problematic then as now. One late eighteenth-century traveller to East Devon found his particularly trying. He wrote 'Am rid of Thomas, thank God! One so viscous & thoughtless was not fit company for me. He was offended on my desiring him to be silent'.[12] His friend's views of their travels together are not known. Another visitor, the Reverend John Skinner, complained that 'If I had known my companion's uncertain movements, and how very little service my travelling with him was in reality, I should have stayed at home and saved my money... Hammond is as able to travel all the world over by himself as any man can be, who only looks to good inns and comfortable accommodations... How very few men are rational companions if tried for a few days together'.[13]

The accounts show the changing modes of transport. John Taylor in 1649 and John Verdon in 1700 both rode on horseback as did many other travellers. Coaches and carriages may have been preferred but the uneven roads made this a difficult choice until the last decades of the eighteenth century when they became more widely available. They remained the main form of transport for several generations until the coming of the railway. Until then expense and ease of travel were the determining factors in choosing the mode of transport. But in the late nineteenth century it became fashionable for some travellers to claim that the speed of rail transport had ruined the pleasures of travel: they reverted to travelling by coach and horses, others walked from London and two in this book travelled by bicycle. Daring or outlandish modes of travel were not confined to the nineteenth century: in the 1590s Richard Ferris, a London gentleman, rowed in a wherry with several companions from London to Bristol.[14] Finally, a significant number of the travellers hesitated to use the ferry across the river Exe at Exmouth and Reverend Skinner, who failed to cross the mouth of the river Axe, had to travel inland several miles in a circuitous route.

12. Basil Cozens-Hardy (ed), *The Diary of Sylas Nevile, 1767–1788* (Oxford, 1940), September 2.
13. See below, the Reverend John Skinner, 1829.
14. Richard Ferris, *The Most Dangerous and Memorable Adventures of Richard Ferris* (1590).

East Devon

Nearly all the writers visited East Devon either during the summer months or in early autumn. The writers show society's changing views of the countryside; whereas Leland in the 1540s praised the rural landscape when it was productive agriculturally, writers from the eighteenth century onwards were passionate about the magnificence of the English countryside. Many enthused about the Vale of Honiton, one even claimed that it was unmatched for its beauty in all of England. In 1788 the Reverend Shaw wrote that it was the 'Garden of Devon'. Others had the typical complaint of the stranger to Devon: the hedgerows obscured the views. Natural history was of interest to several visitors: one writer enthused about the wild flowers at Wilmington Hill and another wrote a full account of the landscape many years after the famous landslip at Axmouth. There are many one-off descriptions, such as of the woollen factory at Ottery St Mary, the building of Swiss Cottage at Bicton, the making of cob and of trout-fishing at Fairmile. An Italian in the seventeenth century noted that the locals lived in mud houses and another visitor, who claimed to be Spanish but was in fact an Englishman, concluded after seeing Devon that England was a paradise for sheep and cattle (whereas, he wrote, Valencia was one for the human race). One visitor was disappointed when he tried to pay homage at Ottery St Mary to Coleridge: he felt the locals had forgotten the poet.

Not every writer was complementary. For example, Topsham was described by one writer in 1798 as 'a dirty and insignificant town' and in the sixteenth century one visitor thought Seaton was 'but a mean thing'. Those travellers who came to East Devon in the late eighteenth and early nineteenth centuries were interested in the carpet factory at Axminster. The visit by the Royal Family in 1789 may have helped make it a fashionable stop but there seemed to be little else of interest in Axminster for visitors to favourably comment on. Invariably, travellers were intrigued by two things in East Devon: the lace making in Honiton and elsewhere and in the seaside resorts, notably those of Sidmouth and Exmouth.

The commentaries on lace were also not always favourable. Some of the early nineteenth-century writers were alarmed by the working conditions of the women and children, the poor pay and the working practices of the employers: later travellers enthused about the lace in romantic terms but some writers deplored it as an emblem of vanity for rich women which was responsible for the wretched lives of many poor children and women. The rise of the seaside resorts coincided with a general increase of interest in travel within England aided by the difficulties of travelling abroad during the Napoleonic Wars. Consequently coastal Devon developed as a holiday destination in much the same way as those places which were situated more conveniently to London such as Margate and Brighton. Tourists wrote about the numbers of fellow travellers on the road visiting the new seaside resorts and also commented on the invalids seeking better health in Sidmouth, Exmouth and other watering places. One diarist, Henry Fitzherbert Stroud, travelled when ill but appears to have been in the South West for evangelistic rather than health reasons. The contents of Knowle, as well as the exotic animals in the garden, also attracted considerable interest partly because it was Sidmouth's leading private house but also because it was such an extraordinary establishment in both its design and contents.

The accounts can also demonstrate the writers' individual interests. Perhaps the most noticeable is the tour by the Reverend Gilpin who was only interested in recording the Picturesque qualities of East Devon. Another good example is the account by John Ashburnham in 1687 who travelled only a few years after the landing of the Duke of Monmouth at Lyme Regis. Ashburnham, a traveller from Sussex, was interested in the local reaction to Monmouth's attempted coup. Some visitors arrived to find particularly unusual or interesting events unfolding such as the annual day of the Otterton Women's Club when the streets were decorated and a band played music in the open air.

Many travellers recounted the history of East Devon in varying degrees of detail and accuracy. It is noticeable that several travellers recited the tale of the burials of early medieval princes along the Axe valley, making it likely that they had access to either guide books or the accounts of previous travellers. The Reverend John Skinner's tour is unusual: archaeology was one of his main interests and he spent considerable time recording the landscape and in gathering oral traditions. His account of Seaton and musings on its Roman past is particularly interesting. Some travellers read William Cimden.

Weather has always been a preoccupation of the tourist, whether it was too warm, wet or even, occasionally, just right. Accommodation is another constant theme in travellers' accounts and among the places they enjoyed in East Devon were the Green Dragon, and later the George, in Axminster, the Golden Lion and the Dolphin in Honiton, the Mason's Arms in Branscombe, the Globe Hotel in Exmouth, the King's Arms in Otterton and the York Hotel and the London Inn at Sidmouth. Food was also frequently noted such as the mutton-chops enjoyed in Branscombe and the delights of tarts with clotted cream at Axminster.

The travellers' tales changed as East Devon was transformed from a thoroughfare to a highly desired destination. Visitors came for the beauty of the landscape, the warm climate and to escape from less desirous parts of the country. Each traveller's account offers a personal view of experiences particular to themselves and uniquely interesting to those concerned with the history of East Devon.

NOTES ON EDITING

Punctuation and spelling has largely been modernised and American English retained. Words in foreign languages appear in italics as do unusual spellings of place names with the modern spelling generally given afterwards, in the first instance, in square brackets. A place of residence, where known, has been given for each traveller. The date given which follows the traveller's name indicates the year in which travel was undertaken. There are further travel accounts on East Devon and these will hopefully be edited as an additional volume.

John Leland *of* St Michael le Querne, London, 1542

Engraving of John Leland from bust formerly in All Soul's College, Oxford

Bodleian Library, MS.Gen.Top.e8–15. There are a number of imperfect manuscript copies of Leland's itinerary. The earliest edition is by Thomas Hearne, *The Itinerary of John Leland the Antiquary* (Oxford, 1710–1712) in nine volumes. The East Devon section appears in volume three, pages 55, 59. However, the following extract is derived from that edited by Lucy Toulmin-Smith, *The Itinerary of John Leland In or About the Years 1535–43* (1907), III, 232, 239–44. The East Devon section was included by Richard Pearse Chope in his *Early Tours in Devon and Cornwall* (Devon & Cornwall Record Society, 1918, reprinted Newton Abbot, 1967), 68–75. There are considerable differences in both the wording and arrangement of text between the Toulmin-Smith and Pearse Chope editions. Also, see John Chandler, *John Leland's Itinerary: Travels in Tudor England*

(Stroud, 1993) who has modernised Leland's language. For example, 'Seaton itself is now a very inconsiderable place inhabited by fishermen, although it used to be much larger when the estuary was good' for 'The town of *Seton* is now but a mean thing, inhabited with fisher men, [but] it hath been far larger when the haven was good.'

John Leland is now principally remembered for his travels but he was also an accomplished writer, and greatly concerned with identifying, locating and collecting, if not rescuing, ancient manuscripts and books. His *Itinerary*, with the lengthy detail on religious houses, would have been of considerable interest during England's Reformation. Leland undertook the tours over the course of some eight years and was about 36 years old when he made this visit to East Devon. He suffered mental illness only a few years later and died in 1552. Some of Leland's terminology differs from modern use, such as the words 'pretty', by which he meant considerable, and 'mean', by which he meant inferior or insignificant.

...Things notable on the east side of Exmouth.

Exmouth, a fisher townlet, is a little within the haven mouth. *Apsham* [Topsham], a pretty townlet on the shore, a 4 miles upper in the haven. Here is the great trade and road for ships that useth this haven: and [e]specially for the ships and merchant men's goods of *Excester*. Men of *Excester* contend to make the haven to come up to *Excester* [it]self. At this time ships come no farther up but to *Apsham* ...[to Exeter en route to Cornwall and returning] From *Excester* to [Clyst] Bridge [is] a 3 miles; under this stone bridge arched runneth a pretty brook, called [damaged. Clyst]. This brook going about half a mile lower runneth by *Clist*, the Bishop of *Excester's* goodly manor place. A 5 miles farther I passed by a ford over a rivulet called Tale, that a mile *dim.* [and a half] lower above *S. Mari Oterey* [Ottery St Mary] town goeth into *Oterey* Water. There is a bridge of stone by the ford of Tale. From this ford of Tale I rode about a 2 miles farther to *Veniton* [Feniton] Bridges, where *Oterey* Water is divided into 4 arms by policy [design] to serve grist and tucking mills. Upon 3 of these streams I rode by fair stone bridges, [but] the first arm of the 4 was the least, and had no bridge that I marked. On the north side of the first bridge was a chapel, now profaned.

St Marie Oterey town is [damaged] from *Veniton* bridges.

From *Veniton b*ridges to Honiton [is] a 2 miles on the east ripe of *Oter* [Otter] River. Honiton is a fair long thoroughfare and market town, belonging to Courteney of *Powdreham* [Powderham] being just xii miles from *Excester* by east in the high way to London. A little beyond Honiton I left London way on the right hand and rode north east 3 miles to Mohun's *Oterey.*

The head and course of *Otery.*

Oterey riseth flat north a 5 miles above Mohun's *Otery* at about a place called *Oterford.* Thence it runneth a 4 miles to a village called *Upoter* [Upottery]. Thence a mile to Mohun's *Oterey*. Mohun's *Oterey* sometime called *Oterey* Fleming. Sir George Carew hath a good manor park at Mohun's *Otery* [in Luppitt].

Sir George Carew told me that this land was not of the lands of Mohuns, Earls of Somerset, but of another Mohun, of whose name there were Barons. He said that Mohun of Somersetshire, the Earl, bore in gold across engrail Sables, and that Mohun of Devonshire gave the arm with the powdered Manche. Much of the land that this Mohun had come by an heir general of one Fleming, that was Lord of Stoke *Fleminges* lordship and the castle at *Dertmouth*. Alanus Fleming was a notable man in that Stoke. Carew married an heir general of the Stoke of Mohun of Devonshire. Carew['s] true name [is] Montgomerik, and he is written thus in old evidence: Motgomerik Dns de Carew. Sir Nicolas Carew came out of this stock. The very ancient arms of the Carew's be 3 lions sable in gold. There was and is a chapel of St Patrike, as I remember, in the castle of *Dartemouth*; and it hath been in times past, as it appeareth, some little cell annexed to some great abbey.

Oterey goeth from Mohun's *Oterey* to Honiton a 3 miles; thence to *Veniton* Bridge a 2 Miles: thence to *S. Mary Otery*. *Otery* goeth from *S. Marie* to Newton Bridge about a mile off; thence to *Oter* Mouth and the very sea a v miles.

Oterton [Otterton] a pretty fisher town, standeth on the east side of the haven, about a mile from *Otermouth*; and on the west side of the haven is *Budelegh* [Budleigh] right almost again[st] *Oterton*, but it is somewhat more from the shore than *Oterton*. Less then a hundreth years since ships used this haven, but it is now clean barred. Some call this haven *Budeley* Haven, of *Budeley* town. The mouth of *Oterey* Haven lyeth south west.

There is a fisher village lower than *Oterton*, even at the very east south east point of *Otermouth.* This village is called *Salterne* [Salterton] and hath been in times past a thing of some estimation; and of this village the haven of *Otermouth* was called Saltern Haven, or peradventure of a creek coming out of the main haven into it.

From Mohun's *Oterey* to *Colington* [Colyton] [is] v miles by good corn, pasture, and some wood. About a mile or [so before] I came to *Colington* I saw from an hill *Shoute* [Shute] a right goodly manor place, a mile off on an Hillside, of the Lord Marquis of *Dorsete*, and by it a goodly large park. The town [it]self of *Colington* is no very notable thing; the personage of it is impropriate to [damaged]. The Bishop of *Excester's* Chancellor is vicar of this town and [has] a fair house there.

Coley River runneth under the rote of an hill that this town standeth on. This brook riseth, as I could esteem, by west north west a [damaged] miles from *Colington*, by the which it runneth; and then as I marked, it passeth by *Colecombe* [Colcombe] Park, hard by *Colington*, lately belonging to the Marquise of *Excester*, and thence going a mile and more entereth betwixt Axbridge and Axmouth town into *Ax* river.

From *Colington* to *Seton* [Seaton], now a mean fisher town, [is] scant 2 mile. I passed over *Cole* [Coly] Water again at *Coliford* [Colyford] or I came to *Seton*. There hath been a very notable haven at *Seton*, but now there lyeth between the 2 points of the old haven a mighty ri[d]g[e] and bar of pebble stones in the very mouth of it, and the river of *Ax* is driven to the very east point of the haven, called Whit Cliff, and there at a very small gut goeth into the sea; and here come in small fisher boats for succour.

The town of *Seton* is now but a mean thing, inhabited with fisher men, [but] it hath been far larger when the haven was good. The Abbot of *Shirburne* was lord and patron of it.

On the west part over an hill beyond *Seton* [in Southleigh] is Wiscombe, a fair manor place, sometime the Lord Bonville's, now belonging to the Marquis of *Dorsete*.

There belonged [to Seaton] and doth yet a chapel to *Seton*, called *Berewood* [Beer] near the shore and there is an hamlet of fisher men. There was begun a fair pier for succour of shiplets at this *Berewood*, but there came such a tempest a 3 years since as never in mind of men had before was seen in that shore, and tore the pier in pieces.

The men of *Seton* began of late days to stake and to make a main wall within the haven, to have diverted the course of *Ax* river, and there almost in the middle of the old haven, to have trenched thorough the Chesil, and to have let out *Ax* and received in the main sea, but this purpose came not to effect; me thought that nature most wrought to trench the Chesil hard by *Seton* town and there to let in the sea.

The west point of Axmouth haven is called *Bereword* [Beer], scant half a mile distant from the very town of *Seton*. Sidmouth, a fisher town, with a brook of that name and a bay, vi miles west [of] *Seton* [damaged] by west above Sidmouth. The east point of Axmouth haven is called White Cliff. These 2 points be almost a mile in distance. The very issue and mouth of *Ax* into the sea at this time is hard under the roots of White Cliff.

I passed from *Seton* at ebb over the salt marshes and the river of *Ax* to Axmouth, an old and big fisher town on the east side of the haven. The Priory of Sion was lord patron here; and here I learned that there is an abbey in Normandy called *Mountborow* [Monteburgh], and this place showeth by writings that Axmouth, Sidmouth, and *Oterton* were cells to it.

The Descent and Course of the River *Ax* from the Head.

Ax riseth a mile east from *Bemistre* [Beaminster], a market town in *Dorsetshir*, at a place called *Ax* Knolle, a ground belonging to Sir Giles Strangwais in a moor on the hanging of a hill: and thence runneth south west a 4 miles to Forde Abbey, standing in Devonshire on the farther ripe of it; and hereabout is a limes [boundary] to *Devonshir* and *Somersetshir*.

Ax then runneth to *Axministre* [Axminster] a pretty quick market town a 3 miles lower *ripa citeriori*; this town is in *Devonshir*. The personage of *Axmister*, so I learned, is impropriate to the church of York. The church of *Axmistre* is famous by the sepulchres of many noble Danes slain in King Æthelstan's time at a battle on *Brunesdoun* thereby, and by the sepulchres likewise [of] some Saxon lords slain in the same field.

Ax thence runneth thorough *Axmistre* bridge of stone about a quarter of a mile lower than *Axmistre* town; somewhat lower then this bridge entereth *Yartey* [Yarty] river, being sometime a raging water, into *Ax* river. *Artey* riseth by north west and entereth into *Ax* by east. There is a stone bridge on *Artey* about half a mile from the place where it entereth into *Ax*; this bridge of some [people] is called Kilmington Bridge [from] a village not very far it. About half a mile lower then *Axmistre* Bridge is Newenham sometime an abbey of Bernardines, of the foundation of Mohun, Earl of Somerset. *Ax* runneth a mile *dim.* lower through *Ax* Bridge of 2 arches of stone; this bridge serveth not to pass over at high tides, otherwise it doth. Thence *Ax* runneth half a mile lower to Axmouth town. And a quarter of a mile lower it goeth under White Cliff into the ocean sea, there called *Ax* Bay...

LIEUTENANT HAMMOND *of* NORWICH, 1635

British Library, Lansdowne 213/27. Edited by L.G. Wickham Legg, *A relation of a short survey of the Western Counties made by a Lieutenant Hammond of the Military Company in Norwich in 1635* (Camden Miscellany 16, 3rd Series, 52), 73 and more recently by Richard Pearse Chope, *Early Tours in Devon and Cornwall* (Devon & Cornwall Record Society, 1918, reprinted Newton Abbot, 1967), 83.

The writer was possibly a member of the Hammond family of Ellingham on the Suffolk border. His travels to Devon extended as far westward as Exeter. The brevity of Hammond's account of East Devon may have been due to an impatience to arrive in Exeter to see his relations or a lack of things of sufficient interest in East Devon. In the previous year Hammond had travelled widely through other parts of England.

...From hence [Lyme Regis] I made speed to Axminster, crossing there a pretty little river, but before I entered the town of *Hunnington* [Honiton] over another river, & from thence by some seats of knights, and gentlemen, with happy guides and fair ways, from that market town *Hunnington*, I ended my five weeks' travel at a quiet inn, the [blank] in the high & chiefest street there of this fair city [Exeter]...

JOHN TAYLOR
of
LONDON, 1649

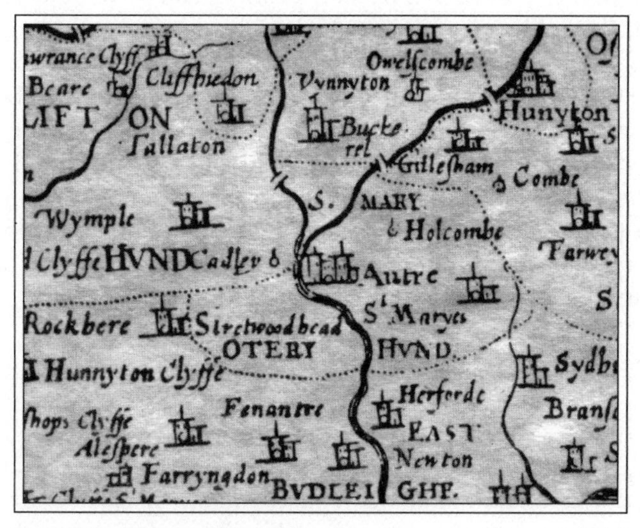

Part of East Devon, from John Speed's map of Devon, 1610

> Frank Graham reprinted in full an edition of Taylor's tour from J.O. Halliwell-Phillipps, *The Literature of the Sixteenth and Seventeenth Centuries Illustrated* (1851) as *John Taylor's Wandering to see the Wonders of the West* (Newcastle upon Tyne, 1967), 25.

Taylor, the 'Water Poet', was a known Royalist and must have had some apprehensions regarding a visit to the South West at the end of the Civil War. He travelled to the far west of Cornwall. Taylor was 69 years old when he visited East Devon and died only four years later. He was well-travelled and this was one of his many publications. Nevertheless, James Davidson, one of East Devon's most industrious historians, wrote that Taylor's financial backers were 'not like likely to be much benefited by his discoveries or his travels if he recorded no more on the other parts of his journey than he has done [about East Devon]': Westcountry Studies Library, James Davidson, Collections for East of Devon, page 171.

...Two hours before *Phoebus* appeared in our hemisphere, I was on footback from Exeter to Honiton, the 27 of July, there I had a night's lodging, and diet of such a homely fashion, as I have no occasion to boast of; there I hired a horse (which proved to be a blind mare) she had two wens as big as clusters of grapes hung over both her eyes, and five or six wens on her shoulders and flanks, all which beautiful ornaments I could not perceive or see till I had rose the beast four mile (for I was mounted before the break of day) but when I saw the comeliness of the beast, between shame and anger I was almost mad at the rogue that owned her; and being near to a market town called Axminster, I dismounted and footed eight miles further to *Broad Winsor* in Dorsetshire where I was better horsed...

COUNT LORENZO MAGALOTTI
of
TUSCANY, 1669

Bridge over the Axe at Axminster, 1669

Lorenzo Magalotti, *Travels of Cosmo the third, Grand Duke of Tuscany, through England during the reign of Charles the second, 1669* (1821), 138–40. See also Richard Pearse Chope (ed.), *Early Tours in Devon and Cornwall* (Devon and Cornwall Record Society, 1918, reprinted Newton Abbot, 1967), 110–111.

Count Magalotti accompanied Cosmos 3rd, Grand Duke of Tuscany, on his travels from Italy to London. He was later Secretary to the Academy del Cimento and was 26 years old on his visit to East Devon.

...On the morning of the 8th, his highness sent Platt to present his compliments to the mayor [of Exeter]. Towards noon, Mr Kirkham and the Messrs. Rolle came to wish him a good journey; after which, having dined, he got into his coach, and departed for Axminster, where he arrived at an early hour. The road was through an uneven country, divided into fields under the plough, and spacious meadows for feeding cows, in which this district abounds. At first we suffered a good deal of inconvenience, because they had to travel a road full of water, and muddy, though not deep. We passed through Honiton, a small but populous village, situated in a valley, and having ascended a hill, from which we could see the sea, we arrived at Axminster, where we found the master of the horse of Henry Howard, brother of the Duke of Norfolk, and of my Lord Philip, grand almoner to the queen, who delivered to Colonel Gascoyne a letter from his master, in which he excused himself for not coming in person to pay his respects to his highness, in consequence of his approaching departure on his embassy to Fez; and informed him that he had sent his carriage to Salisbury to be at the service of his highness. The master of the horse was admitted to an audience by the serene prince, and departed that same evening for London. His highness then went out to walk, and passed the evening in seeing some ancient medals, which had been dug up in this neighbourhood, and were brought for his inspection by the minister of the church.

Axminster is a collection of two hundred houses, many of which are made of mud, and thatched with straw. It contains nothing considerable, except the parish church, which has a tower, in which are bells so well tuned, that their sound is exceedingly harmonious and agreeable. The trade of the inhabitants consists in the manufactory of woollen cloth.

On the 9th, having travelled twelve miles through a country more cultivated, pleasanter, and more fertile than on the preceding day, we arrived at Hinton St George...

JOHN ASHBURNHAM
of
ASHBURNHAM, SUSSEX, 1687

Axminster, overlooking the Axe, 1669

East Sussex Record Office, ASH 933.

Two years after the tour he was created Baron Ashburnham.
Ashburnham was on a tour through East Devon to Exeter.
He was then thirty-one years old and died in 1710.

Tuesday the 14th of June 1687
We set out from Dorchester about 9 in the morning to go to

Axminster, which is about 22 miles from it. This Dorchester is not above 6 miles from Weymouth from whence they have their Wines and a great many other good things. Dorchester was formerly a town of great Trade, but the Trade is now decayed and gone westward towards Exeter. We went through a very fine Valley of Corn and after that through an enclosed Country to Bridport from thence through Stony Lanes to Charmouth, from thence we went to see Lyme [Regis] which is but a mile out of the Exeter Road. It is the famous place where Monmouth landed. We went to see the place where he first came in to the Town, which was Westward near the Bowling green and from the Bowling green we saw the places where he set up his standard which lyeth Eastward of the Town. The Country is exceedingly hilly here about, the Lanes narrow and very stony. From Lyme we came 4 Little Miles to Axminster to the sign of the Green Dragon, the road is very stony and bad. We came in about 6 in the evening, they told us Monmouth camped here at Axminster and that when he was proclaimed King at Taunton, the Rabble asked him what Religion he would maintain, he replied the Church of England as his Father had done, upon which they were disgusted, and forsook him in great numbers pretending several frivolous things in excuse. They expected he should have here declared for liberty of conscience. Here is excellent kerseys made at Axminster, it is 4 miles within Devonshire.

Wednesday the 15th of June 1687

We set out from Axminster about 9 in the morning and passing through a hilly, and some part enclosed country came to Honiton, near which is Sir Thomas Putt's house. Honiton is a pretty market town and 10 miles from Exeter, from thence we came through a very good country well enclosed and most upon downs, about 2 miles from Honiton is a new house [Escot] built by Sir Walter Young, and there Mr Isack met us, we went on through a very good road and country and came to Exeter about 4 in the afternoon...

Miss Celia Fiennes
of
Newton Toney, Hampshire, 1698

Axminster, from the Axe, 1669

The many editions of her *Through England on a side saddle in the time of William and Mary* (1888) include Christopher Morris, *The Journeys of Celia Fiennes* (1947), 244–5, 271–2. The East Devon extract was included by Richard Pearse Chope in his *Early Tours in Devon and Cornwall* (Devon & Cornwall Record Society, 1918, reprinted Newton Abbot, 1967) on pages 111 to 112 and 136 to 137.

Fiennes was on an extensive tour from London into the north of England and then southwards to Cornwall before returning to London. She travelled on horseback accompanied by several servants. Fiennes was thirty-six years old when she visited East Devon and died in 1741.

...I entered into Devonshire 5 mile off from Wellington just on a high Ridge of hills which discovers a vast prospect on each side full of enclosures and lesser hills, which is the description of most part of the West; you could see large tracts of grounds full of enclosures, good grass and corn beset with quicksets and hedge rows, and these lesser hills, which are scarce perceivable on the ridge of the uppermost yet the least of them have a steep ascent and descent to pass them.

Culimton [Cullompton] is a good little Market town, [with] a Market Cross and another set on stone pillars (such a one was at Wellington but on brick work pillars); here was a large Meeting of near 4 or 500 people, they have a very good Minister but a young man, I was glad to see so many tho' they were but of the meaner sort, for indeed its the poor [who] receive the Gospel, and there are in most of the market towns in the West very good Meetings. This little place was one continued long street, but few houses that struck out of the street.

From thence 10 mile to *Exetter* up hills and down as before till one attains those uppermost ridges of all which discovers the whole valley, then you sometimes go a mile or two on a Down till the brow of the hill begins in a descent on the other side; this City appears to view 2 mile distant from one of those heights, and also the River Ex which runs to *Topshum* [Topsham] where the ships comes up to the bar; this is 7 mile by water, from which they are attempting to make navigable to the town which will be of mighty advantage to have ships come up close to the town to take in their serges, which now they are forced to send to *Topshum* on horses by land which is about 4 mile by land; they had just agreed with a man that was to accomplish this work for which they were to give 5 or £6000, who had made a beginning on it...[continuing west to Cornwall and returning] from Exeter I went to Honiton 15 mile, all fine gravel way the best road I have met withal in the West; here it is they make the fine Bone lace in imitation of the Antwerp and Flanders lace, and indeed I think its as fine, it only will not wash so fine which must be the fault in the thread; Honiton is a pretty large place, a good Market house, near it a good Church with a round tower and spire which was very high and a little peculiar in its form, somewhat like a pigeon house roof; here is a very large Meeting of Dissenters.

Thence I went to Axminster 7 mile more, but not so good way being much in lanes, stony and dirty, and pretty much up and down hills, like the other parts of these counties: beyond Axminster where I passed over the river *Ax* on a pretty large bridge I came to Somersetshire again (this Axminster is a little market town) and the London Road by Chard...

JOHN VERDON
of
EAST DEREHAM, NORFOLK, 1700

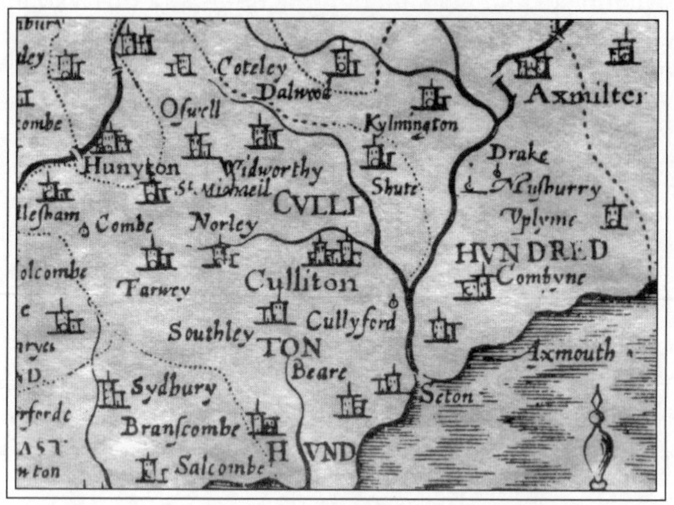

Part of East Devon, from John Speed's map of Devon, 1610

Verdon had travelled extensively through England in the previous year and this appears to have been his first visit to East Devon. He and his companions had intended to tour Scotland but, as he explained, their reasons were as numerous as those men that give for drinking. He left his home in Norfolk at four in the morning on July 10 and arrived in Devon nearly three weeks later.

[July 29th]

About half a mile from this is a place on a hill called *Uplime* [Uplyme], which parts Dorsetshire & Devonshire, & here it was that first of all we saw men carrying their corn (for 'twas Harvest time) upon crooked sticks laid cross a horse, which with their Art would carry about hour hundred weight, & here likewise first appeared that monstrous sight of Gambados instead of boots, which all the country rejoice in & here likewise appeared (I mean about 15 miles further [presumably Honiton]) an honest Gentleman, one Mr Powel, a lace-man, whom I must in gratitude record for his unheard of kindness, & that was that he not only proffered me, but was very pressing, to supply me with what moneys or Bills in any great Town where I should move, that I would accept of, which friendship was contracted in spending a shilling, which was all our reckoning & I paying it and saying it exactly nicked me being all the moneys I had (meaning silver) he thereupon offered the kindness above said, which I thought unusual from one I have never seen before, not my companion, but once in a public house seven years before this time. This Gentleman afterwards (which I hope I sha'nt forget to mention in its proper place) continued his Friendly Offices to me, tho' at a distance from me. After we parted with him we had eight miles to Exeter, all extraordinary good road...

DR WILLIAM STUKELEY
of
LONDON, 1724

Portrait of William Stukeley

William Stukeley, *Itinerarium Curiosum* (1776), 156–9. Also see Richard Pearse Chope (ed.), *Early Tours in Devon and Cornwall* (Devon & Cornwall Record Society, 1918, reprinted Newton Abbot, 1967), 137, 142–5.

Stukeley, one of the founders of the Society of Antiquaries just a few years before in 1718, was also interested in medicine and Druidism. His publications include *Stonehenge, a temple restored to the British druids* (1740) and *Palaeographia Britannica* (1743–52) in three volumes. He was aged thirty-seven on this visit to East Devon and died more than forty years later.

...Beyond Chard to Honiton is a very bad road of stones and sand, over brooks, spring-heads, and barren downs. From the hill-tops about Stockland I first had sight of the southern ocean; a most solemn view, a boundless extent of water thrown into a mighty horizontal curve. Beyond Honiton the scene of travelling mended apace, and the fine Devonshire prospects entertained the eye in a manner new and beautiful; for here the hills are very long and broad, the valleys between proportional, so that the vastly-extended concavity presented an immense landscape of pastures and hedge-rows distinct, like a map of an actual survey, and not beyond ken; these are full of springs, brooks and villages, copses and gentlemen's seats; and when you have passed over one hill, you see he like repeated before you, with Nature's usual diversity. They told me of a great cairn, or heap of stones, on Black Down, called Lapper-stones; probably a sepulchral monument...Leaving Exeter, my farthest western longitude at present, I steered my course back again along the sea-side, enwrapped in contemplation with the poet,

> *Undæ quæ vestris pulsatis littora lymphis,*
> *Littora quæ dulces auras diffunditis agris!*
> VIRGIL

Nor could I think myself alone, when so much new entertainment was presented to me every minute. Much rock-samphire grows upon these cliffs. The Roman road seems to have crossed the Otter at Hertford. At Woodbury is a camp. I passed by Sidmouth, and came to Seaton, a little village upon the mouth of the river *Ax*. This Mr Camden conjectures to have been the Roman *Moridunum*, and with reason. It has been a great haven and excellent port, of which they still keep up the memory; the river runs in a large valley, having high ground on each side; the shore is rocky, high and steep, consisting of the ends of hills which here run north and south; the ground at bottom under the rocks is marly; the waves wash it down perpetually, undermining the strata of stone, which from time to time fall down in great parcels. At present this haven mouth, which is a good half mile over, is filled up with beach, as they call it; that is coggles, gravel, sand, shells, and such matter as is thrown up by the roll of the ocean: so that the river water has but a very narrow passage on the east side under the cliff. The beach was covered over with *papaver luteum corniculatum*, now in blossom: the people in the isle of Portland call it *squat maw*, i.e. bruise herb, and use it in that case, no doubt, with good success, where both intentions are answered, of dissolving the coagulated blood, and easing pain. On the west side, near Seaton, upon a little eminence is a modern ruined square *pharos* built of brick; they remember it sixteen foot high; and two guns lie there. They say there were formerly many great foundations of houses visible nearer the sea than the present town, but now swallowed up; and in all likelihood there stood the Roman city. More inward toward the land, beyond the great bank of beach, is a marsh which the sea has made, landing itself up when its free flux is hindered; this is full of salt-pans, into which they take the sea-water at high tides. When they dig these places they find innumerable keels and pieces of vessels, with nails, pitch, anchors, etc., six or eight feet deep, because it was formerly part of the haven; anchors have been found as high as Axminster and beyond it, though now there is no navigation at all: so great a change has Time produced in the face of Nature, upon these confines of the two great elements always opposing each other.

Sic volvenda ætas commutat tempora rerum.
LUCR. V.

Half a mile off, upon higher ground, on the western side is a castle in a pasture, but formerly tilled, called Honey Ditches: it is moated about, and perhaps walled; for they dig up much square stone there. The place is an oblong square, containing about three acres: I guess it to have been the garrison of the port. Just by the present haven-mouth is a great and long pier or wall, jutting out into the sea, made of great rocks piled together to the breadth of six yards. They told me it was built many years ago by one Courd, once a poor sailor, who, being somewhere in the Mediterranean, was told by a certain Greek, that much treasure was hid upon Hogsdon hill near here, and that this memorial was transmitted to him by his ancestors; Courd, upon his return digging there luckily found the golden mine, which enriched him prodigiously, so that at his own expense he built this wall, with an intent to restore the harbour. The people hereabouts firmly believe the story, and many have dug in the place with like hopes; and as an argument of its truth, they say some of his family are still remaining, that live upon their estate got by him.

A mile higher on the same western side of the river is *Cullyford*, where was the ancient road from London to Exeter passing over at Axbridge, which is now a stony ford, with two bridges that traverse the valley and the river, once a haven. Here have been many inns and houses, and a considerable town. They talk of great stone vaults being found; so that is probably arose from the destruction of *Moridunum*, as *Culliton* [Colyton] adjacent, from it. Further it was a corporation, and they now keep up their claim by an annual choice of a mayor, who has a mace too, but I suppose not of great elegance.

I suppose the Foss road went on the east side of Chard, and so by Axminster and *Culliton*, to Seaton or *Moridunum*, where properly it begins; whence if we measure its noble length to the sea-coast in Lincolnshire, at Grimsby or Saltfleet, where I imagine it ends, it amounts to 250 Roman miles in a straight line from north-east to south-west. Your lordship (Lord Pembroke) presented me with an oyster, found a little northward of Axminster, where the very fish appears petrified with its cartilaginous concretion to the shell, all in their proper colours...

Seaton (*Moridunum*), as published by Stukeley in 1724

DANIEL DEFOE
of
STOKE NEWINGTON, LONDON, 1724

The church of Ottery St Mary from the south west, 1832

G.D.H. Cole (ed.), *A Tour Through The Whole Island of Great Britain* (1927), I, 221–2. Defoe's tour was originally printed in three volumes during the 1720s. The most recent edition is by P.N. Furbank and W.R. Owens (New Haven, 1991). The extract edited by Richard Pearse Chope in his *Early Tours in Devon and Cornwall* (Devon & Cornwall Record Society, 1918, Newton Abbot, 1967), 145–7 omits some of Defoe's text.

Defoe, originally Daniel Foe, may be better known as a novelist than as a journalist. His *Moll Flanders* and *Robinson*

Crusoe appeared before this tour and he published several hundred works in total. Trade and commerce were among Defoe's particular interests to note while touring. He was about 63 years old when in East Devon and died only seven years later.

...From thence [Chard] into the same road I was in before at Honiton. This is a large and beautiful market-town, very populous and well built, and is so very remarkably paved with small pebbles that on either sides the way a little channel is left shouldered up on the sides of it, so that it holds a small stream of fine clear running water, with a little square dipping-place left at every door; so that every family in the town has a clear, clean Running River (as it may be called) just at their own door, and this so much finer, so much pleasanter, and agreeable to look on, than that at Salisbury (which they boast so much of), that, in my opinion, there is no comparison.

Here we see the first of the great serge manufacture of Devonshire – a trade too great to be described in miniature, as it must be if I undertake it here, and which takes up this whole county, which is the largest and most populous in England, Yorkshire excepted (which ought to be esteemed three counties, and is indeed, divided as such into the East, West, and North Riding). But Devonshire, one entire county, is so full of great towns, and those towns so full of people, and those people so universally employed in trade and manufactures, that not only it cannot be equalled in England, but perhaps not in Europe.

In my travel thro' Dorsetshire I ought to have observed that the biggest towns in that county sent no members to Parliament, and that the smallest did; that is to say, that *Sherborn*, Blandford, *Winborn-minster*, Sturminster, and several other towns choose no members, whereas Weymouth, *Melcom* and Bridport, were all burgess towns; but now we come to Devonshire, we find almost all the great towns, and some smaller, choosing members also. It is true there are some large populous towns that do not choose, but then there are so many that do, that the county seems to have no injustice, for they send up six-and-twenty members. However, as I say above, there are several great towns which do not choose Parliament men, of which *Bidiford* [Bideford] is one, Crediton or Kirton another, *Ilfracomb* [Ilfracombe] a third; but, those excepted, the principal towns in the county do all choose members of Parliament.

Honiton is one of those, and may pass not only for a pleasant good town, as before, but stands in the best and pleasantest part of the whole county, and I cannot but recommend it to any gentlemen that travel this road, that if they please to observe the prospect for half a mile till their coming down the hill and to the entrance into Honiton, the view of the country is the most beautiful landscape in the world – a mere picture – and I do not remember the like in any one place in England. Tis observable that the market of this town was kept originally on the Sunday, till it was changed by the direction of King John.

From Honiton the country is exceedingly pleasant still, and on the road they have a beautiful prospect almost all the way to Exeter (which is twelve miles). On the left-hand of this road lies that part of the country which they call the South Hams, and which is famous for the best cider in that part of England; also the town of St. Mary *Oterey*, commonly called St. Mary *Autree*. They tell us the name is derived from the river Ottery, and that from the multitude of otters found always in that river, which however, to me, seems fabulous. Nor does there appear to be any such great number of otters in that water, or in the county about, more than is usual in other counties or in other parts of the county about them. They tell us they send 20,000 hogsheads of cider hence every year to London, and which is still worse that it is most of it bought there by the merchants to mix with their wines – which, if true, is not much to the reputation of the London vintners. But that by the by…

An Unknown Male Traveller *from* Nanswhyden near Newquay, Cornwall, 1741

Devon Record Office, 64/12/29/1/13

The account is from the papers of the Quicke family of Newton House, Newton St Cyres near Exeter. In the late eighteenth century the daughter of Elizabeth, sister of the Earl of Godolphin, married into the Quicke family; it is likely that this travel account came into the family papers through this Cornish connection. The unknown male was on a journey to London from Nanswhyden, home of the Hoblyn family, between Newquay and St Columb Major in Cornwall. He was part of a large party.

...Walked to the Southernhay, but the rain drove us back. Dined at 11 but waited till almost 3 for the coach being mended, then set out. Mrs W. on horseback. Quite dark when we got to Bradninch which [is] the oldest corporation in England. Walked up a bad hill into the T[own] & up another at the end. Very merry & dirty, stuck in a narrow lane, met many coming from Cullompton Fair when we came to that T[own]. Found the inn full. Eat [sic] some of their Fair provisions for supper, had private lodgings. Very bad roads that day.

Thursday wet.

All 5 in the coach till we came to M Down. Bad road to Maiden down pretty well to Wellington. Miss B. rode...

Dr Richard Pococke
1750

Lane's Chapel, Cullompton church, 1861

British Library, 15,800. The Exeter section was included by J.J. Cartwright in his *The Travels through England of Dr Richard Pococke, successively Bishop of Meath and of Ossory during 1750, 1751, and later years* (Camden Society, 2nd series, 1888, Vol. 42), 99–101. There are only two minor differences with the original text in the extract edited by Richard Pearse Chope, *Early Tours in Devon and Cornwall* (Devon & Cornwall Record Society, 1918, reprinted Newton Abbot, 1967), 178–80, 214–215.

Later Bishop of Ossory and Meath, Pococke was widely travelled before this visit to East Devon; he had already toured the Alps and eastern Mediterranean including to Egypt, Palestine, Cyprus and Greece. He was aged forty-six when he travelled to East Devon.

...September 20. From Lyme [Regis] I went four miles almost directly north to Axminster on the river *Ax* in Devonshire, the bounds between the two counties being a little to the west of Lyme. This place is in the high road from London to Exeter. In the church they show two tombs, which they say are of two Saxon kings; and they have a tradition in the country that a battle was fought in Kingsmead near Mestern, in which one of them they say was killed. The account we have is, that they are the Saxon princes slain by the Danes, in the battle of Brunaburg; and King Athelstan in remembrance of the victory built a minster here for seven priests to pray for the souls of the slain. One of the tombs is on the north side of the quire with long robes, the head is off, but there are some remains of what looks like a coul. This, I was told some antiquaries said, was a bishop. The other is in the north isle, and both under niches; it has a coul over the head, and something in both hands which might be a crucifix, it looks very much like the statue of a woman. Digging lately at the west end of the church they found bones fill'd with lead, but no lead on the outside of the bones. I saw one of them. There is a chapel to the north of the church which is very old, and is now used as a school, and the south door of the church is very ancient; and what is particular, across the inside of the arch are eleven reeds cut in stone about two inches diameter. The capitals in the church are four angels holding shields of arms and their wings meeting the corners.

Going to Honiton I went over a hill of gravelly soil and came to a small stream which falls into the *Ax*, and crossed two more hills of clay and came to Honiton on the *Autre*; the east side of this town was burnt down four years ago. We went on in the afternoon and came to *Venne* bridges, over some rivulets that fall into the *Autre*, which rise to high that the roads are sometimes impassable for a few hours. Here King Edward the VI's army under S[r] John Russel and Lord Grey defeated the Cornish and Devonshire rebels. Coming to Fair mile I saw the seat of Sir Wm Young, and going up the hill saw the town of *Autre* [Ottery St Mary] and had a glorious view from the top of it of the hills to the east of *Autre* fringed at top as in a strait line with the heathy ground, and then into the vale in which the *Ex* runs, and several rivulets that fall into it, and of the city of Exeter. When we came to the bottom of this hill I found it a red sandy soil all the way to Exeter. The river *Ex* rises near the north coast of Devonshire, have no considerable town on it but Tiverton, Exeter and Topsham; Dulverton, Bampton, and *Samford* are on rivulets that fall into it; two large streams join it from the north-east, *Columbton* having a town on it of the same name, and Bradninch; and from the north-west the river *Credy*, on which stands Crediton...[to Exeter]

I went on to Star Cross, and crossed over the river to Exmouth, situated near the place where the *Ex* empties itself into the sea, and is chiefly inhabited by fishermen and publicans, it being a place to which the people of Exeter much resort for diversion and bathing in the sea, and the situation is so pleasant, having beautiful little hills to the east finely improved, and a view of the fine country on the other side, that some persons of condition have come to live at the place, which they are improving by a gravel walk to the river, that is to be planted, and they are going to make a bowling green. Sir John Colliton has a garden full of curious plants, chiefly from [southern] America, where he has a son settled. He has the magnolia or lawrel-leav'd tulip in blossom, and also the Carolina sword blade aloe; he has the trumpet tree, the Carolina raspberry tree, the anemony tree, and Carolina kidney bean tree, the artichoke or orange myrtle, the flowers of which are in clusters and of a reddish cast, a beautiful turn cap'd Carolina martagon, which is red and white, the motle-leav'd tulip tree, which seems to be only the occidental plane-tree, the serpentine euphorbium, the coat of which resembles the scales of a serpent, but it is very much raised.

Directly east of Topsham is *Clyst St Maries*, where the Parliament forces barricaded themselves up by laying trees across the way and planting their ordnance; but when they heard Lord Russel was at Woodbury they endeavoured to surprise him; but he routed them, pursued them to this place, and then to the heath, and entirely defeated them...[through to Cornwall and then returning to Devon]

October 20. I went on eastward, the road being exceeding good, in a sandy soil, and I saw *Columbton* on the river Columb, which falls into the *Ex*. It was the demesne of the King of the West Saxons, and Alfred left it to his youngest son Ethelward. Coming towards the borders of this country I saw West Leigh and the quarries of limestone in the hills near it, which is a bluish stone with white veins in it, and is the only limestone in all this country. To the east of it is *Hulcombe*, where there is an old castle. All the prospects here are very delightful of a rich, well inhabited country, and fine hills to the south-east.

Passing over a common we came at the bottom of the valley into Somerset shire. All the country to the south from *Totness* to Plymouth is called *Southam* [South Hams] which is so famous for cider, but by the introduction of the Herefordshire redstreak of late years they make far better cider near Exeter. They let the apples fall, and put them in heaps in the orchard to rot and ferment, and then grind and press them out. They have an apple called the bitter-sweet, which gives a fine flavour to the cider; the management afterwards is drawing off frequently...

MISS CAROLINE GIRLE
of
LONDON, 1760

Portrait of Mrs Philip Lybbe Powys, *née* Caroline Girle

Emily J. Climenson (ed.), *Passages from the diaries of Mrs Philip Lybbe Powys of Hardwick House, Oxon., A.D. 1756 to 1808* (1899), 65–6, 77–8.

The following account is part of the 'Plymouth Journal' in which Miss Girle noted that 'if the rusticity of a dull pen, like a piece of rough marble, may be polished by exercise, then (as I've scribbled over much paper), may I in time, perhaps, have the honorary title of an expert journalist'. She travelled through East Devon while en route westwards to Plymouth and was part of a small party which included her father. She was then twenty-one years old and two years later she married Philip Lybbe Powys of Hardwick House, Oxfordshire. She was also familiar with Gloucestershire, Oxford, East Anglia, Derbyshire and Yorkshire.

...reaching that night Axminster. We found ourselves in a town of a very poor appearance, nothing in it worth a stranger's notice, except the carpet manufactory to see; that is indeed well worth while; the weaving of it is extremely curious, and gave us ladies the more pleasure, I believe, as our sex are here admitted to be artists – an uncommon privilege at this time of day, when the men seem to engross every possible branch of business to themselves. Axminster is on the great Western road, and the first town in the county of Devon. We were led by Camden, and curiosity to take an inside view of the church, he having told us of the monuments of two Danish princes slain at the battle of Bruneburg in this neighbourhood, fought by King Athelstane, with seven princes, over whom he obtained victory; but really the sight of their highnesses afforded us great entertainment, nor should I have had the least notion by their present clumsy appearance such uncouth lumps of stone were once designed to represent royalty. We left Axminster next day. Near it is a seat of Mr Tucker's, so sweetly situated that none can, I fancy, exceed it. Indeed the country here is most amazing fine, and the Vale of Honiton, a few miles farther, so far exceeds any idea one can form of a landscape, that 'tis in vain to endeavour at the description. The inhabitants of Dorsetshire, they say, pique themselves on what Charles II said of their county, which was, "that in or out of England he never saw its equal;" but sure he had then, I should imagine, never been in Devonshire; the former is very charming, but still in my opinion exceeded by the latter. At *Hainton* [Honiton] we made a stay of some hours. 'Tis really a very pretty town. Five miles from it is a seat of Sir William Young's, which we passed that day in our way to Exeter... [travelling to Plymouth and then returning to Exeter]

... reached Exeter early on Friday, stayed there the whole day, and got the next morn by twelve to Honiton. When we before were at this town, knowing we were to return thro' it, we deferred till then seeing the making of bone lace; so now, as soon as we had breakfasted, went to view this their chief manufacture, which really gave us great pleasure, and much more to see 'twas our own country-women that could arrive at such perfection in this work, as I hope will prevent our ladies from forming the least wish to have the right Flanders; for really, on comparing two pieces, ours had the first preference; and if so, how cruel not to encourage the industrious poor of our native land. After seeing the lace-making we went to the broad-cloth weaving, which, tho' in a different way, is still curious; and from thence, it being market-day, we strolled round inquiring the price of several commodities, and, ignorant Londoners as we were, quite astonished to hear we might have a couple of fine chickens for sixpence, a pound of veal for three-halfpence, and other provisions in proportion cheap. What a surprising difference from the Metropolis! From the market we went back to our inn, and there, for the remainder of our stay, amused ourselves with the transcription on the wainscot, which, at such places, I think every idler seems to subscribe their unit for the entertainment of the next idle gazer. I found the following four lines, which perhaps by many have been found too true in their pursuit of grandeur:–

"How wretched is our fate,
What hazards do we run;
We are wicked to be great,
And great to be undone."

After a stay of nearly five hours at Honiton, we pursued our journey; and having mounted one of those hills which surround this pretty town, we had again in view the fine vale I've mentioned before, than which I think no prospect of the mind can surpass in beauty. We that night lay at Axminster, and from thence, to have the pleasure of variety, the next morn we took the other road to Salisbury from that we came. Soon after we got out of Axminster we came into Somersetshire...

The Reverend William Gilpin *of* Boldre, near Lymington, Hampshire, *c.*1778

'View over the estuary of the Ex' by William Gilpin

William Gilpin, *Observations on the Western Parts of England, relative chiefly to Picturesque Beauty* (1808), 268–80

Gilpin's *Observations on the River Wye* of 1770 opened up the debate on the Picturesque in Britain. Shortly afterwards he published other descriptions of the country, including the Lake District, Hampshire, Sussex, Kent and Scotland, but he waited some twenty years to publish his visit to Devon. In 1798, when the tour was dedicated, Gilpin appears to have no knowledge of the work of the Reverend John Swete, the county's leading exponent of the Picturesque. This is partly explained by Swete only becoming interested in the Picturesque Movement in about 1789. Gilpin dedicated his book to Henry Addington, Speaker of the House of Commons, and first Viscount Sidmouth. Addington's principal residence was at Upottery. Gilpin noted that during the years in which the tour was in manuscript he had been able to improve it and wrote that 'how variously Nature works up the same modes of scenery in different parts of the world'. Gilpin was about 54 years old when he visited East Devon and died in 1804. Unusually, Gilpin had travelled first on Devon's north coast before coming to Exeter and East Devon.

...From the mouth of the *Ex* the coast affords nothing very interesting, till you come to the mouth of the Sid. This river opens into the sea between high promontories; that on the west is particularly lofty, and much broken, though not rocky, and is represented as affording many picturesque views. But here is no bason opening into the land, as in the other rivers of this coast. The Sid is a mere rural stream, and preserves it character pure to the very shores of the ocean.

The valley through which it takes its course, is a scene of peculiar construction. It forms a gentle descent towards the sea between two steep hills which leave little more room at the bottom, than what the road and the river occupy. So that, in fact, it has hardly the dimensions of a valley, but might rather be called a cleft in the higher grounds, running down to the sea. The hills, however, which compose its sides, are not (like the narrow valleys of a mountainous and rocky country) abrupt and broken; but consist chiefly of rich pasturage, and are covered with flocks and herds. They are adorned too with wood; and though in their course they now and then wind a little, they generally lead the valley in a straight line from north to south.

Through this narrow valley you rise slowly near the space of nine miles. So long an ascent, though in all parts gradual, raises you at length to a great height. At the conclusion of the valley, you find yourself on a lofty down; from whence you have some of the grandest views which this country, rich in distances, affords. You look chiefly towards the west, and take in an amazing compass; indeed all the district on both sides of the *Ex*, as far as the sea. These high grounds formed that *hard edge*, and made that peculiar appearance, which we observed in the road between Exeter and Honiton. From these lofty downs you descend gently into Honiton, where these two different routes from Plymouth unite.

As we left Honiton, the obscurity of a hazy morning overspread its vale; the picturesque beauty of which we had heard so much commended. If, therefore, it possesses any, (which from the analogy of the country may be questioned,) we are not qualified to give any account of it. A misty morning, in general, gives new beauty to a country; but we must catch its beautiful appearance, as we do all the other *accidental* appearances of Nature, at a proper crisis. We left Honiton at too early an hour in the morning to see the full effect of the mist. It rather blotted out, than adorned, the face of the country. The most picturesque moment of a misty morning is just as the sun rises, and begins its contention with the vapours which obstruct its rays. That appearance we had soon after, and in such profusion, that it gave a beautiful effect to a landscape, which seemed not calculated to produce much effect without it.

We have a striking picture of a morning-sun, though unaccompanied by mist, in the short account given us of Lot's escape from Sodom. We are told, *The sun was risen upon the earth, when Lot entered into Zoar.* Descriptive poetry and painting must both have *objects of sense* before them. Neither of them deals in *abstracted ideas*. But the same objects will not always suit both. Images, which may shine under the poet's description, are not perhaps at the same time picturesque; though I believe every picturesque object is capable of shining as a poetical one. The passage before us is both poetical and picturesque. A relation of the plain fact would have been neither. If the passage had been coldly translated, *Lot arrived at Zoar about sun-rise*; the sense had been preserved, but the picture would have been lost. As it is translated, the whole is imagery. The first part of the expression, *the sun was risen upon the earth*, brings immediately before the eye, (through the *connection* of the sun and the earth), the rays of a morning sun striking the tops of the hills and promontories; while the other part of the expression, *Lot entered into Zoar*, brings before us (through the same happy mode of raising and connecting images) a road, the gates of the town, and the patriarch approaching it. Not, by the way, that we should wish to introduce the *story* of Lot's retreat, with any *distinction* into the picture. The principal part would be the *landscape*; and Lot could only be a distant figure to adorn it, and in that light unnecessary. *History* introduced as the *ornament of landscape* appears absurd. In Bassan, and some other masters, such introductions are frequent. We consider, therefore, the passage before us merely as *landscape*, and lay little stress on the *figures*. Reubens has thrown a fine glow of colouring into a picture on the subject, in the possession of the Duke of Marlborough. But Reubens has introduced, as he ought, the figures on the *foreground*, making the landscape entirely an *under-part*. I forget whether he has given his picture the full effect it might receive by throwing the back scenery into that grand shade, suggested by the words of scripture, the *smoke of the country went up as the smoke of a furnace*. The atmosphere also might have a good effect, tinged with the ruddy glare of fire blended with the smoke.

As the mist cleared away, and we saw more of the country around, its picturesque charms did not increase upon us. If the hills and dales, however, of which the whole country is composed, possess little of this kind of beauty, they possess what is better, the riches of soil, and cultivation in a high degree. If any valleys can be said to *laugh and sing*, these certainly may. Nothing can exceed either their tillage or their pasturage.

Among the beautiful objects we occasionally met with in this country, the cattle, which everywhere grazed its rich pastures, were worthy of remark. Most of those we saw seemed to be of a peculiar breed, elegantly and neatly formed, rather small, generally red, growing gradually darker towards the head and shoulders. Their horns, which are short, are tipped with black; their coats are fine, and their heads small.

At Axminster the carpet-works are worth visiting. Some of them display a very rich combination of colours; but in general, they are so gay, that furniture must be glaring to be in harmony with them. Of course they are too gay to be beautiful.

No carpeting, perhaps, equals the Persian in beauty. The Turkey carpet is modest enough in its colouring; but its texture is coarse, and its pattern consists commonly of such a jumble of incoherent parts, that the eye seldom traces any meaning in its plan. The British carpet again has *too much meaning*. It often represents fruits, and flowers, and baskets, and other things, which are generally ill represented, or awkwardly larger than the life, or at least improperly placed under our feet. The Persian carpet avoids these two extremes. It seldom exhibits any *real forms*, and yet, instead of the disorderly pattern that deforms the Turkey carpet, it usually presents some neat and elegant plan, within the compartments of which its colours, though rich, are modest. The texture also of the carpet is as neat and elegant as the ornamental scrawl which adorns it.

From Axminster we left the great road to visit Ford-abbey.

In a sequestered part of the country, where Devonshire and

Dorsetshire unite, lies a circular valley, about a mile and half in diameter. Its sides slope gently into its area in various directions; but are nowhere steep. Woody screens, circling its precincts, conceal its bounds; and in many parts connecting with the trees, which descend into the bosom of the valley, form themselves into various tufted groves. Through the middle of this sweet retreat winds a stream, not foaming among broken rocks, nor sounding down cataracts; but mild like the scene it accompanies, and in cadence not exceeding a gentle murmur. From this retreat all foreign scenery is excluded. It wants no adventitious ornaments; sufficiently blessed with its own sweet groves and solitude.

> — Such *landscape*
> Needs not the foreign aid of ornament;
> But is, when unadorned, adorned the most.

This happy retirement was once sacred to religion. Verging towards one side of the valley stand the ruins of Ford-abbey. It has never been of large dimensions, but was a model of the most perfect Gothic, if we may credit its remains, particularly those of a cloister, which are equal to any thing we have in that style of architecture. This beautiful fragment consists of eight windows, with light buttresses between them, and joins a ruined chapel on one side, and on the other a hall or refectory, which still preserves its form sufficiently to give an idea of its just proportions. To this is connected by ruined walls a massy tower. What the ancient use of this fabric was, whether it belonged to the ecclesiastical or civil part of the monastery, is not now apparent; but at present it gives a picturesque form to the ruin, which appears to more advantage by the pre-eminence of some superior part.

At right angles with the chapel runs another cloister, a longer building, but of coarser workmanship, and almost covered with ivy. The river which enters the valley at the distance of about half a mile from the ruin, takes a sweep towards it, and passing under this cloister, opens into what was once the great court, and makes its exit through an arch in the wall on the opposite side.

> This venerable pile,
> — clad in the mossy vest of fleeting time,

and decorated all over with a variety of lichens, streaming weather-stains, and twisting shrubs, is shaded by ancient oaks, which, hanging over it, adorn its broken walls without encumbering them. In short, the valley, the river, the path and the ruins are all highly pleasing; the *parts* are beautiful, and the *whole* is harmonious.

They who have lately seen Ford-abbey will stare at this description of it. And well may they stare; for this description antedates its present state by at least a century. If they had seen it in the year 1675, they might probably have seen it as it is here described. Now, alas! it wears another face. It has been in the hands of *improvement*. Its simplicity is gone; and miserable ravage has been made through every part. The ruin is patched up into an awkward dwelling; old parts and new are blended together, to the mutual disgrace of both. The elegant cloister is still left; but it is completely repaired, white-washed, and converted into a green-house. The hall too is modernized, and every other part. Sash-windows glare over pointed arches, and Gothic walls are adorned with Indian paper.

The ground have undergone the same reformation. The natural groves and lawns are destroyed; vistas and regular slopes supply their room. The winding path, which contemplation naturally marked out, is gone; succeeded by straight walks, and terraces adorned with urns and statues; while the river and its fringed banks have given way to canals and stew-ponds. In a word, a scene abounding, with so many natural beauties was never perhaps more wretchedly deformed.

When a man exercises his crude ideas on a few vulgar acres, it is of little consequence. The injury is easily repaired; and if not, the loss is trifling. But when he lets loose his depraved taste, his absurd invention, and his graceless hands on such a subject as this, where art and nature united cannot restore the havoc he makes, we consider such a deed under the same black character in matters of picturesque beauty, as we do sacrilege and blasphemy in matters of religion. The effect of superstition we abhor. Some little atonement, however, this implacable power might have made in taste, for its mischiefs in religion, if it had deterred our ancestors from connecting their mansions with ruins once dedicated to sacred uses. We might then have enjoyed in perfection many noble scenes, which are now either entirely effaced or miserably mangled.

Before we leave these scenes, I must relate a story of the monks of Ford, which does great credit to their piety. In happened (in what century tradition says not) that a gentleman of the name of Courtney, a benefactor to the abbey, was overtaken at sea by a violent storm; and the seamen having toiled many hours in vain, and being entirely spent, abandoned themselves to despair. "My good lads," (said Courtney, calling them together, and pulling out his watch, if watches were then in use,) "My good lads, you see it is now four o'clock. At five we shall certainly be relieved. At that hour the monks of Ford rise to their devotions, and in their prayers to St. Francis, we will be sure to remember me among their benefactors; and you will have the benefit of being saved in my company. Persevere only one hour, and you may depend on what I say." This speech reanimated the whole crew. Some flew to the pump, others to the leak; all was life and spirit. By this vigorous effort, at five o'clock the ship was so near the shore, that she easily reached it; and St. Francis got all the credit of the escape.

From Ford-abbey we were obliged to return to Axminster...

The Reverend Stebbing Shaw *of* Cambridge, 1788

Honiton church, 1793

Stebbing Shaw, *A tour to the West of England in 1788* (1789), 338–41, 441–5. The extract edited by Richard Pearse Chope, *Early Tours in Devon and Cornwall* (Devon and Cornwall Record Society, 1918, reprinted Newton Abbot, 1967), 215–216, 231–3 rewrote and omitted significant sections of Shaw's East Devon description.

Shaw's tour began and ended in London. He was a Fellow of Queen's College, Cambridge and later published *History and Antiquities of Staffordshire*. Shaw was twenty-six years old when he visited East Devon.

...Early next morning the sun's bright beams gave a more serene aspect to the sky, and we journeyed on the next stage to *Columpton*, situate on the river Columb. The general tenor of the country was rich, hilly and extensive. About halfway near the bleak hill of Maidendown, we pass the division of the two counties and enter Devon north east. The soil is various, the hills in these parts naturally barren, and the lower grounds fruitful, but the whole much improved by manure. The air is mild and healthful in the latter but very sharp on the former, which we now felt; and arrived at *Columpton* well prepared to enjoy a comfortable breakfast. This is a larger and better market town than the last, and displays more of the woollen manufacture. King Alfred bequeathed it to his youngest son Ethelward, with other lands in this county, Somerset and Hants.

From hence to Exeter we passed much hilly ground and through a very picturesque village of moss-clad houses, called Bradninch. Next saw on our right, Sir Thomas Ackland's at Columb-John, a very neat white mansion, beautifully situated under a wood-crowned knoll, surrounded with a park of deer, and a fine vale in front, graced with the pleasing objects of a lofty village tower, and distant hills. From the summit of Stockhill, two miles from Exeter, you have a glorious circular prospect, the ground gradually falling every way from this centre into a deep and beautiful vale, enriched with various seats, villages, and the fair city; the vast circumference rising again to a noble range of verdant mountains, heaped and intersected in most variegated order; while on their distant tops the sea-mark towers distinguish its frontier country, and the river *Ex* opening towards the south winds broadly to the channel. The common traffic and business of this country is mostly done by horses with panniers and crooks; the former are well known every where, but the latter are peculiar to the west, and are simply constructed, with four bent heavy sticks in the shape of panniers, but the ends awkwardly projecting above the rider's head; with these they carry large loads of hay or garden vegetables. The country people ride in a prodigious large boot of wood and leather hung instead of stirrup to the horse's side and half open, which they call gambados. Query whether [Henry William] Bunbury did not from hence take the idea of his burlesque horsemanship of Geoffry Gambado?...[travelling west to Cornwall and then returning to Exeter]

...In order to complete the remainder of our tour, much resembling in its outlines a figure 8, we now directed our course south east towards Dorchester. About half a mile from the city we pass the ancient and extensive pile of the laudable work-house or hospital before described; two miles beyond this, where the Topsham road parts to the right, is Heavitree gallows (so named from the adjacent village), with a square piece of ground enclosed by a strong wall, for the burial of sufferers; a plan I never remember to have seen before. The road now in a more gravely soil was excellent and uninterrupted by tedious hills; the surrounding enclosures of arable and pasture, glowed with fertility; while the happy seedsman, scattering round his showers of grain, hailed the smiling season with the voice of melody. Thus we journeyed on till we came within six miles of Honiton, from the brow of which hill we were presented with the sweetest scene of cultivation I ever held. This may be called the garden of Devon, not only from its own intrinsic superiority, but the beauteous order in which it is disposed; a fine amphitheatre of meadow and arable enclosure gradually ascending towards the south, in the highest cultivation, up to its natural boundary of open hills, ranged in all the uniformity of a perfect wall; to the east and north appears a similar circular defence, but not so strongly marked. Descending into this lovely vale, we saw on our left *Escott*, the seat of Sir George Yonge, a fine old place of good architecture and beautifully situated. A little farther the river Otter forms a sweet winding canal, where we pass a very picturesque scene of cots and ivy-mantled bridges. This spot, now only a decayed village called *Veniton*, is famous for a battle fought against the Cornish rebels in the reign of Edward VI. We now met numbers of market people with panniers, crooks and gambados.

Honiton is a neat market town situate on the river Otter; the country around it is beautiful. It was held before the conquest by Drago, a Saxon; in the Norman survey, it is described under the title of *Terra Comitis Moritonensis*, or lands belonging to Robert, Earl of Morton, half brother to the Conqueror, to whom he gave great possessions in these parts, and made him Earl of Cornwall. We afterwards find these lands bestowed by Henry I, on Richard de Redvers, created Earl of Devon, Lord of Okehampton, &c. From this family the title and lands of the Earls of Devon came to the Courtenays. This manor therefore being bestowed by Hugh Courtenay, upon his 5th son Philip, of Powderham Castle, near Exeter, has continued in his posterity, and is now part of the possessions of Viscount Courtenay, of that beautiful place. This town sends members to parliament, under the government of a portreeve, chosen annually at the court of the lord of the manor, who makes the return of the members elected by all the inhabitants, called burgage-holders. The present condition of this town is indebted to a dreadful fire, which broke out on July 19th, 1747, and reduced three parts of it to ashes, to the great distress of several hundred industrious inhabitants. The houses now wear a pleasing aspect, and the principal street extending from east to west is remarkably paved, forming a small channel well shouldered up on each side with pebbles and green turf, which holds a stream of clear water with a square dipping place opposite each door; a mark of cleanliness and convenience I never saw before. The first manufacture of serges was introduced into Devonshire at this town, but at present it is employed chiefly in making lace. It may be worth remarking, that the market day was here held before the reign of King John on Sunday, but changed by his direction it still continues on Saturday, which we now saw. After dining at an excellent inn, we proceeded over vast hills surrounded with beautiful vales; from the top of Honiton hill the landscape may vie with any part of this Kingdom.

Axminster, where we now arrived to repose, is a considerable market town, situate on the rive Axe, from whence, together with a minster erected here by King Athelstan, it has its name. This foundation was for seven priests, but afterwards reduced to two, for whom a portion of land was allotted, called priest-aller; which with the parsonage now belongs to two prebendaries of York, to pray for souls buried here, who were slain at the battle of Brunaberg, in a field, which is at present called King's-field. The manufacture of this place is chiefly carpets, and esteemed superior to the Wilton, being worked by the pliant fingers of small children, from patterns and colours laid before them. Thirteen shillings per yard is the lowest price, and from thence their value may be increased almost to any sum.

Leaving this town, we soon entered Dorsetshire...

EDWARD DANIEL CLARKE
of
LONDON, 1791

Coach by St Margaret's chapel, Honiton, 1795

Edward Daniel Clarke, *A Tour through the South of England, Wales and part of Ireland made during the summer of 1791* (1793), 48–50.

A traveller and son of Edward Clark, another noted traveller. He subsequently toured the continent and the mid-east. Clarke was later professor of mineralogy at Cambridge and university librarian. This tour was 'respectfully addressed' to 'those who can feel interested in the rambles of an Englishman, who can survey with pleasure a simple delineation of British scenery'. He travelled from London through Devon to Cornwall before visiting Wales, Ireland and the north of England as far as Lancashire. Clarke was aged twenty-two when he visited East Devon.

...From Bridport we came to Axminster, famous all over Europe for its carpet manufactory. I was surprised to find such a little, paltry place, the origin of so much magnificence. The manufactory is all the property of one man. The work is chiefly done by women. We saw forty of these employed; the pattern lays before them, and with their fingers they weave the whole. This they execute with great quickness, and it is amusing to observe how fast the most elegant designs are traced out by the fingers of old women and children. They were then employed in weaving a large carpet for Lord Harewood, late Mr Lascelles, which was to cost one hundred and forty pounds. A workshop is also building, solely for the purpose of making a single carpet for the Empress of Russia.

Leaving Axminster, we proceeded to Honiton, and descending a hill into the town, had for a mile and a half, one of the finest prospects in England. Indeed, from the great richness and fertility of the country, Devonshire abounds in beautiful prospects. Honiton is populous and flourishing. The manufactory of serges is carried on here to a considerable extent. By this means, the poor of every age, and sex, find employment, and the whole wears an appearance of industry and frugality. A stream of clear water passes on each side, through all the principal streets, a circumstance of essential utility to the inhabitants, and should they be subjected to a similar calamity, which befell them by fire, above forty years ago, the dreadful effects of it might be, in some measure, avoided.

After leaving Honiton, we reached Exeter about four o'clock in the afternoon...

William George Maton
of
Salisbury, 1794

Lane's aisle, Cullompton church, 1842

William George Maton, *Observations relative chiefly to the natural history, picturesque scenery and antiquities of the Western Counties of England, made in the years 1794 and 1796* (Salisbury, 1797), I, 80–85, 311–316. The extract by Richard Pearse Chope in *Early Tours in Devon and Cornwall* (Devon & Cornwall Record Society, 1918, reprinted Newton Abbot, 1967), 233–5, 273–4 omits extensive and significant sections from the East Devon description.

Maton became a Fellow of the Linnaean Society in the year of his tour to the West Country. He was appointed physician-extraordinary to Queen Charlotte in 1816 and to the Duchess of Kent and the infant Princess Victoria in 1820. Maton was twenty years old when he visited East Devon.

...Sidmouth being our next place of destination, on this day's journey we entered Devonshire. Not only another county, but a new scene, opened to us as we approached that town. Unlike the wide downs and frequent wastes, silent with desolation, in the county we had just left [Dorset], every part of the landscape now in view seemed, from the plenitude of its population, the extent of its cultivation and enclosures, and the luxuriance of its vegetation, almost itself alive.

— The roving sight
Pursued its pleasing course o'er neighbouring hills
Of many a different form, and different hue,
Bright with ripe corn, or green with grass, or dark
With clover's purple bloom.

Scot's *Amwell*

The mind dwelt with peculiar delight on the broad space in which the hands of man had been so industriously employed, and in which nature promised to remunerate him with plenty. We had now lost all vestiges of chalk, and from the fertility before us easily conceived how rich a change the soil had undergone. The former seemed to terminate about ten miles beyond Lyme, and is succeeded by a red sand. We quitted the high road about three miles from Sidmouth and descended into the town from one of the lofty ridges that command it on each side and bound a most charming vale.

Sidmouth is situated close to the sea, which is reddened by reflecting the colour of the cliffs. These are composed of sand, tinged by the red oxide of iron, and partly calcareous. Sand and pebbles have choked up the port, so that pleasure-boats and fishing-smacks are the only vessels that can touch at the shore. At the time of a clear summer sky, Sidmouth is intensely hot; its low situation, a broad bed of pebbles, and the glare of the lofty red cliffs act like so many reverberators. It is much frequented, however, in the bathing season, and many families continue their residence even during the winter. The situation is certainly a very delightful one. In our botanical excursions about Sidmouth, we found *Anchusa sempervirens* growing abundantly. The little *Arenaria rubra (marina)* literally covered the front of the cliffs on the shore, but unaccompanied by any other plant.

Taking leave of the coast for the present, we proceeded towards Exeter, through Ottery St. Mary. The red oxide of iron continued to tinge the soil the whole way, and, added to the richness of the surrounding scenery and the romantic winding of the road, exhibited a novel and agreeable effect. We descended into Ottery under the umbrage of widely-spreading trees; the branches of which screened the town from our view until we arrived close to it, but the venerable towers of the church sometimes peeped through the foliage.

Ottery St Mary is a place of some trade, manufactories of flannel, serge, &c. having been lately established here, through the laudable exertions of Sir George Younge, and Sir John Duntze, Barts. The town has certainly much to recommend it to attention, particularly the church, which is a fine ancient fabric. It was dedicated to St Mary. The manor and hundred were given by Edward the Confessor to the church of St Mary at Rouen, in Normandy. This prince, it will be recollected, was much attached to Normandy, on account of having been so long resident there; his mother too was a Norman princess. The chapter of Rouen afterwards sold the whole to John Grandison, Bishop of Exeter, who established a quarter college for a prior and secular priests, and built the present church, after the plan of St Peter's at Exeter. This took place in the reign of Edward III. The north porch of the church was built in the reign of Elizabeth, but the body of it and two fine square towers are part of the original structure. Narrow windows, more like loop-holes than any thing else, seem to have been in fashion when this church was built, though in the west front there is a noble circular one, ornamented with a good deal of tracery work. Several monuments were pointed out to us, belonging to very distinguished personages interred here. We did not view without interest an old mouldering turret, the only remains of a house once inhabited by the great Sir Walter Raleigh. There is another building deserving of notice just without the church-yard, where the old convention-room of Oliver Cromwell is shown to the traveller.

The road to Exeter is a broad, flat, dusty turnpike, augmenting the glare of the sun's rays by the redness of its surface. Clay now begins to preponderate in the soil, but a considerable portion of sand still remains mixed with it, so as to constitute a very rich loam, which seems to originate from the decomposition of a compact dark-coloured stone that lies very little below it. A new tribe of plants appeared; *Cotyledon Umbilicus*, *Hieracium subaudum*, *H. umbellatum* and *Polypodium Filix mas* were in profusion by the road sides…[travelling on to Exeter and Cornwall before returning]

Quite to Honiton the landscape continues uninterruptedly rich, and some of the highest hills are decorated to their summits with wood and luxuriant verdure. Arable, meadow, and pasture lands seemed to be in pretty equal proportions. Separation of property is made by hedge-rows, from which rise tall, slender elms pared almost to mere poles, it being the practice to strip them of their branches to a great part of their height. The multitude of villages scattered on all sides conspire with this sweet scene of cultivation (how deficient so ever it may be considered in picturesque effect) to produce on the mind the most pleasing impressions imaginable.

Honiton is situated in a most delightful vale watered by numberless streams and brooks. The river Otter flows through the town, which consists of a broad, handsome street running from east to west, and well paved. The parish church is half a mile distant, but there is a chapel, called Allhallows, within the place. A manufactory of lace is the only flourishing branch of business, yet Honiton is by no means deficient in population. It is a borough by prescription, and all the inhabitants who pay scot and lot are entitled to votes.

Axminster enjoys equal conveniences, in regard to water, with Honiton, the River Axe (from which it takes its name) running through the middle of the parish. The high road to Dorchester whither we were now proceeding led us through this neat, healthy town. From the reported antiquity of its foundation, we felt some curiosity to view the church, which is a heavy, but venerable structure, and has undergone various alterations at very different periods, as is evident from the various styles of architecture which it exhibits; no part of it, however, can be of so early a date as the reign of (its supposed founder) Athelstan. This monarch is said to have erected a minster here for seven priests, who he appointed to pray for the souls of some Saxon chiefs slain in the bloody battle of Brunenburgh, in Northumberland, and interred here. Unless the removal of a corpse to so distant a place of interment was in those times considered as the greater mark of respect, one can scarcely credit a story that assigns to the above personages graves at Axminster, even when supported by the authority of a Camden – see Gibson's first edition, page 23. It seems much more probable that the warriors to whom Athelstan paid these honours lost their lives on a subsequent occasion, when he came to quell a rebellion (of which William of Malmsbury makes mention) in these parts.

Axminster is famous for a manufactory of carpets, the process of weaving which is very different from any other that I have seen. They are woven in one entire piece, several hands being employed in conjunction at the same loom.

Seven miles north-east from Axminster, and four miles from Chard, stands *Ford* Abbey, the seat of J.F. Gwynn, Esquire. It was founded by Adelesia, Countess of Devonshire (the sister of Richard de Brioniis, and daughter of Albreda, niece of William the Conqueror), for monks of the Cistercian order – Grose's *Antiquities*, vol. 2, page 62. This building, beautifully situated on the banks of the river Axe, appears to have been converted into a mansion house at the time of the Dissolution. The south front is very extensive, and exhibits a curious and magnificent remain of monastic grandeur. The dormitory and cells of the monks, the cloister, (which is one hundred feet in length), the refectory, and a chapel are all entire and in fine preservation; the porch was built soon after the Dissolution, in the style of architecture that prevailed during the reigns of Edward VI and Elizabeth. In other parts the windows have been modernised, and some additions and alterations made. The furniture of many of the apartments seems to be coeval with the first secular inhabitants; *some* rooms, however, are fitted up in a more recent style, and Mr Gwynn is about to introduce other elegancies and conveniences of modern times. There are a few good portraits, though not disposed to the best advantage, and a picture (by Caracci) of Martha preparing for our Saviour. The gardens are laid out in the old taste, with hanging terraces and fish-ponds. A broad gravel walk extends a considerable way beyond the front of the house. The park contains sixty acres, and is well wooded with chestnut, beech, fir, and oak. Many of these trees appear to have stood for centuries. The hand of taste might still be employed with success – little else seems wanting to render *Ford* Abbey one of the noblest residences in the west of England, and it is certainly one of the most perfect *monastic* structures that time, depredation and fanaticism have left in this kingdom.

The chert with which the road is covered between Honiton and Axminster announced to us that we were not far distant from chalk, and at length, beyond Bridport we found the grand tract of it that stretches over the bleak downs of Wilts and Dorset. About Axminster indeed hills and ridges of chalk partially appear, and calcareous matter seems to commence not far eastward from the river Otter. There is limestone about Stockland, and quarries of it are worked at Beare near the coast…

The Reverend Thomas Rackett *of* Spettisbury, Dorset, 1794

Dorset Record Office, D/RAC:NU181, letter to his wife. See H.S.L. Dewar (ed.), *The Thomas Rackett Papers, 17th – 19th centuries* (Dorset Record Society, no. 3, 1964).

Rackett was rector of Spettisbury for more than sixty years. He was on a tour through Devon to Cornwall. Rackett was thirty-seven years old when he visited East Devon.

Exeter, August 15th

My dear love,

As I think you will like to hear how we go on, I write from hence to tell you that from Jone's we went to Lyme [Regis] where we stayed one night, it being too hot to travel for more than a few miles in one day. From thence we went to breakfast at Sidmouth, a very pretty bathing place in a very romantic situation, but as we did not travel for the sake of the amusements to be found at those places, we walked out horses after breakfast to Ottery, where we dined, & this morning we arrived here [Exeter] where there is a fine cathedral & the country round about us is very beautiful…

The Reverend John Skinner *of* Camerton, Somerset, 1797, 1829

Budleigh Salterton from the sea, *c.*1855

British Library, Add. MSS 28793/45–8 and Somerset Record Office, DD/SAS C/1193/10. The Somerset copy has been edited by Roger Jones, *West Country Tour: Diary of an excursion through Somerset, Devon and Cornwall in 1797* (Bradford on Avon, 1985), 25–8. There are considerable differences between the two manuscripts.

Skinner was greatly interested in archaeology and was twenty-five years old on this first visit to East Devon and fifty-seven on the second. Skinner was the incumbent of Camerton in Somerset from 1800 until his death (by suicide) in 1839. He may have wanted to be remembered, as one of his namesakes before him, as 'a burning and shining light'. He bequeathed his manuscripts to the British Museum. Skinner's publications include *Ten days' tour through the isle of Anglesea [in] December 1802.*

1797

Somerset Record Office, DD/SAS C/1193/10

[September 27]...From Exeter I proceeded to Sidmouth, the place of my destination, fifteen miles distant, to dinner: the roads rough, but the views interesting. The place from its low situation on the beach is sheltered and warm, it being surrounded on every side except towards the sea, by high hills; the pleasantness of its situation of late years, has attracted many bathers, though its beach is by no means so well adapted to the purpose, as a more shelving sandy shore, it being a bank of shingles, or large pebbles, and the sea deep, and at times very rough near the coast. At present, there are but four machines employed, and the gentlemen and ladies, engage them indiscriminately. To remedy in some measure the inconvenience of the loose beach, the inhabitants, have formed a gravel walk nearly a quarter of a mile in length, facing the sea, which is the usual resort for the company, also a thatched building to shelter them in bad weather, and a billiard table. They have besides, a spacious assembly and card room, where they meet six evenings in the week, during the season, which are in general well attended, the subscription being half a guinea, and two shillings on coming into the room on a ball night. There is a good inn called the London Inn kept by civil people where there is a *Table d' Hote* at a moderate expense.

September 28

I took lodgings at 18s per week and agreed for my horse at 12s. Met Mr Amyatt of Hampshire who is staying here with his wife and daughter on telling me it was his intention to visit Exmouth and Teignmouth the following day I accepted the invitation of accompanying them being desirous of seeing these watering places to form a comparison between them and Sidmouth.

September 29

Left Sidmouth at seven this morning after passing a mountain almost perpendicular called Peak Hill and traversing a good deal of uneven ground arrived at Exmouth about two and whilst the horses were preparing to cross the ferry walked with Mr Amyatt to a gentleman's house of the name of Evans when on entering this room we were surprised to meet with Sir John D'Oyly just returned from taking leave of his son who had been detained for nearly two months on his passage to India by contrary winds in Torbay. We here were very hospitably entertained and it was fortunate for us that we laid in some stock of provender as we did not arrive at Teignmouth till after eight o'clock.

Exmouth in point of situation and extent is superior to Sidmouth and the beach is much better adapted for bathing. The river *Ex* when the tide is in affords beautiful scenery. Lord Courtnay's, Mr Baring's and many other gentlemen's seats being on the banks. At low water the smell of the mud must be very unpleasant. I understand the company who frequent this place live more to themselves than they do at Sidmouth and in many respects it appears preferable. Passed over the ferry between five and six o'clock which indeed is not a little dangerous in the manner they contrive it. The carriage being placed in a boat so very much confined that the wheels and part of the perch hang over the water and should any sudden blast have taken the side of the carriage in that situation it would be in great danger of oversetting. I think they charged Mr Amyatt 7s 6d for passing besides the horses...

1829

British Library, Add.33714, fos 272–4, 285–99.

[October 20]...Arriving at Cullompton, which arrives [sic] its name from its situation between two streams. We baited the horse at a small inn and took the opportunity of visiting the church, which is a curious old building with a chapel attached to it, which a black lettered inscription round the walls informs us, was built in the year 1525, by a person of the name of Lane, who appears to have been a Clothier, the emblems of shears &c &c represented represented [sic] in the buttresses; also vessels and commercial emblems: the inscription as follows:

In honour of God, and his blessed Mother Mary: remember the soul of John Lane...(*wap at nil anacre*), the soul of Tomlyn his wife, to have in memory with all other their children and [?]pends of your own charity which were founders of this chapel: and here lyeth in sepulchre the year of our lord God II thousand five hundred six and twenty. God of his grace on their both souls to have mercy and finally [send] them to the eternal glory Amen for Charity.

I also copied an inscription on a flat stone near the Chancel door, fixed against the wall to the memory of William Skinner, Vicar of Cullompton, who died in 1643; it is as follows, Mr William Skinner, Master in Arts, sometime Pastor of this place, who deceased December 10, *Ann. Dom.* 1643. The Epitaph within the border on which the inscription was cut is as follows:

Where zeal with knowledge meet there's light and fire
Light to discern what's fit ardent desire
Th' one darting ray's, th' other its heat on far our
Friend's great parts in soul on others shone.
With zeal did warm inflame more hearts than one
justly affirm they that knew Skinner might
He was a burning and a shining light
In a separate compartment was inscribed:
He was a burning and a shining light.

There was some ancient carved work and painted oak on the screen and roofing of the church, but I noticed no old monuments, if we except a representation of skulls and bones, which used to [be] placed near the entrance door, as a *memento mori*, but it has been removed and placed on the pavement. We left Cullompton a little after two, and had a delightful drive to Exeter, the river Culm accompanying us a great part of the way, flowing in a rich meadow to the right of the road; Culm implies the enclosure of the ic, made by the water, the river deriving its name from the settlement between the streams at Cullompton. Before we arrived at Poltimore, the seat of Sir George Bamfylde, we noticed the beautiful well wooded Park of Sir Thomas Ackland to the left. The house is well placed on the side of a verdant hill, well sheltered with woods: the bright autumnal tint on the trees, heightened by the glow of a fine and cloudless sky, set off the rich scenery to the greatest advantage: the name Poltimore seems to betoken a place situated near the Portway or waterpass leading to Exeter. The church in this village is a fine old structure, and the incumbent, one of the Bampfylde family, at present occupies the Manor House. We got to Exeter about four o'clock...

...Leaving Exeter, I proceeded along the Honiton road through *Heavytree* Turnpike Gate. I suppose *Heavytree* is a corruption of Abertre or avytre, that is, the tre or residence near the Portway or passage to the water. *Clist* (*ie clys et*) Honiton, and Rock Bere (crocber) indicate the same things, namely, outposts on the line of the public road. I arrived at St Mary Ottery, or Ottery St Mary, a little after eleven, and went immediately to the Old Church dedicated to St Mary. The term *Ot er ii* implies the Oet or water settlement of the *erii,* or road leading to the water. The Church seems to have been constructed in imitation of Exeter Cathedral, having two Towers at the transepts, very small lancet windows light the side aisles. There are two Monuments, apparently about the time of Edward III, under gothic canopies. My conductor said they were called Gog and Magog. Having read on a monumental inscription the name of a place called Cadhay, I asked whether the house was far from Ottery? and learnt it was not more than half a mile. I engaged my learned guide at the church to conduct me thither, being assured from the name it was an outpost to some stronghold, Hay signifying a fort or enclosed port, and Cad a camp, or stronghold. The house is now occupied by the parson who rents the estate, formerly the family of the Haydons were owners of the place for many generations. Query, does no the name Haydon given from the place they occupied, it being synonymous with Cadhay; since dun implies a stronghold, as well as Cad; but this by the way. Having made a sketch of the old mansion, I was returning back to Ottery, when the person who rents the property overtook us and on enquirying of him whether there was no some strong camp in the neighbourhood of his house? He answered in the affirmative, and pointed to an eminence on a ridge of hill about a mile distant from his residence, where he said were some high banks round the top of the hill, which was called the Castle (Cadsle); that a bank was extended from the summit, for a great length, nearly a mile, which joined the Turnpike: that the house he inhabited was much more ancient inside, than it appeared to be from the point I took it: that there was a very long room with small windows, which looked into a Court, which was called the Queen's Court, because the Statues of Queen Elizabeth, her sister Mary, and Brother Edward, were in that Court; also one of Henry VIII their father: these were in good preservation he informed me and would have been most happy to have shown them to me. He moreover said, that the Castle (or Cadsle) belonged to Sir John Kennaway, who lived in a house called Escot Lodge, not far distant (es cad); that he had occupied this place ever since the house he purchased of Sir George Younge had been burnt down. How well I remember calling on this gentleman with Mr Amyatt nearly thirty years ago. Lady Kennaway was Mr Amyatt's daughter, and I believe god-daughter to my Mother. The old baronet is quite blind. His wife is alive, as also his wife's sister, Mrs Philips. Had time permitted, I would certainly have paid my respects to them, but the weather being very uncertain I wished to make the rest of my way to Seaton. There is a fine stream which runs under Ottery St Mary, and a brook which passes through the streets and flows into it. The animal called Otter derived its name from having its et or seat on the au or o, namely water.

Leaving St Mary Ottery, followed an interesting road for three miles to the bottom of *Chinway* [Chineway] Hill, where I was obliged to dismount and walk my horse to the summit. Chin way seems to be improperly pronounced, from the Saxon Cynpez, implying the main or principal way from the coast, probably to Exeter; as it is to be remembered that the Bay of Seaton was the principal harbour on the Coast, even till a late period, I mean within these 500 years, and in all, probability there was a Roman road ran on the line of the present Turnpike or nearly so. The summit of *Chinway* Hill is clothed by a dark heath. Slowly getting into cultivated plantations of Scots Firs, occasionally skirting the road; from one point I made a sketch of an opening at the extremity of the valley above Sidmouth, which will convey a tolerable idea of the hilly district between Exeter and the Channel. A large party of gypsies, with no less than five horses and donkeys, moreover formed an appropriate accompaniment to this heath scenery. Having gained another acclivity, I found the road across Honiton, which pointed towards Roncombe Turnpike house, running the whole way through groups of barrows, some of them 100 yards in circuit, and planted with firs. As this road traversed Farway (Feppez) Parish, which implies the way or road of the fer or passage, I became fully assured that I was on the line of the original road. Never have I seen so many tumuli within the space of a mile, as on this hill near Roncombe Turnpike house. There is a deep valley running towards the Coast in the direction of Sidmouth. Beyond this, I sketched two Barrows of large dimensions; one measuring 120 yards in circuit at the base, the other about 90. The road passes between them. As the sea is full in view in front of the Barrows, signals might have been conveyed inland from them. I cannot help thinking from the level surface of that marked B, that fires were sometimes made thereon as signals. My sketch will best explain the appearance of these remains. The road, as it descends from the heights, passes through a deep valley covered with wood, and soon emerging again, proceeds to the left at a point where one branch diverges to go to *Bere* [Beer], the more westerly arm of the Bay. It rained with great violence, the whole way as I descended the hill to Seaton, which prevented my sketching the high land on the opposite side of the *Ax* river, which I doubt not was the *Moridunum*, not Seaton; for the banks are steepened by art and the range of hill terminates in an abrupt cliff above the sea. Having put up my carriage at the Inn, and the weather holding up, I walked on the beach and fully ascertained the harbour between Axmouth and Seaton. The southern termination of the cliff before mentioned is still called by the inhabitants Heaven Cliff, that is, Haven Cliff, the place of passage. The Dunum must have been situate above this river Ax, exactly similar to Old Mixton Hill, above the river Ax, in Somersetshire; and both these rivers had their denomination from flowing beneath the stronghold.

I returned to dinner before five, and had afterwards sufficient light to walk to Seaton Church, which is built, if I mistake not on a Fort, close to which the vessels lay, when the level was covered with water. The field next adjoining the Churchyard rises with a steep bank above the level, and is called at the present day The Merchant's Road, but of this more tomorrow. I made two sketches in order to show the situation of Seaton Church nearly opposite to Axminster Church, with the Bay between, and having penned in my sketches and brought up my Journal to this time, I went to bed.

October 23

I left my bed ere the Sun rose, and as soon as I could leave the house, proceeded to the shore with the intent of visiting the ridge of high ground on the further side of the *Ax* river, where it empties itself into the Sea. The line of beach from Seaton to this point cannot be less than half a mile; a bar of shingles having choked up the Bay, in which they formed a walk for the company who visit the place, but no bathing machines. Having crossed the river in a Ferry Boat I enlisted a lad who conveyed me over, to accompany me to the *Dunum*, for such I found it was. A little above the Ferry, we ascended by the ancient pass between, leading to the Heaven: the division of this towering hill, nearer to the Sea, is called Heaven, or rather Haven Cliff; that position, running towards Axmouth, of the *Dunum,* whose banks are as steep as the roof of a house, is denominated Ball Haven; that is, the Bal, or fortified place, above the passage: the road passing straight up this defile, was called, as my conductor pronounced it, Worn higher land: Waren, or Faren would indicate an ancient way, and this I doubt not was the Portway by which the Britons passed from the *Moridunum* or strong settlement above the Sea to the Port. This lane I found, on subsequent inquiry joined the road leading to Lyme, about two miles beyond. The sketches I made 1, 2, 3, and 4, will best explain the well guarded pass from the top of the Haven

Cliff. I saw three towering hills; one contiguous to the *Dunum*, called Oxen Hill, that is, the en, or projection of the oic or ox, the fortress over the water.

My guide said there was a large camp on this hill, and that people had found money, and various articles; indeed a superstitious opinion seems to prevail that treasures are there hidden under the guardianship of evil spirits; since the boy assured me, that one 5th of November, when they made a bonfire on the hill, large stones were thrown by some invisible hand, and if they had not dispersed, their arms or their legs would have been broken moreover, that a man who lived at Axmouth, had permission to take as much as he would from one hoard, on condition that he told no one of the circumstance; but he could not conceal it from his wife; after which, although he went frequently to the place he could not find it again. Deriving very different conclusions from these stories, and supposing that some Roman Coin had been found within the Camp in times past, I made an agreement with my guide, who seemed to be an intelligent lad, to meet me at Axmouth in the course of an hour and a half; and I returned across the beach to my quarters. I forgot to mention that the cliff on the extremity of this *Moridunum* or height above the Sea, seems to be separating, and in the course of a short time, I doubt not but a large mass will fall to the great joy of the collectors of Antediluvian fossils.

While on the beach, before I turned off, to pass through the village to the Inn, I stopped to make a sketch, showing the heights I had just quitted and the level on which the tide once flowed. Some admirer of Sea Views, has lately erected a house on the shingly beach: the windows facing the ocean. Such a person might as well pass his days in guardship: *sed de gustibus nil disputandum*. Had it been low water, my horse and carriage might have crossed the *Ax* by a ford, as the boy informed me, which would have saved me five miles: as it was, I was constrained to drive to Colyford Bridge, upwards of two miles from Seaton, where is a causeway across the level. Coly implies the Hill above the water; that is, the towering heights above Axmouth. Doubtless the passage was performed at low water in ancient times, across the level from Axmouth to Seaton, near the Church, perhaps a considerable portion of the level might then have been traversed at low water, and the river crossed by a Ferry boat.

As I again passed Seaton Church, I again made observation on the field called Merchant's road. If the Romans had a settlement or outpost at Seaton, I think it must have been at this place, but I could not meet with any indications of pottery in the newly made graves, or of Roman bricks in the Church Yard walls: some of the stones seemed better squared than what one might have expected in so rough a work: but there were no tokens one might depend on to fix their actual residence here. On arriving at the Turnpike gate, instead of taking the Lyme road to the left, I turned off to Axmouth, to the right, passing a square built mansion, called *Stitcombe* [Stedcombe] House, the residence of a Mr Hassel. *It ys et combe*, implies the seat in the Valley, leading to the water. A road from hence appears to have ascended the North side of Oxen hill, leading to the camp, as I have endeavoured to describe in my sketch. The lower road, by which I drove to Axmouth, had been made I imagine at a much later date, then the time of the Romans and Britons. Having met with my former guide, and under his direction, put up my horse and carriage at a Farm House, I walked to the church, since I generally find that in all places the Church stood in the midst of the fort station or settlement of the ancients, and for this plain reason, because the roads usually centred there. There is nothing interesting in the exterior of the edifice, like at Seaton: there is a square embattled tower, which might occasionally have been used for defence, as well as for a Belfry, but the windows in the body of the Church are not perhaps more ancient than the time of Henry VII. The door way may boast a higher antiquity of three or four centuries, being the Anglo Norman form employed in Henry Irst's reign. The pillars are circular which support the roof of the Nave; but the arches are pointed. Since I have seen the Churches in Normandy, I am assured that the pointed arch was used as early as the time of the Conqueror, since they are to be found in the Church he built at Caen; but whether they were introduced into England before the time of Stephen, I cannot take upon myself to determine. This I know, that Furness Abbey, in the North, was built by him, when Count de Blois, has pointed arches; but of this en passant. Having made my sketch of the doorway, and finished my perambulation of the Churchyard, in order to see whether there was any appearance of an ancient fortress, indicated by banks and walls, but to no purpose.

I retraced my steps in order to ascend the Castle Hill, which was indeed an arduous undertaking; since my young guide led me up a steep, as precipitous as the roof of a house; so that I was frequently obliged to put my hands to the ground to prevent slipping. The fortress occupied the extremity of the lofty ridge, facing the West, and was surrounded by an agger from ten to twelve feet high, to the land side; that is, where a transverse branch was made to guard the approach over the ridge. The bank cannot be less than forty feet on the slop of the bottom of the ditch. Beyond this again, there was another bank about a hundred yards to the eastward: this has very much from the appearance of a Roman work; but I could meet with corroborative testimony that the Camp was occupied by these Conquerors: the are within the lines is from seven to eight acres, and has been in tillage time out of mine; indeed two yokes of oxen were then engaged in turning up the soil, which is flinty and by no means dark. The farmer who was overlooking his men, could give no information of Roman coins or pottery having been picked up here; but he has the same story as the [lad] related of treasure trove.

I could clearly trace the old road, passing obliquely from *Stidcombe* on the north side of the Castle Hill. It entered the Fosse at the North side of the Castle Hill and continued under the steep bank to the East: descending the south east side of the hill and apparently crossing the Dunum, which I noticed this morning before breakfast, but now had an opportunity of assuring myself of its being really such; as all the banks are strongly guarded by banks rising one above the other on the slope of the hill: the road which descended from Castle Hill, after crossing the valley above Axmouth and the old road to Lyme ascends to the Dunum near a Farm House called the Steps (that is, place of passage). My sketch will best show the side of the Dunum, as it appears from Oxen Hill Camp, which to all appearance was an outpost to this strong and extensive settlement of the Britons. Had time permitted, I would have traced the road which led to it from the East, and descended to the haven. There might have been a settlement of the Romans among the Britons upon the Dunum, which from situation, and the several trenches attached to it must have been the Moridunum, since Seaton can have no possible claim to this denomination. Having a farewell sketch of the lofty agger to the East, which reminded one of that risen on Maes Knole Camp in Somersetshire, I descended to where I had left my carriage, and was soon on the road to Lyme. This place was so named from *el y on* or water enclosure, hence the Greek λτμνυς harbour. I had not proceeded above two miles up a steep hill, when I stopped to make a sketch of a towering height called Musbury (*quasi* Maesbury) hill, on which are the lines of a stronghold, and the appearances of a British road running toward Oxen hill. I doubt not but all these British holds were connected by the public roads: in fact they guarded the passes through the country. If the Romans had a station at Axminster, they might have had a vicinal way to the coast, leading at the base of this ridge of hill, instead of passing from one fortress to another, over this Alpine Country...

George Lipscomb
c.1798

Gateway to Shute House, 1803

George Lipscomb, *A Journey into Cornwall through the counties of Southampton, Wilts, Dorset, Somerset & Devon interspersed with remarks, moral, historical, literary and political* (1799), 140–51, 343.

Lipscomb began his journey at Portchester and travelled through East Devon en route to Cornwall. He wrote that his journey was originally intended 'solely with an intention of affording some amusement for the leisure hours of a Friend, he feels a considerable degree of embarrassment in exposing it to the public eye'. Lipscomb explained that his book was adapted from a series of letters and edited to remove remarks that were too personal for publication. He undertook the tour, with several companions, sometime between 1796 and 1798 when he was appointed Deputy Recorder of Warwick. He was born in 1773, making him in his mid twenties on his travels through East Devon and died in 1846. Lipscomb was trained as a surgeon and had worked at St Bartholomew's Hospital in London. Among his other publications were *The History and Antiquities of the County of Buckingham*, *A description of Matlock Bath* and *A Journey into South Wales*.

...Pursuing the road to Axminster through a narrow lane, we met with vast quantities of that celebrated diuretic fox-glove, the *Digitalis purpureus* of *Linnaeus*; and remarked, that this plant appears to grow to a much larger size in Devonshire, than in any other part of England which we had seen.

A close road brought us to a Common abounding with plovers; and at the extremity of it passed a fine clear stream, flowing into a valley on the left, and emptying itself into the sea at the very point where an opening to the water has been already noticed.

The church of Axminster presents itself to your view, when at the distance of about two miles from the town. You now meet with several branches of the river *Ax*, one of which is so rapid as to turn a mill.

There is a small neat habitation of white stone chequered with flints, upon an eminence on the right, before you enter the town, called *Clocum* [Cloakham].

Axminster is a most miserable town. The houses are extremely mean, and many of them covered with thatch. They are in general built with a rugged kind of stone, produced everywhere in this part of the country.

The Church stands in the middle of the town, and is an irregular building of some antiquity, as appears by the entrance on the south side, which is under a Saxon arch, now, in no good condition.

This building has suffered considerably since it's first erection. There is at present one aisle, attached to the north side, with a parapet highly ornamented; but the Saxon arch above-mentioned opens immediately into the body of the Church; there being no aisle on that side.

There is a gravel walk with some rows of elms around the churchyard, which would have a pleasing effect if it were not cooped up in an enclosure of the most shabby houses I ever saw.

All the streets are narrow, crooked, and in the highest degree inconvenient and disgusting: there is, indeed, a most excellent Inn, at which, with the best provisions the country affords, the traveller may console himself, for the scarcity of objects without doors, deserving his curiosity or attention.

Here, we had a good dinner and a handsome desert, and first tasted that luxury of the west called clotted cream, which is always served up with their tarts. This delicacy is made by scalding the whole of the milk as it is drawn from the cow, and then exposing it to the air for several hours. I must not omit to mention the carpet manufactory, which is certainly well worth seeing; and this branch is brought to so great perfection, that the carpets made here, are equally durable and elegant as the Turkey carpets imported.

We saw several, under the hands of the different labourers, the colours of which were wonderfully clear and beautiful: the price varies from thirteen shillings to twenty-five and upwards, per yard. The persons employed are Women and Children, and it is really astonishing to see with how much facility the latter are brought to the knowledge of this kind of work, by which so many are enabled to earn their bread, who would not otherwise be capable of contributing in any degree, towards their own maintenance and support.

In one of the rooms at the Inn above mentioned, is hung up, a copy of an Epitaph on Mr Walter, formerly a representative in Parliament for Devonshire, which though not remarkable for it's elegance of composition, conveys so handsome a compliment to the memory of a worthy and distinguished character that I felt a strong impulse to transcribe it.

Unspotted by an imputation of deviating from the strictest independency in Parliament, nor blindly attached to any set of men, he, with those principles of inflexible justice, which first recommended him to the honor of a seat for this County, persevered in support of, or opposition to measures, as they appeared conducive or destructive to the trust in him reposed.

The loss of the private Gentleman is universally felt, as his virtues were universally expanded. To the indigent around his mansions, he extended his beneficence; to the industrious labourer he contributed daily support. Public charities testified his liberal assistance; and the channel of friends conveyed (unconfined by party) alleviation to private distress. Christianity excited his incessant attention: conspicuous by private example in his own family; and by many enlarged subscriptions to dilate it's influence. Without ostentation but with a conscious pleasure in his duty, he hath gained to himself, through the one Mediator, an immortal reward. So valuable a character being now no more, we have this consolatory prospect, that his virtues with this fortune, will descend in a like copious stream.

Reader!
To whom Virtue! To whom Piety!
To whom your Country is pleasant,
Stop!
much to be lamented by thee,
fell,
John Rolle Walter, Esq.
Of noble lineage
Nobler by Virtue!
A Man!
A Friend!
Fairer than whom the Earth did ne'er produce!
A Brother most brotherly to all!
In the British Parliament,
Perhaps not so splendid
Nor greedy of fame,
But just, firm, and resolute,
Amongst base and corrupted Ministers,
Of the Province of Devonshire
He best deserved.
He was a Man much to be praised
And
Much to be lamented.
He died the 27th of November 1779.

The road from Axminster to Honiton, after passing through the small village of *Kilverton* [Kilmington] crosses a heath from whence there is a view of Axminster. A little further on, an irregular hill half a mile to the right of the road, affords a most picturesque and entertaining prospect; the declivity being covered with small verdant fields of cattle, interspersed with coppices, and here and there, a rural farmhouse.

This hill appears part of the boundary of a remarkably fine valley of great extent, where the wandering eye is soon lost in the shades of the woods, and the approximation of those most distant, to the horizon itself. As you descend into the valley there is an entrance, on the left, to Shute House, the seat of Sir John De-La-Pole Bart. The horned cattle here, are extremely beautiful, but of a small size; their colour is most commonly a dusky red, or brindled, and the horn short and blackish.

Before you reach Honiton, the road takes a serpentine course, and gives an enchanting view of that town and the hills which shelter it: and on the right is an ancient encampment, upon an eminence which commands the road from Chard.

There is a large white house just beyond Honiton, and the prospect is not a little improved by the neatness of the turnpike-house, which is a building in the form of a Roman D; having its walls stuccoed and surmounted with battlements.

Honiton is a handsome town, with a noble high street very broad and well paved; but it is at present much disfigured by an old decayed Market House, standing in the middle of the street.

The reason for this nuisance being permitted to remain, is, that an old gentleman enjoys a lifehold estate in it: but it is said, that the Lord of the Manor, Viscount Courtenay, has obtained an Act of Parliament, enabling him to remove it on the death of this person; which will make so great an improvement in the street, that it may then vie in breadth and elegance with almost any one, out of the Metropolis.

Honiton being in the direct road from London to Exeter, and only one stage from the latter, has an amazing thoroughfare for carriages and passengers, by whom it is constantly enlivened.

A roman military way formerly ran through Axminster and Honiton to Exeter: it came from Cirencester in Gloucestershire, out of Akeman Street way, and united at Bath-Easton with a smaller road called *Via Badonica*; but the place where it falls in with the turnpike, between Crewkerne and Axminster, is not now so easy to be discovered.

About four miles from Honiton, we passed three small bridges, over as many rapid streams. The country people call this place Minnyberges, a corruption of Fenny bridges. The hamlet is in the parish of Ottery. Two miles beyond it, stands *Escott*, a large old house, with fine trees about it, at some distance from the road. It was formerly the residence of Sir George Yonge, K.B. many years one of the representatives for Honiton; but now the property of Sir John Kennaway.

The cross roads in this part of Devonshire being close, and inconvenient for the passage of wheel carriages of all kinds, the produce of the land, as well as merchandize, is chiefly carried by horses upon a sort of frame called a Crook; which is made of wood, bent in a peculiar manner, so as to be capable of having packages tied upon it.

These horses are not secured with traces, but run loose in troops, consisting of five or ten, having either one or two men mounted upon other horses, to drive them. When they are in small numbers, the driver is commonly seated on the top of the load, and trots, or sometimes, even gallops along, with the greatest unconcern, up hill and down, and over the roughest ground; perfectly regardless of every thing he meets with, and without the least apparent apprehension on his own account, notwithstanding he is elevated so high, as to be in eminent danger of suffering considerable injury, if the animal should make one false step.

Loads of straw, hay, wood, and furze, are all conveyed in the same manner, and the horses which carry them are no small annoyance to any unfortunate passenger whose steed may happen to be restiff [stationary or refusing to go forward], or who may, by chance, approach too near the crooks, which in these narrow roads it is very difficult to keep clear of, with the utmost circumspection.

I observed in the vicinity of Exeter, that the loose gravely soil assumed a redder colour, and before we came into that City, the road, which is cut through high banks of sand, is covered with loose stones like the rust of iron...

...We travelled over the same ground we had before passed, to Axminster, of which, from the unfavourableness of the weather, we did not at all increase our good opinion: although it certainly afforded us both reason and opportunity to strengthen what was before advanced in praise of the accommodations to be met with at the George Inn. The road from Axminster to Bridport is very hilly...

The Reverend Anthony William Glynn *of* Kingston, The Isle of Wight, 1798

Isle of Wight Record Office, OG/TT/71.

The Reverend Glynn was on a tour through Dorset to Cornwall. He was rector of Kingston on the Isle of Wight but his family was Cornish and hailed from Glynn near Bodmin. He died in 1819.

The country from Wooton to Axminster is barren & unpleasant but becomes more fertile toward Honiton which is situated in a very rich vale, and from Honiton to Exeter the road runs thro' a fertile, well-wooded country.

Axminster is a dirty little town. A large carpet manufactory is carried on there. Honiton is a bad town – between that town & Exeter on the right is *Escott*, the seat of Sir George Young. & near Exeter a fine view on the left down the river Exe to Topsham &c…[to Exeter and return] From Exeter the road lays thro' a very rich & beautiful country, which is well wooded & watered by the river *Ex* to Tiverton, an indifferent town. About 4 miles from Exeter on the right (I suppose about two miles from the road is [Killerton] the seat of Sir Thomas Ackland). The country continues very rich & fine from Tiverton to Holcombe. From Holcombe to Nettlecombe the country is very rich…

ROBERT SOUTHEY
of
WESTBURY, 1799, AND KESWICK, 1802, 1824

St Margaret's chapel, Honiton, 1795

Southey made a number of tours through the West Country partly because of his friendship with Samuel Taylor Coleridge. Accounts of two of these tours, in 1799 and again in 1824, were written in Southey's personal papers while the third, of 1802, was composed, and published, as if written by a Spanish visitor. Southey was less than complementary, but at least consistent, as will be seen by comparing his private writings with the public descriptions. He died in 1843.

1799

John Wood Warter (ed.), *Southey's Common-Place Book Fourth Series* (1850), 522.

A week after his travels in East Devon in 1799 Southey, then aged twenty-five years old, wrote from Exeter to his younger brother Thomas 'We could get no lodgings at Seaton, Sidmouth or along that coast so we housed ourselves at Hobson's Choice at Exeter': Kenneth Curry (ed.), *New Letters of Robert Southey* (New York, 1965), I, 199. The following year he visited Cullompton and noted that it was 'one of those towns where the innkeepers have enough business to make them procure good accommodations, and not enough to render them negligent': Warter, *Common-Place Book*, 524.

Tuesday, August 27

To Taunton twelve [miles], to Honiton eighteen. At Honiton they put the Coleridges into a chaise with cart-horses. We were told that the towns-people there are remarkably dishonest, and have been so ever since the borough has been venal. On the road is one rich view over the vale of Taunton.

Wednesday, 28

To Seaton twelve. A hilly and uninteresting road, for some miles over an open heath so luckily lonely that we found our trunk, which fell off some half mile before it was mist. At Seaton no lodgings were to be had. It is a high, open, naked Dorsetshire sort of country, with nothing to make me leave it with regret or remember it with pleasure. To St Mary Ottery, twelve. The church here is very beautiful, the place itself remarkable as the birth-place of Gower, and Browne the Pastoral Poet and Coleridge.

From Ottery I walked with S.T. Coleridge to *Budley Salcome*; on the way we past the mansion of Sir Walter Raleigh. In Lord Rolle's park are the finest beeches I ever saw, one in particular which is quite dead, but in its ramifications even more beautiful than the summer trees; it branched into three great branches, one of which shot immediately into three smaller ones. The Otter enters the sea at *Budley Salcombe*. I forded it at its mouth. The scenery upon the river is tame and soothing; like all the Devonshire rivers it often overflows.

Also we went to Sidmouth, a nasty watering place, infested by lounging ladies, and full of footmen. [then to Exeter and Plymouth. Two months later he visited Honiton and noted 'The vale rich and beautiful.']

1802

Don Manuel Alvarez Espriella, *Letters from England* (1814 edn), I, 29–34. The edition by Richard Pearse Chope, *Early Tours in Devon and Cornwall* (Devon & Cornwall Record Society, 1918, reprinted Newton Abbot, 1967) on pages 309 to 310 has minor differences with the original.

Southey's *Letters from England* was published under his pen-name. Southey was already established as an author by the time of his *Letters* and had previously visited Spain and Portugal. He was 28 years old on this visit to East Devon.

...We departed [from Exeter] about noon the next day; and as we ascended the first hill looked down upon the city and its cathedral towers to great advantage. Our stage was four leagues, along a road which, a century ago, when there was little travelling, and no care taken of the public ways, was remarkable as the best in the West of England. The vale of Honiton, which we overlooked on the way, is considered as one of the richest landscapes in the kingdom: it is indeed a prodigious extent of highly cultivated country, set thickly with hedges and hedge-row trees; and had we seen it either in its full summer green, or with the richer colouring of autumn, perhaps I might not have been disappointed. Yet I should think the English landscape can never appear rich to a southern eye: the verdure is indeed beautiful and refreshing, but green fields and timber trees have neither the variety not the luxuriance of happier climates. England seems to be the paradise of sheep and cattle; Valencia of the human race.

Honiton, the town where we changed chaises, has nothing either interesting or remarkable in its appearance, except that here, as at Truro, a little stream flows along the street, and little cisterns or basins, for dipping places are made before every door. Lace is manufactured here in imitation of the Flanders lace, to which it is inferior because it thickens in washing; the fault is in the thread. I have reason to remember this town, as our lives were endangered here by the misconduct of the innkeeper. There was a demur about procuring horses for us; a pair were fetched from the field, as we afterwards discovered, who had either never been in harness before, or so long out of it as to have become completely unmanageable. As soon as we were shut in, and the driver shook the reins, they ran off – a danger which had been apprehended; for a number of persons had collected round the inn door to see what would be the issue. The driver, who deserved whatever harm could happen to him, for having exposed himself and us to so much danger, had no command whatever over the frightened beasts; he lost his seat presently, and was thrown upon the pole between the horses; still he kept the reins, and almost miraculously prevented himself from falling under the wheels, till the horses were stopped at a time when we momentarily expected that he would be run over and the chaise overturned. As I saw nothing but ill at this place, so have I heard nothing that is good of it: the borough is notoriously venal; and since it has become so the manners of the people have undergone a marked and correspondent alteration.

This adventure occasioned considerable delay. At length a chaise arrived; and the poor horses, instead of being suffered to rest, weary as they were, for they had just returned from Exeter, were immediately put to for another journey. One of them had been rubbed raw by the harness. I was in pain all the way, and could not but consider myself as accessory to an act of cruelty: at every stroke of the whip my conscience upbraided me, and the driver was not sparing with it. It was luckily a short stage of only two leagues and a quarter. English travelling, you see, has its evils and its dangers. The life of a post-horse is truly wretched:– there will be cruel individuals in all countries, but cruelty here is a matter of calculation: the postmasters find it more profitable to overwork their beasts and kill them by hard labour in two or three years, than to let them do half the work and live out their natural length of life. In commerce, even more than in war, both men and beasts are considered merely as machines, and sacrificed with even less compunction.

There is a great fabric of carpets at Axminster, which are woven in one entire piece. We were not detained here many minutes, and here we left the county of Devonshire, which in climate and fertility and beauty is said to exceed most parts of England: if it be indeed so, England has little to boast of. Both their famous pirates, the Drake and the Raleigh, were natives of this province; so also was Oxenham, another of these early buccaneers, of whose family it is still reported, that before any one dies a bird with a white breast flutters about the bed of the sick person, and vanishes when he expires...

1824

Kenneth Curry (ed.), *New Letters of Robert Southey* (New York, 1965), II, 261–2.

Southey spent several days with friends and acquaintances in East Devon before travelling on to Exeter and Crediton. He was then 50 years old.

[11 January, letter to Miss Edith May Southey]

...After a journey with no discomfort and only one misadventure, I was landed at the Kennaway's door [at Escot] at one o'clock. The misadventure consisted in overturning a market cart, with a woman and two men in it. The tilt saved them from any harm, but I suppose the butter and the eggs suffered, and they were in such a rage that they would not suffer us to give them any assistance, so we left them on the road, vowing vengeance. It afterwards appeared that their anger was increased by an unlucky mistake of the Guards, who in the half morning twilight thinking to help the woman out from the tilt by her arm, took hold of her knee! It is supposed that there will be a law suit about it; but I believe they were to blame for keeping directly in the middle of the road, and not drawing on one side when they saw us coming.

Sir John Kennaway doses his guests and his servants with family worship, of which too much is worse than none. He edified Dr [Edward] Copplestone [provost of Oriel College] as well as myself on the Sunday evening by reading a sermon and a long prayer after it; and with equal want of judgement he made his two little girls (nice creatures they are) show off by repeating verses and extracts from Mr Irving. They are about the size of Kate and Bel, and waltzed together very prettily. Only think of their calling one Gussy!! Whose name is Augusta. Lady K. paints. Her husband ought to choose the chapter about Jezebel for his reading and commenting. They were very obliging and hospitable to me, Charles as good humoured as ever. He appears to remember with great pleasure every little circumstance that occurred at Keswick. The most interesting person in the family is a brother of Sir Johns who is almost blind, a well-informed, mild, patient man, whom it is impossible not to like and compassionate.

On Monday I removed to Ottery. Henry Coleridge (the *Amans amantis* of Sara's book) speaks and laughs so like Edward, that I could have supposed he had been Edward if my eyes had been shut. But he is neither so tall nor so handsome. I liked him well and his brother Frank also. The Colonel [James Coleridge] seems the only fortunate one in the family in his sons. George, tho' very well disposed, appears to be much inferior to them in understanding, and Edwin is a sort of Tony Lumpkin upon whom education has been thrown away. The Colonel is suffering from a spasmodic affection of the stomach, which has I fear a serious appearance.

Tuesday to Mr Marriotts. There I met Mr Barker, almost heartbroken by his son's conduct, and Dr Miller of Exeter, who married one of Mr Hewitt's sisters. Hewitt is in orders and serves the curacy of Downton, about four miles from Mrs May's house at Hale [in Hampshire]. Wednesday to Exeter...

THE REVEREND RICHARD WARNER
of
BATH, 1799, 1808

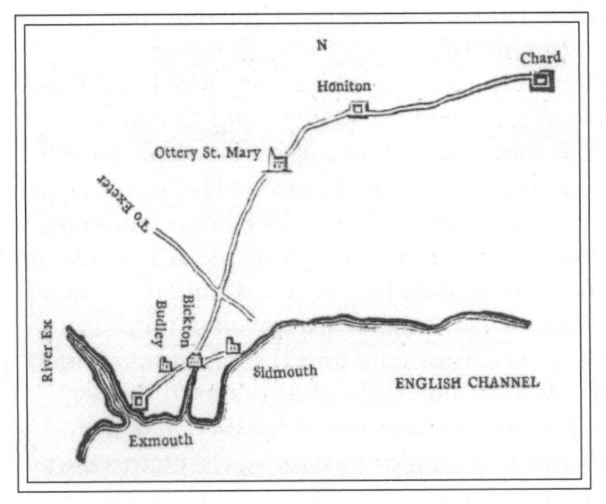

Map of the Reverend Warner's travels in East Devon, 1799

Warner's tours were written as a series of letters to a friend, William Johnston. Warner travelled alone in 1799. The tour of 1808 was made, he wrote, because in 1799 he had travelled westward only as far as the border of Cornwall. Warner travelled with a companion, only identified as 'W—', who 'promises to direct my curiosity, and assist my enquiry, will enliven every incident what may occur and spread a sunshine over the excursion'.

1799

Richard Warner, *A Walk through some of the western counties of England by the Revd Richard Warner of Bath* (Bath, 1800), 196–201. The following account is derived from two letters written on 17 & 19 September.

[September 17 1799]

...Exmouth, (from whence I date this) lying three miles to the eastward of Dawlish, on that side of the river Ex, is by no means liable to the criticism which I have just ventured to throw out on the latter place. It is a town of some extent; and, therefore, neither simplicity, nor picturesque beauty, are looked for in it: the houses may be grouped into any forms that fancy suggests, without the builder's incurring the censure of having spoiled the scene by incongruous architecture.

The variety and grandeur of the view which the houses near the shore command, is seldom equalled. Old Ocean opens his heaving bosom to the south, and the *Ex* comes sweeping down in a broad sheet of water, from the opposite point. This estuary, sprinkled with shipping, enclosed between hills, which are ornamented with groves and mansions, castles and cities, presents, at full tide, and under a calm sky, the picture of an Italian lake. Limited in time, I could only visit, by a distant view, scenes which promise much gratification on a closer inspection – Topsham, and the beautiful country around it; Exeter and its venerable cathedral; the bold, broad, commanding summit of *Hall-Down*; and the magnificent seat and grounds of Mamhead, which ornament its eastern declivity. Powderham-castle is immediately opposite to me, but I do not regret my inability to visit it, since its situation is low, and the grounds about it are uninteresting. Besides, I have no passion for *magnificence*, unless it be united with a little *taste*; and should therefore receive no sort of pleasure in contemplating such gew-gaws as a silver grate plastered over with gold, and three window-curtains, on each of which has been lavished the enormous sum of seven hundred guineas.

The cheerful society and courteous hospitality of some kind friends, whom I accidentally met at Exmouth, rescued me from that *ennui* which a solitary wandered like myself would otherwise have experienced in a strange place, and shut up during a public-house in one of the most inclement days I ever witnessed. The morning, however, of to-day, falsely flattering, tempted me to quit Exmouth, where (as

Johnson observes) I had drunk Lotus, and commit myself to the capriciousness of the present season, unlike any other in the annals of meteorology. But I have been severely punished for the folly of deserting social comfort by an uninterrupted rain, which has fallen with the most obstinate perseverance for eight long hours. You must content yourself, therefore, with little more than the bare names of the places through which I passed, since the day has been but ill-calculated for enquiry or investigation.

Had the weather permitted, I should have led you through the grounds of Bicton, the seat of Lord Rolle, about six miles from Exmouth, where the *patula fagus*, the wide-spreading beech, rising to an enormous size, indicates to the planter the propriety of cultivating a tree so evidently congenial to the soil of the country. I would have carried you into the woollen-manufactory of Newton [Poppleford], a few miles further on. You should have also visited the old conventual church of Ottery St Mary, built by John de Grandison, bishop of Exeter, who, by wonder-working eloquency totally unknown in these days, persuaded the clergy of his diocese to surrender into his hands a considerable part of their property during their lives, and to leave the remainder of it to him after their deaths, for the purpose of endowing churches, building colleges, and establishing hospitals!! But of these places, and Honiton to boot (remarkable for holding its market on a *Sunday*, till the reign of King John) I must refer you to those more fortunate tourists who have trodden the same course with myself under smiling heavens. Sufficient for me be it to say, that I am safely housed at Chard, the first town on the borders of Somersetshire, after a journey which threatened me more than once with the pains of drowning...

1808

Reverend Richard Warner, *A Tour through Cornwall in the Autumn of 1808* (Bath, 1809), 26–7. The following account is derived from his first letter, addressed from Ashburton on 25 July 1808.

...Quitting Somersetshire, about three miles from Wellington, we entered Devonshire at Blewets' cross; and after a further progress of ten miles, reached the town of Cullompton; remarkable for its handsome church, with the beautiful chapel it contains, built by John Lane, a wealthy clothier, in the fourteenth century; a structure one should have thought far beyond the means of an humble tradesman, had we not recollected that the woollen manufacture was first established in these parts, and confined to them for a long period, during which time immense fortunes were made by those who preserved the monopoly of this lucrative branch of trade. We were also much struck by a venerable house in the town, a well-preserved specimen of the architecture of the fifteenth century.

The magnificent scenery of Devonshire now opened upon us; sweeping hills and broad luxuriant valleys, backed to the north and west by the dark irregular summits of Exmoor. The picturesque effect, too, of the high banks which occasionally bounded the road on either side, was not lost upon us; where the combination of the red highly-carbonated earth, and the green foliage spread over its face, produced a most agreeable harmony of colouring. The vivid vegetation of the low parts of Devonshire is indeed almost proverbial with artists; and the chief of English painters, Sir Joshua Reynolds, used to assert that the verdure in the neighbourhood of Exeter, Bath, and Bristol, was the richest in the kingdom.

In the happiest part of this scenery stands Killerton, the elegant mansion of Sir Thomas Acland, screened to the north-east by a superb tract of wood, and commanding a view, if not extensive, at least beautifully diversified...

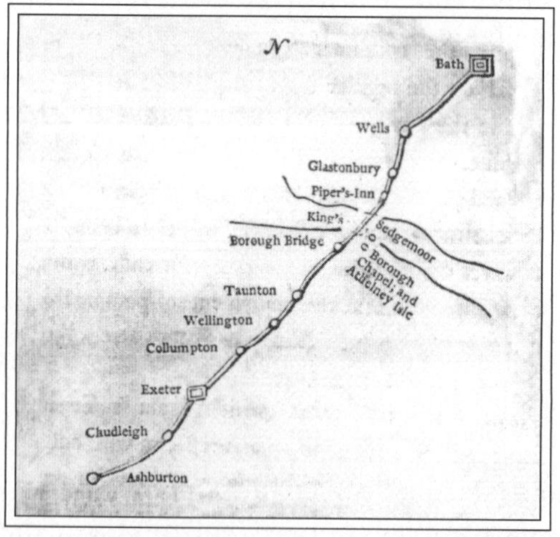

Map of the Reverend Warner's travels in East Devon, 1808

Martin Dunsford
of
Tiverton, *c.*1800

Portrait of Martin Dunsford, *c.*1800

Martin Dunsford, *Miscellaneous Observations, in the course of two tours* (Tiverton, 1800), 5–13, 83–6.

Dunsford is better known as the author of *Historical Memoirs of Tiverton*. His interest in history is immediately apparent from the *Miscellaneous Observations* with his comments on the works of other older historians such as John Hooker and Samuel Isacke and in his lamenting the lack of historical research since. Dunsford gave several reasons for this travel account in writing that he was accustomed to ride for his own recreation, health and 'variety of entertainment' but added that 'a love of truth guided his observations on the characters and opinions of men...the manners and customs of other individuals and communities'. He also wrote that he felt restricted by living in a small community and hoped travel would 'enlarge his view of mankind'. Dunsford died some seven years later. The following account comes from his second tour which he made along Devon's south coast.

...The passage, about a mile across the river to Exmouth, in the evening was at this time boisterous and dangerous, the boat was aground on the sand several times, and we reached the passage house late, and with great difficulty; the wind was so high, the boatmen thought it unsafe to return that night to Topsham, and continued at Exmouth till the morning. Several instances were remembered, and told me, of the loss of pleasure boats and company, as well as larger vessels, in navigating this river at improper seasons; and particularly in attempts, to pass the narrow channels between the sand banks, and crossing the bar at its mouth, which the masters of loaded vessels will not risk, without able pilotage.

Exmouth is one of the most frequented watering places on the Devonshire coast, it is irregularly built in groups of houses, some of which are good modern buildings, erected of late years chiefly by the inhabitants of Exeter, several of whom have their annual summer residence there; many elegant and convenient houses, have been built also, to provide lodgings, for the numerous families that yearly visit this place: there are some pleasing walks shaded by high trees, in what is called the square, a large open place in the centre, between the scattered groups of buildings.

Tho' the walks to the river side, and sea shore, over the loose sand, are troublesome to invalids, those on the cliffs are highly pleasant, and salutary, and easy of access; they afford an extensive sea prospect – much of the south coast of Devon – the course of the river with its variegated banks – and the amusing view of the passing vessels of trade...Powderham – the Belvedere towering above a thick wood – the village of Star cross – and distant view of *Halldown* hills on the opposite side of the river, exhibit grand, interesting, and diversified pictures, of nature and art beautifully combined. We find nothing of Exmouth in antiquity, but of its being a small fishing town, composed of mariners and fishermen's dwellings, which are now chiefly confined to one or two narrow streets on the side of the hill, where the females are generally employed in the manufacture of lace.

On leaving Exmouth, I crossed the river to Star cross...

JOHN EVANS
of
ISLINGTON, LONDON, *c.*1803

Portrait of John Evans, 1816

John Evans, *The Juvenile Tourist: or, Excursions through various parts of the island of Great Britain; including the west of England, midland counties, and the whole of Kent; illustrated with maps, and interspersed with Historical Anecdotes and Poetical Extracts; for the improvement of the rising generation in a series of letters to a pupil* (1816 edn), 30–40,78–82.

On the title page Evans was noted as 'Master of a Seminary for a limited number of Pupils, Puffins Row, Islington'. Evans' account was written as a series of letters to a student. He travelled, with another unidentified friend, as far west as Exeter via Devon's south coast and returned to London via Honiton. At Sidmouth Evans stayed with the Reverend Edmund Butcher, author of a tour through East Devon in 1803. Some of this text has not been included, mainly where he digressed on general natural history and the moral nature of the sea. Evans was in his mid-thirties when he visited East Devon and died in 1827.

...We left Lyme, encircled by the shades of evening, and, passing through *Culliton* [Colyton], a snug little place, reached Sidmouth at a late hour, when its inhabitants were peacefully reclined on their beds:

Tempus erat quo prima quies mortalibus segris
Incipit, et dono divum gratissima serpit.

'Twas in the dead of night, when sleep repairs
Our bodies worn with toil, our mind with cares.

We soon, however, got access into the house of our friend, a gentleman of respectability, who entertained us with his accustomed hospitality.

I cannot help remarking with what different sensations we travel after sun-set in those parts of the country which are remote from the Metropolis. Neither footpad nor highwayman haunted our imaginations. The darkness of the night, and the retiredness of the roads, would, in the vicinity of a great city, conspire for our destruction. Whereas here we were only exposed to the dangers incident to night-travelling, and of course were better able to secure our personal safety. In this respect the Country reminds us of the golden age, when Innocence and Peace joined hand-in-hand to render men happy; whilst the huge over-grown metropolis nourishes in her bosom miscreants of every description; whence they issue with desperate intentions, the pest and disgrace of society! Laws, human and divine, are insufficient to restrain them. Every returning winter invites these men to the perpetration of deeds of violence. We are fearful of walking abroad – we are not suffered to rest quiet in our habitations. Whatever boasted advantages, therefore, Cities may possess, for peace, quietness and safety, give me some retired spot in the Country. And why this essential difference?

Man made the Town, God made the Country!
Cowper

In my next epistle I shall send you an account of Sidmouth and its vicinity. I remain Yours respectfully.

Letter III

Dear Sir,

Having in my last two Epistles delineated my route to Sidmouth, I now proceed to give you an account of this place and its vicinity. Of late years it has become the resort of genteel persons during the summer season. But at a former period it used to offer the valetudinarian, in addition to the softness of the sea-breezes, all the pleasures of retirement.

The friend who had admitted us beneath his hospitable roof, possessed a spot remarkable for the neatness of its appearance and the felicity of its situation. I eagerly availed myself of the light of the ensuing day, to ascertain the nature of the place whither I had arrived amid the shades of midnight darkness. The house I found was enclosed by a garden, highly cultivated, abounding with fruit, and furnishing a prospect both of the ocean and of the surrounding country. The scene had all the gloss of novelty: at one of its extremities lay a summer-house, into which we ascended by a flight of steps, and from which The Sea burst upon the eye of the spectator with uncommon grandeur. Its hoarse resounding murmurs were even thence distinctly heard by the listening ear: and struck with the contemplation of so immense a body of water, I was ready to exclaim with [James] Thomson:

> And, thou, majestic main,
> A world of secret wonders in thyself,
> Sound his stupendous praise, whose greater voice
> Or bids you roar, or bids your rearings fall!

...Instead of attempting to describe Sidmouth with my own pen, I will present you with an account obligingly drawn up by my friend, the Rev. Mr H[arri]s, who accompanied me in this journey. His residence at the place for many years, joined to the inquisitive turn of mind which he is known to possess, well fitted him for the delineation.

'Sidmouth is seated at the bottom of the immense bay which is formed by the two noted headlands, Portland Point and the Start Point. It was, formerly, a place of considerable note, and possessed an ample harbour for shipping, and an extensive trade: but such have been the encroachments of the ever restless ocean upon this part of our coasts, that its port is now lost, and its trade annihilated.

Different geographers, speaking of this place, tell us that its harbour is now choked up by sand; but this is palpably an inaccuracy, as the harbour was certainly *not* formed by any inlet of the sea, and consequently could not be filled up by the accumulation of marine substances. The fact is, the land to the westward of the town, formerly projected far beyond its present boundary into the sea, and probably formed a Bight-Bay, or natural pier, within which vessels sought refuge in times of danger. This supposition is the more plausible, as immense rocks are now seen at low water, stretching far from the point just mentioned, in a southern direction, and pointing out to the observing eye an eligible basis for the re-erection of such a work: nay, more, there are those who can recollect a chain of rocks similar to the very picturesque one which yet rears its head and defies the buffetings of the waves which followed each other to the southward, till they were lost in the depths of the ocean! But though no trace of the port now remains, and even the remembrance of it is swept away by the tide of time, this is by no means the case with respect to the commerce and spirit of enterprise which once animated this place. Tradition tells us that the pilchard fishery, that immense source of national wealth, was once carried on to a great extent by the natives of Sidmouth: that its hardy sons, with every returning season, sought their finny stores, and pursued them along the coasts of Cornwall, round the Scilly Isles, and even up the northern shores of their native country.

Unhappily two succeeding unfavourable seasons overtook them, their boats were all cast away, their crews overwhelmed in the ocean returned no more. Where the bustle and gaiety of business had adorned every countenance with smiles, nothing was seen but sable weeds – nothing was heard but sighs and lamentations! The spirit which had animated this enterprising spot was quenched at once, and for all its former celebrity, nought remained but the apparatus in which its merchandise had been prepared for the market; the memory of what it once was, and the ecclesiastical records, which detail to future incumbents the plenteous tithe which their forerunners had collected from the deep!

It ought not to be forgotten that this spirit of enterprise was not the consequence of their peculiar situation: it is said, that when no longer able to find refuge for the busy craft among their native rocks, the inhabitants of Sidmouth set on foot a liberal subscription, and with it erected a quay at Torquay; and hence their vessels, boats and craft of every description, take shelter from the tempest there, in time of distress, without paying the customary port duties which are exacted of all others.

At present, Sidmouth is only known as a place of resort for the valetudinary and the dissipated; and to each of these it presents attractions peculiarly inviting. Seated on the base of the two lofty mountains which form its charming vale, and closed up on the north by the Honiton hills, it presents its bosom only to the southern ray, and to the southern zephyr, and fanned by the pure breeze of the ocean alone, must, of course, be well calculated to redress the injury which filthy cities, crowded rooms, and mephitic vapours, entail upon mankind. In this respect Sidmouth claims a decided superiority over all its competitors for public resort. Here no filthy lagoons impregnate the atmosphere with poisonous miasma; no stagnant pools here putrefy in the solar ray; wherever there is water, it flows, and constantly crossing the traveller's path, tempers the sultry gale, gives fresh verdure to the luxuriant herbage which fringes its tinkling course, cherishes the thousand plants and flowers with which every hedgerow is garnished, embalms the air, and revives the fainting energies of nature. The charming diversity for which Devon is famed, seems here to be collected into one point. Does the sated mind turn from the monotony of the ocean? In the vale behind it, every thing is rich, luxuriant and variegated, calculated to awaken the softest and most tranquillizing emotions in the bosom; the trees are seen here flourishing even to the water's edge, with a verdure and luxuriance which is elsewhere unknown.

Along the banks of the Sid, which, bursting at once from beneath a mighty rock, meanders its three-mile-course to the ocean, we meet with all that beautiful variety of scenery which Fenelon so richly describes in his *Telemaque* – meadows embroidered with flowers, fields waving with corn, orchards laden with fruits, while every turn in its fantastic windings presents us with the delicacies of the landscape in some new point of view, adds some fresh tuft of trees, some little murmuring water-fall, some straw-thatched cottage to the picture. Upon the mountain, the half-suffocated victim of fashion and midnight orgies, breathes the pure aetherial atmosphere; and while his path is strewed with flowers, gazes upon nature in some of her most elegant attitudes, and catches at one glance an extent of prospect, a variety of scenery, which is almost unrivalled.

It has been debated to which of the adjacent summits the palm of excellence in this respect is due, but the point can alone be determined by the peculiar taste of the beholder. From the eastern high lands the vale of Sidmouth is certainly seen to the most advantage; the perspective is undoubtedly confined, but it teems with luxury. The ravished eye looks down upon a landscape stretched out like a carpet beneath it, which centres within itself as much picturesque beauty as is collected within an equal boundary in any country upon the earth!

Here every thing necessary to an enchanting picture seems to be concentrated. Lands, rich and well-cultivated, hedge-rows amply furnished with forest trees; mountains tipped with copse, bespotted with sheep; here glowing with the gilded blossoms of the furze, and there finely tinted with the numerous varieties of the heaths, which flourish on their slopes; the whole decorated, not with the frowning awe-commanding mansions of the great, but besprinkled with cottages, villages and hamlets, with their white-washed spire peeping through the orchards that envelope and almost hide it from view! On the precipices which terminate either hill, the picture is uncommonly sublime and striking; from the eastern summit the eye ranges over a vast extent of country, and is only bounded at the distance of forty miles, by the rugged tors upon the forest of Dartmoor. Beneath we see the *Halidown* Hills, the Start Point, the Berry Head, Torbay, with its ever shifting fleets; and in the cliffs we have 'Pelion upon Ossa' and 'Caucasus upon Pelion' in tremendous massed heaped upon each other! From the Peak we gaze upon the white cliffs of Albion (and here take out leave of them) the south-western coast of Dorset, the Portland Isle, which, like a bully, projects itself into the channel, and seems to hurl defiance against the opposite shores.

'In Sidmouth itself we have nothing which is worth noticing, if we except the Church tower, which is certainly a fine piece of masonry. The modern erections are many; among the rest there is an excellent inn, a large and convenient assembly-room, billiard-room and reading-room. On the beach, a gravel walk of about one-third of a mile in length, has been constructed for the accommodation of the company; the bathing is commodious, and, for the convenience of the infirm, warm salt-water baths have also been erected. Here the naturalist may find an ample field of investigation. The hills abound with plants, many of which are rare. In the cliffs numerous spars of different kinds are to be collected; nor are the rocks deficient in materials for study and amusement.

Beautiful specimens of the Pholen are found imbedded in the marly foundations of the hills; and blocks of free-stone, which have been broken from the summits of the cliffs, abound with *echinae marinae*, petrified coral, and many other productions of a similar description. In the basons, worn by the action of the waves in the rocks, elegant corallines abound; and not unfrequently that singular production of nature, the animal flower, vulgarly called the sea anenome.'

From this entertaining account of Sidmouth, by my friend, you will have it in your power to form a satisfactory idea of the spot at which we were now arrived...

Wandering one day on the beach of Sidmouth early in the morning, I met with an aged fishermen, seated under the cliff of a rock, and employed (like James, the son of Zebedee, and John his brother, of old) in mending his nets. I entered into conversation with him, and learnt from him many things with which I was unacquainted.

Among other particulars, he told me, that these coasts had, of late years, been, in a measure, deserted by the finny tribe. For this fact no satisfactory reasons could be assigned. This spirit of emigration, by no means uncommon, at present, amongst the human species, has, it seems seized the piscatory race; not is it yet ascertained to what shores they have betaken themselves. I gave this son of misfortune a trifle, for which he appeared grateful. Indeed I pitied this poor old man, who lamented the desertion, as it had been the occasion of narrowing the means of his subsistence. On his brow was indented many a furrow, and his physiognomy assured me that he had, oftentimes, borne 'the pitiless pelting of the storm'.

Mackerel, however, are caught here in abundance. I saw a draught brought ashore one evening, and poured from the net into a basket. I was struck with their appearance, and handled them, for their colours were beautiful. The silvery white was shaded by purple dyes, and the agonies of dissolution produced a thousand variations, marked by exquisite delicacy! Upon my return from this scene, I found the band belonging to the Sidmouth volunteers playing on the beach, which, combined with the murmurs of the 'wide weltering waves' generated pleasing sensations. The company were parading backwards and forwards, and [the] sun rapidly setting in the west, while the approaching shades of darkness admonished us that day was closing upon us, and the empire of night was about to be resumed. Indeed, at that instant, to adopt the language of a celebrated female author, 'I contemplated all nature at rest; the rocks, even grown darker in their appearance, looked as if they partook of the general repose and reclined more heavily on their foundations.'

The purport of my visit to Sidmouth was to enjoy the company of my valuable friend, the Rev. Mr. B[utcher], who, on account of indisposition, had been obliged to quit the metropolis, and chose to retire into this part of the country. Him and his amiable family I found embosomed in a vale (they are since removed to Sidmouth) which, for the softness of its air and the richness of its prospect, cannot be exceeded. Their mansion was neat and commodious; their view on the left extended towards the sea, and on the right was terminated by a rising hill; whilst the declivity of the opposite mountain, intersected by enclosures, and spotted with sheep, imparted a picturesque scene to the eye of the beholder. Near the foot of the door ran a rivulet; which by its murmurs soothed the ear, and by its transparency gratified imagination. About the distance of two fields above the mansion, the sea beautifully unfolded itself to view between the hills, and vessels were appearing and disappearing, not wholly unlike the objects passing through a magic lantern; though certainly the scene had no connexion with the ludicrous, nor were the objects transmitted with equal rapidity. At the top of the hill was an ancient encampment; but whether of Roman or Danish origin cannot be ascertained with certainty. There is no doubt, however, that these coasts were infested by the enemy in the earlier periods of British history. From this eminence we looked down on the other side into the little village of Sidbury, and its clustered cottages suggested to the mind those flattering images of felicity, which we usually connect with rusticity.

My abode was at the house of my friend. Thence we often sailed forth to survey the adjacent prospects; but the weather was by no means favourable to our excursions. One fine day, however, we ascended the opposite eminence, Beacon Hill, clambering up its side with difficulty. But its summit recompensed the toil which we had endured. Though unaccustomed to the art of drawing, yet seating myself upon a hillock, I was tempted to take a rough sketch of the cottage we had left, and of the hills with which it was surrounded. The whole scene before me might be likened to the representation of a *camera obscura*, where the reflected images of objects are exhibited with neatness and accuracy. In our wandering onward, we stooped down and plucked many a ripe whortle-berry from amidst the prickly furse which covered the ground, and the gathering of which affords to many poor persons the means of maintenance. We at length came to the brow of the hill, and stopping at the beacon, we, for some time, surveyed with astonishment the divine prospect which burst upon us from every quarter of the horizon! Nor could it be pronounced altogether unlike the eminence whither Adam was led by the archangel Michael to show him what lay hid in the womb of futurity:

> — A hill,
> Of paradise the highest, from whose top

The hemisphere of earth, in clearest ken
Stretch'd out to th' amplest reach of prospect lay!

Before us the wide ocean extended itself, where, could our vision have been invigorated, we should have spied the islands of Guernsey, Jersey and Alderney, together with the opposite coast of France. On the left lay Sidmouth, whose venerable tower alone was visible to us, and beyond projected the Portland Isle, reminding me of the unfortunate Haleswell East Indiaman, whose fate is fresh in every mind. Behind, was seen a fine extent of country, from the centre of which the smoke of Exeter ascended, thus enabling me to ascertain the spot in which the western metropolis was situated. Beneath us was a wood, whose embrowned appearance imparted a solemnity; and it seemed, indeed, fitted for our Druidical ancestors, who were attached to these sylvan recesses. On the right, at the extremity of our prospect, Torbay presented itself; and we could descry the little rock by which its entrance is characterised.

This group of objects, which, from this eminence, filled the eye and exhilarated the heart, I was unwilling to relinquish; it was the finest sight that I had ever beheld, combining the sublime and beautiful in perfection! Descending from this point, therefore, with lingering step, I stole many a farewell look, feeling the reproach suggested in the words of the poet...

...After a fortnight's stay in this part of Devonshire, I with regret bid my friend the Rev. Mr B[utcher], and his family, an adieu; for they remind me of the group delineated by Thomson, who are said to have been blessed with:

An elegant sufficiency, content.
Retirement, rural quiet, friendship, books,
Ease and alternate labour, useful life,
Progressive virtue and approving heaven!

I remain, dear Sir, Yours...

[next 'letter']

...Quitting Exeter, I reached Honiton, at the distance of fifteen miles, a pleasant town, being one long street, in which are to be found many good houses. In the midst of it, however, stands a row of tottering shambles, which, were they shouldered down, would heighten the beauty of the place. Through the town runs a stream of clear water, with a little square dipping place at every door. The first serge manufactory in Devonshire was in this town; but it is now employed in the manufacture of lace, which is made broader here then anywhere else in England; and of which great quantities are sent to London. A specimen of lace has been shown, the thread of which it was fabricated cost the manufacture upwards of *ninety guineas* a pound at Antwerp; also ladies' veils are made and sold from *ten* to *seventy* guineas! A dreadful fire happened here 1747, by which three-fourths of the town were consumed. By this, and similar accidents, however, the place has been eventually benefited; for the houses which are rebuilt are said to be neater in their appearance and more commodious to the inhabitants. This was the case, indeed, with *London*, which was nearly consumed in the terrible fire of 1666, – it rose like a fair and beautiful Phoenix out of its ashes!

The parish-church of Honiton stands pleasantly on a hill above the town, whither I had an agreeable walk; the edifice presented an antique appearance, and there were tombs within the walls, which contained the bones of persons of distinction. Around one of the pillars was entwined the following sentence: *Pray for the soul of* — the name was almost obliterated. It had evidently been inscribed there in the days of Popery, previous to the period of the Reformation. The church-yard was crowded with graves; and at the entrance of one of the side-doors was shown me the spot where lay the remains of the Rev. Dr. *William Harris* (who died 1770,) author of *The Lives of the Stuarts*. He resided in Honiton for many years, and sustained a character of respectability. He published an Historical and Critical Account of the Life of James the First, of Charles the First, of Oliver Cromwell, of Hugh Peters, and of Charles the Second, in two volumes. He began the life of Jams the Second; but the materials left behind him were too scanty for publication. I have thus enumerated his publications, because his *Life of Charles the Second* is omitted in the list of his productions, with which we are furnished, in the late new edition of the Biographical Dictionary. The plan of these lives is similar to that of Bayle's Dictionary, where the text is short, but accompanied with notes, including copious illustrations. Mr Hollis, his munificent patron, has thus characterized his labours – 'All his works have been well received, and those who differ from him in principle, still value him in point of industry and faithfulness.'

This country church-yard seems to have been of that rustic cast which might have inspired the muse of a [Thomas] Gray. In walking round it my eye was fixed on a row of graves, over which was fixed the grassy turf, and on which the setting sun shone with splendour!

During my stay at Honiton, I had an opportunity of being present, one Sunday evening, at a meeting of itinerant Quakers. Curiosity drew together a crowd of people who poured into the General Baptist place of worship, which was lent the Friends for that purpose. Two women and a man, from America, held forth on this occasion. One of the women spoke well: indeed her countenance conciliated attention. Her features were marked by a pleasing solemnity, and her manner, though not free from the usual tone, was characterized by simplicity. The harangues of the two others were tedious, and the audience discovered signs of impatience by indecently beating their feet on the floor, long before the meeting came to a conclusion.

In spite of the eccentricities of the Quakers, we cannot but admire their hatred of war, and their detestation of Slavery:

> The purest wreaths which hung on glory's shrine,
> For empires founded, peaceful PENN! Be thine;
> No blood-stain'd laurels crown'd thy virtuous toil;
> No slaughter'd natives drench'd thy fair-carn'd soil.
> Still thy meek spirit in they flock survives,
> Consistent still their doctrines rule their lives;
> Thy followers only have effac'd the shame
> Inscrib'd by slavery on the Christian name!
>
> More

The *only* in the last line but one, is now happily incorrect, as the British Parliament has also *effaced the shame* by the abolition of the slave-trade.

At Honiton, Mrs H[?arris], the worthy niece of the late Dr William Harris, showed me a curious Latin book of her uncle's, printed in the time of the Protectorate, and executed with typographical beauty. It contained an extravagant panegyric on the character of Oliver Cromwell, and was decorated with a striking likeness of that celebrated man on horseback. The resemblance between the two Latin terms, Olivus, an olive tree, and Oliverus, Oliver, is the foundation of this very complimentary performance. Accordingly the frontispiece exhibits a fine lofty olive tree, on the trunk of which, near the root, is inscribed in large letters, Oliverus; and on its numerous branches, stretching themselves forth on either side, are engraven the chief virtues which adorn humanity. The author having informed us, at the commencement of the treatise, that by the trunk is meant Oliver Cromwell, a whole chapter is assigned to each of the virtues, showing that they are all, in their plentitude, centred in this great man; and that, therefore, he is entitled to universal admiration! This curiosity convinced me, that an excessive adulation of men in power, is by no means peculiar to monarchical governments.

Nor must I omit to inform you, that a gentleman in this neighbourhood, at whose house I passed an agreeable day, favoured the company with a sight of some fossils, in which the taste of the selector was conspicuous. By particular request, several botanical sketches were also brought out for inspection. The investigation of the beauties of nature is a laudable employ; to the supreme Author such an exercise of our powers is a tribute of praise, and to the contemplator of them it yields an heartfelt satisfaction. When we thus rise from fossils to vegetables – from vegetables to animals – from animals to Man, it amounts to a full proof of Diety. To talk of Chance insults the human understanding – it is a term invented to conceal our ignorance. Can Chaos produce spontaneously this fair form of nature? Can Fate arrange the various movements of the material creation with such delicacy and harmony? Can a mere nullity conduct and sustain a system thus operating with design and regularity?...

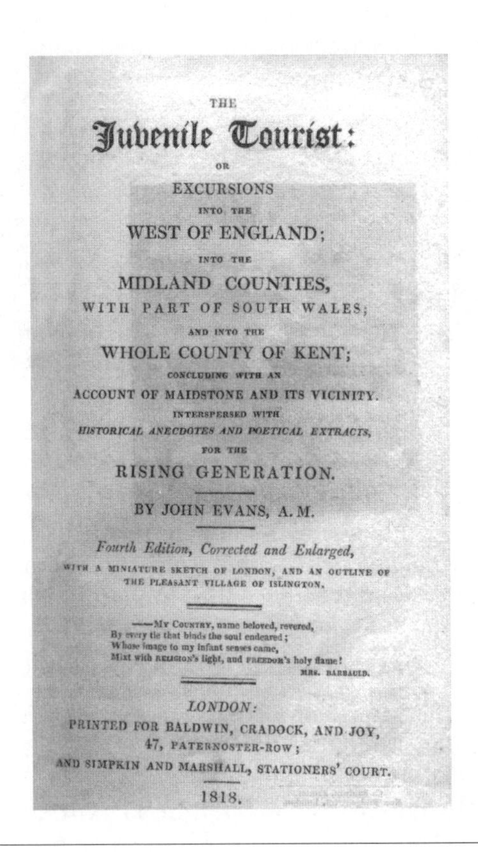

THE
Juvenile Tourist:
OR
EXCURSIONS
INTO THE
WEST OF ENGLAND;
INTO THE
MIDLAND COUNTIES,
WITH PART OF SOUTH WALES;
AND INTO THE
WHOLE COUNTY OF KENT;
CONCLUDING WITH AN
ACCOUNT OF MAIDSTONE AND ITS VICINITY.
INTERSPERSED WITH
HISTORICAL ANECDOTES AND POETICAL EXTRACTS,
FOR THE
RISING GENERATION.

BY JOHN EVANS, A. M.

Fourth Edition, Corrected and Enlarged,
WITH A MINIATURE SKETCH OF LONDON, AND AN OUTLINE OF THE PLEASANT VILLAGE OF ISLINGTON.

——My Country, name beloved, revered,
By every tie that binds the soul endeared;
Whose image to my infant senses came,
Mixt with Religion's light, and Freedom's holy flame!
MRS. BARBAULD.

LONDON:
PRINTED FOR BALDWIN, CRADOCK, AND JOY,
47, PATERNOSTER-ROW;
AND SIMPKIN AND MARSHALL, STATIONERS' COURT.

1818.

The Reverend Edmund Butcher *of* Sidmouth, 1803

Sidbury, 1817

Edmund Butcher, *An Excursion from Sidmouth to Chester, in the summer of 1803, in a series of letters to a lady, including sketches of the principal towns and villages in the counties of Devon, Somerset, Gloucester, Monmouth, Hereford, Salop, Derby, Stafford, Warwick and Worcester* (London and Exeter, 1805), 1–15, 447–62.

The Reverend Butcher, a Unitarian minister in Yorkshire and London from 1789 to 1797, resided at Burscombe, situated to the west of Sidbury, in about 1794 to recover his health. He retired to Sidmouth from 1798 to 1820 and was a friend of John Evans, author of *The Juvenile Tourist*, who visited him at Sidmouth sometime between 1805 and 1809. The two extracts printed here form part of a larger tour to the Midlands. Butcher wrote that his three motives for this tour were the improvement of health, the attainment of 'innocent pleasure' and the renewal of old friendships. He also wrote that he was familiar with the accounts by Reverends Warner and Gilpin. Butcher's account was written as a series of letters to an unidentified woman. His first letter, number seventeen, was composed at Bristol and dated 6 July. The second extract printed here is from his final letter written on his return to Sidmouth. It has been included although he was not a stranger to Sidmouth because it formed part of his general tour. Butcher travelled with his wife and three of their children. He was 46 old when he made this journey and died in 1822. His other publications included *Sermons for the Use of Families* and *Moral Tales for Youths*.

...As it was our object to reach Bristol the first day, which is a distance of 75 miles, it was necessary to go a stage before breakfast; indeed this was what I wished to effect the whole journey, and what, as the inclinations of my companions tallied with my own, I was in general able to effect. How smoothly does not only an occasional excursion, but the great journey of life roll on, when those who are embarked in the same vehicle have a sincere wish to accommodate and oblige each other. I need not tell you how much this is my happy lot.

The clock struck five on the morning of July 5, 1803, when we left our own door. A veil of thick clouds obscured the rays of the sun, and a driving rain, the relics of a heavy shower, which for some hours before had drenched our neighbourhood, attended us for three or four miles: the hedges and banks, however, between which we were passing, poured streams of fragrance on both sides of us.

You are well acquainted with a Devonshire cross-road. The foliage upon the trees and high banks was now at its acme of luxuriance; except, therefore, at a gate, or other casual opening, we could only see right-a-head. The lane of leaves through which we were riding, in many places so narrow that two carriages could by no means pass each other, has also a number of little bendings and curves, so that to see far, even before us, was impossible. On the right and on the left, however, we knew that we were passing a rich variety of rural beauty, and frequently we caught rapid glimpses of it as little apertures presented themselves on either side. The river Sid, which, though it has only the short distance of about six miles to carry its tribute, to the ocean, gives name to three places in its course, Sidbury, Sidford and Sidmouth, was rolling its then troubled current on our right hand, and on the left rose the hills, in the bosom of which lies the little hamlet of *Burcombe*. Sweet is the recollection of this place to my heart; there it was that six years ago, in a cottage which still bears the appellation of White-house, I sought that health which several years residence in the metropolis had greatly impaired: Thanks be to HEAVEN I did not seek it in vain! Two years abode in this charming and tranquil spot poured fresh oil into the lamp of life, enable me to taste with new relish the domestic comforts with which I was surrounded, and at length to resume the duties of that profession, which, as it was the deliberate choice of my heart, it has been my highest pleasure to discharge.

Sidford is the first place through which our road lay: it is a small hamlet, most of the houses of which have an air of neatness about them. Almost at right angles to the direction in which we came lies the turnpike road from *Lime* [Regis] to Exeter, which passes over a small bridge, the arches of which are beautifully ornamented with ivy. A small distance from this bridge is the middle point of the road betwixt *Lime* and Exeter; fourteen miles is the distance marked to each of these places. Salcombe-hill, over which the road to *Lime* passes, with its well disposed masses of trees rising to the very top, hounded our view on the right hand, and on the left were the cultivated divisions and the hanging woods of the Core and Castle hills.

Something more than a mile from Sidford lies Sidbury. It is a scattered and irregular village. The parish church, which is an ancient edifice, without anything particular to distinguish it, and a humble dissenting meeting, are the two places in which the religious services of its inhabitants are carried on. The situation is uncommonly beautiful; embosomed by a circle of well-wooded and cultivated hills, it offers to the heart which loves retirement, and delights in contemplating the simple beauties of nature, a variety of spots in which such views may be fully gratified. The business of lace-making employs most of the females of Sidbury. Some very costly and beautiful patterns are worked here; but is a melancholy consideration that so much comfort and health are sacrificed in producing these, after all, unnecessary articles of female decoration. The sedentary nature of this employment, and the early age at which multitudes of children are confined to it, make a terrible havoc of life and health. The sallow complexions, the rickety frames, and the general appearances of languor and debility, which numbers of these young women exhibit, are sad and decisive proofs of the pernicious nature of the employment: the small, unwholesome rooms, in which numbers of them, especially during their apprenticeship, are crowded together, are great aggravations of the evil. It is no wonder that the offspring of such mothers are, in a majority of instances, a puny, feeble, and frequently short-lived race. Perhaps these remarks apply universally to manufacture, and particularly to those in which numbers of children are employed early in life, and to some in a much higher degree than to that of lace-making, in which the material made use of had nothing pernicious in it. The confinement, however, of the children, is by far too rigid; ten hours in the day in the time for which they are commonly kept at work; and even then, if they have not completed their task, they are not released, but deprived of the little pittance of time in which they should be regaining the use of their cramped limbs. In the case of the children employed in the cotton manufactories, the legislature has interfered, I hope to some good purpose. I trust the situation of these little lace-makers will soon be brought under its notice. Society, if only from self-interest, should be as sparing of its hands as possible.

Another hardship in the case of the Devonshire lace-makers ought not to pass unnoticed, and that is the manner in which they are generally paid for their labour. Their employers keep hucksters' shops, and oblige them to purchase whatever they deal in, and, frequently, articles which they do not want: if the poor creatures insist upon money, a penny is unfeelingly and unjustly deducted out of every shilling on that account. There is an act of parliament expressly forbidding such extortion, but as acts of parliament cannot execute themselves, this is of little importance. To such masters of any description, however, as make a profession of religion, it may not perhaps be utterly in vain to remark, that there is a book, in which, amongst many other passages of a similar nature, these words are to be found:

'Go to now, ye rich men, weep and howl for your miseries that shall come upon you; your gold and silver is cankered, and the rust of them shall be a witness against you, and shall eat your flesh as if were fire. Behold, *the hire of the labourers* who have reaped down your fields, *which is of you kept back by fraud*, crieth; and the cries of them which have reaped are entered into the ears of the Lord of Hosts.'

Continuing the route to Honiton, we pass a pleasantly situated and good house, belonging to Mr Jenkins; here, also, we cross the little river Sid, which from this time flows on the left hand. The road now begins to ascend, and the valley, which thus far lay on the right, now runs on the left hand of the traveller. The road is narrow, and the prospect confined, but in every other respect is most delightful. The foliage is so rich and various, the undulations of the valley so picturesque, and the verdure so bright, that a pleasanter path for a ride on horseback can scarcely be conceived.

About six miles from Sidmouth, Gittisham-hill, over which the road is carried, becomes extremely steep. The zig-zag, by which its abruptness is in some degree counteracted, has almost acute angles; this, however, soon ceases; and a fine broad road over the hill compensates the toil and alarm which the ascent of Pinhill sometimes occasions to persons not accustomed to mountainous roads.

As we approach Honiton, the pretty village of Gittisham opens on the left hand, and soon after the rich, extensive, and highly cultivated vale of Honiton is fully developed. The white church of Up-Ottery is a principal feature in the distance, and several large and handsome single houses are scattered over the sylvan and verdant scenes which stretch before us, to the borders of Somersetshire, and on the left hand to Exeter, the western metropolis of England. Several clumps of firs ornament the broad back of Gittisham-hill, and, in sultry weather, afford shelter to the stock, which, for the greater part of the year, are browzing the short sweet grass which it produces, and inhaling the fine salubrious breezes which, from its proximity to the ocean, are constantly sweeping its lofty summit. From one of these clumps, just before the road descends on the Honiton side of the hill, we gain a view of the town, stretching itself in the vale below, and apparently running away from its church, which, in solitary state, is perched upon a hill, about half a mile from the town. The smoke, which was just rising from many of the chimneys, and which, when illuminated by the morning sun, adds not only a variety, but a beauty to the general picture, was, on another account, a pleasing exhibition to me and my party; it indicated a preparation for breakfast, which our stomachs informed us would be no unpleasant addition to our materials of enjoyment. About seven o'clock we found ourselves in the house of a hospitable friend. They knew of our coming, and they greeted us with all their accustomed affection. The 'Indian beverage' smoked in our cups, the gifts of Ceres and Primrose loaded our plates, and a variety of conversation, principally upon the excursion before us, filled up the hour that we had allotted for this regale.

The situation of Honiton is delightful; its neighbourhood is the finest part of Devonshire; it is surrounded with fine arable and pasture lands. The river Otter, which runs near it, is but small, but its windings enrich the landscape. It is a populous well-built town; it consists chiefly of one long street, and is well paved with broad flagstones. A stream of fine clear water runs through the town, with dipping places before every door. In the middle of the street are shambles for the sale of meat, vegetables &c but these, which were never judiciously placed, are now become, from their age and the reparations which from time to time it has been necessary to give them, an absolute nuisance to the place: the property should be purchased, and a new market erected in some other situation at the general expence of the town. When I make such a remark, however, I am very sensible that the expences of the state are an objection to local improvements, except in large commercial places, which it is very difficult to obviate. What a melancholy reflection, my dear friend, is it, that the infatuation of mankind, century after century, is such, that while millions are spent in spreading misery and death amongst each other, the arts that would embellish, and the schemes that would add to the comfort of life, are obliged to yield to the imperious demand for the mere necessaries of existence!

The parish church being so inconveniently situated, in 1743, a new chapel, a plain handsome stone edifice, was built, nearly in the middle of the town; besides this, there are two dissenting meeting-houses. Here was the first serge manufactory in Devonshire; but now the making of lace is the principal employment of the inhabitants. Great quantities of this article are sent to London; and, it is said, that broader laces are made here than at any other place in England.

A peculiarity in the ancient history of Honiton is, that before the reign of King John, its market was kept on a Sunday. A charity school for thirty boys was opened here in 1713. A small hospital stands upon the Exeter road, about a quarter of a mile from the town, which, with a chapel, was founded and endowed for four lepers, by one Thomas Chard, an abbot. By a regulation made in 1642, other poor persons are admitted as well as lepers. Honiton has been unfortunate in fires. In 1747, three-fourths of the town were consumed, and damage done to the value of £43,000. In 1765, and 1797, also, terrible fires took place. Several substantial houses, erected by the Phoenix Fire-Office, both add to the beauty of the town, and prove the utility of such institutions.

Honiton is a place of great antiquity; it once belonged to one Drago, a Saxon, and in Doomsday Book it is termed *Terra Comitis Moritonensis,* ie 'The Lands of the Earl of Moriton'. This nobleman was also earl of Cornwall, and brother to William the Conqueror. This estate being forfeited by his son, for rebellion against Henry I was given to Richard de Rivers, earl of Devonshire.

The principal inns are the Dolphin and the Golden Lion, both which have good accommodations. The delightful situation of the place is thus noticed by the poet [John] Gay:

> Now from the steep, 'midst scatter'd farms and groves
> Our eye through Honiton's fair valley roves.

At about eight o'clock, recruited with our breakfast, and gratified with the kindness of our friends, we again entered our chaise, and pursued our route towards Taunton. The morning, which till now had been wet and gloomy, cleared up, the clouds broke away in all directions, and the blue expanse, which was soon almost entirely unveiled, was irradiated with the beams of a bright sun. 'Such,' I involuntarily exclaimed to my dear companions, 'was the morning in which our fortunes were indissolubly blended with each other: a clouded sky and a succession of showers attended our passage to the church, but soon after the ceremony was over, the gloom dissipated; the little excursion on which we entered was cheered with a sunshine, which has proved no bad emblem of the happiness which, for above thirteen years, had blest our union – thus, if it please the Author of all good, may it still continue.'

We were now winding along a road full of beauty: on the right stretched a succession of vales and hills towards Dorsetshire, and, at a little distance, on the left, rose Woodbine-hill, the neat and friendly mansion of Admiral Sir Thomas Graves.

The small church of Monkton, which, surrounded with firs, stands close by the road side, with only a mere cottage in its vicinity, gives one a vivid sensation of that modesty and quiet in which the religious sentiment best flourishes. The road itself is so narrow and secluded, that is proximity does not seem in the least to interrupt the stillness of the place. The little cemetery, which surrounds three sides of the edifice, is in perfect unison with the whole scene, and seems to offer a place of repose so perfectly secure, as almost to extort a wish that after the toil of life is ended this might be the place of rest.

In the little hamlet of Luppit, which lies also on the left hand, there is a small dissenting place of worship, which for many years was the scene of the labours of Dr William Harris, well known in his day as author of several pieces of biography, written in the manner of Bayle, the peculiarity of which is, that the notes are considerably more bulky than the text. As books of reference, such productions are very valuable; every assertion is established by its proper authorities, and a great number of anecdotes are generally introduced, which an historian, writing in the common way, would omit. Dr Harris in this manner wrote memoirs of James I, Charles I, Oliver Cromwell, Hugh Peters and Charles II. The meeting in which he officiated is still occasionally used, but has not settled minister or congregation.

From this place the road rises all the way to the little village of Up-Ottery, which stands upon a considerable eminence, and, in very direction, commands not very extensive, but very charming views of the surrounding country. A neat church and a tolerably good inn are ornament and accommodations to this little place, which is also further distinguished by a neat farm-house and estate belonging to the present prime minister of England, the Right Hon. Henry Addington: it is, I have been informed, his paternal estate.

From *Up-Ottery* the road still continues to ascend, and, at length gaining a level, winds round what may be termed the artificial and upper base of a considerable hill; the valley on the right hand continues extremely beautiful, and of considerable extent. Some dilapidated walls, and firs planted in an avenue form, indicate the relics of departed and at least comparative greatness. A rude cottage or two are now the only habitations on the spot. After a descent of some length, the road again rises, and brings us to the extensive level across which the boundary line between Devon and Somerset is drawn, called Blackdown. The name indicates the general sterility which marks this extensive and elevated common: a thin coat of black mould supports a scanty covering of short and extremely dark-coloured grass, sprinkled in tolerable plenty with the yellow and purple flowers with which most of our heaths are both adorned and perfumed. A considerable number of small sheep are scattered over this wide expanse, and procure a sustenance from it which gives to their flesh a peculiarly delicate flavour.

From this lofty down the road dips with unavoidable abruptness into the rich valley of Taunton Dean…

Sidmouth, October 30 1803

Once more, my dear Madam, I address you from what, after all my wanderings, I am truly glad to see – my *own home*. To the lover of domestic joys what magic is there in this little word; and how truly are those to be pitied who have no relish for the peaceful, virtuous delights of their *own* fire-side.

Dulce Domun! Charming sound!
What sweet ideas crowd around
When o'er the mind those pictures come,
Which mem'ry sketches far from home.
The glowing fire, the elbow chair,
Those sweet reliefs from cold and care;
The clean-swept hearth; the frugal board;
The shelves with various authors stor'd;
The pratt'ling babes, the cheerful wife,
That sun-shine of domestic life;
A study, where the musing mind
Can intellectual treasure find;
A parlour to receive a friend,
And from severer cares unbend;
A little, flowery, green retreat,
Where health and moderate labour meet;
A respite form the world's vain jars,
Its noise, its nonsense, and its wars –
These, these are things the bosom cheer,
And render *Dulce Domun* dear.

For some months before it took place, the little tour of which I have given you an account in these letters, was an object of pleasing expectation to us all. That excursion has now been over for a considerable time, and, like all past events, has faded into a sort of vision, the images of which are every day becoming less distinct. All, however, is not forgotten. Memory retains some traces of the objects it presented, and gratitude has added some names to the tablet of friendship, and deepened the lines with which she had formerly engraven others. We have to record the superintending Providence of our HEAVENLY FATHER through all the stages of our journey – and to look forward, with hope, to the season when, under our own roof, some of our friends, at least, will give us an opportunity of expressing our sense of their kindness.

I shall dedicate the remainder of this closing epistle to a sketch of the place in which, perhaps, I may terminate my earthly pilgrimage.

Sidmouth, a small but rapidly increasing town, lies in the Channel, about midway betwixt *Lime* and Exmouth, and at the bottom of that vast bay, the extremities of which are Portland and the Start points. It has a bold, open shore, and many of its newest houses are ranged upon the beach, which is defended from the attacks of the ocean by a natural rampant of pebbles, which rises in four or five successive stages from the surface of the sea at low water. With every tide the exterior parts of this shifting wall assume some different situation; are sunk either higher or lower, or are driven to the east or west, according to the strength and direction of the wind. At low water, considerable spaces of fine hard sand are visible – these afford a pleasant walk, but are frequently interrupted by collections of stones, and streams which find their way through the pebbles to their parent ocean – in dry weather, however, these streams are very inconsiderable. At the head of this shingly rampart, a broad, commodious walk, which is called The Beach, has been constructed, and furnishes a delightful promenade. It is nearly a third of a mile in length, is kept well rolled, and furnished at the extremities, and in some other parts, with convenient double seat, from which either the land or the sea may be contemplated with every advantage. Close to the walk, and about the middle of it, is a tolerably spacious covered retreat, called *The Shed*, in which, as it is benched all round, and open only to the sea, a most convenient view of that sublime object may at all times be obtained. Large parties are frequently chatting in this recess, and the weak invalid here finds a spot in which, defended from every wind but the salubrious south, he can inhale those breezes which so frequently suspend the ravage of disease, pour fresh oil into the lamp of life, and send him back a renovated being to both the cares and joys of mortality. What a melancholy thought is it, that many of these renovated beings, when the blessing of HEAVEN has recruited their emaciated frames, strung their nerves with fresh vigour, and made them a new gift of existence, go back into society only to repeat former scenes of folly and excess, and finish the climax of their infatuation and ingratitude, by wasting the precious boon which they have obtained.

As a watering-place, Sidmouth, in its natural advantages, yields to none of the retreats of *Hygeia*. An air mild and salubrious, a soil uncommonly fertile, the purest water continually flowing, and a situation defended from every wind but the south, give it a pre-eminence over most of those places on our coasts which are resorted to fro the purposes of health or amusement. The beautiful vale in which it stands is bounded on both sides by long, lofty mountains – these form its eastern and western sides, and towards the north it is screened by the Honiton hills. Viewed from the beach the vale has the appearance of an immense land bay, if I may use such an expression, the curve of which is formed by a perfect amphitheatre of hills. Most of these are cultivated nearly to their tops – the enclosures are numerous, and present a rich variety of arable and pasture grounds; where there is no cultivation, they are covered with a short sweet grass, mixed with furze and heath, whose yellow and purple flowers beautifully diversify the landscape. The herbage feeds great numbers of sheep, and the furze supplies with fuel many a cottage and baker's oven.

In the hedges a great number of forest trees are interspersed – elms, ashes and oaks are the chief; but several other varieties are to be med with – and a multitude of orchards are scattered in every direction. In the spring and summer the numerous lanes which intersect and divide this rich valley are truly delightful – the country then seems a universal garden – innumerable are the flowers that perfume the air with fragrance, and delight the eye with their manifold shapes and colours: the deep banks are literally covered with these vegetable gems. The trees are many of them very lofty; and the foliage, even of those which grown almost at the edge of the sea, extremely luxuriant. Great quantities of holly and ivy enliven the dreary months of winter, and, with myrtles and other evergreens, shed a perpetual verdure over this charming spot. As the vale is but narrow, there is but little absolutely flat surface – slopes and swells, bright with constant verdure, every where greet the eye; and pellucid streams, running from almost every declivity, refresh and decorate the landscape through which they flow. The whole eastern side of the vale is watered by the serpentine Sid, which enters the ocean close under the marly rocks at the east end of the beach – in summer this in an inconsiderable stream, but in winter, or any part of the year, when swelled by an accession of rain, it is a foaming torrent, which then disdains to creep through the pebbles, but driving them to the right and the left, opens itself as an unincumbered passage to its parent deep.

Since Sidmouth has been growing into fame as a watering place, a great number of new houses have been erected – this very year has added no less than seven to the number, and still the Crescent, which is a row of houses called The Fortfields, remains unfinished. The houses on the western cliffs are so much detached and elevated, that I think if a few more were added they might assume the appellation of Clifton.

Not only is the town greatly enlarged within these few years, but a great number of single houses are scattered around it, and adorn, not merely the flat part of the vale, but the slopes of the hills which bound it on either side. The two most distinguished of these mansions are the houses of Emmanuel Baruh Lousada and George Cornish, Esquires. The former forms a beautifully neat object on the western declivity, and the latter one equally interesting on the eastern slope. From the grounds of Peak House, the spectator has a fine reach of the ocean, the white cliffs of Charmouth, and Bridport, and the bold promontory of Portland – and from Salcombe Hill, Mr Cornish's mansion, an excellent nearer view of the town, the little bay in which it is secluded, the deep-ribbed side of the high peak, the western wing of the ever memorable Torbay, and the Start-point, which appears plunging into the distant waves, and beginning the line of demarcation betwixt the sky and the land. From each of these elevated stations, a rich and picturesque view of the valley is to be obtained. Specimens of every kind of rural beauty are here collected; and, as the seasons of the year revolve, a landscape, frequently varying its hues, but always luxuriant and beautiful, courts and gratifies the eye of the spectator. The most extensive land view is to be had from the eastern or Salcombe hill – the eye ranges over a distance of above forty miles, and rests in farthest ken upon the most elevated points of Dartmoor.

To this eastern hill, which rises abruptly from the river, Mr C. has lately made a very convenient and truly picturesque walk – to overcome in some degree the steepness of the ascent, it takes a zig-zag form, and its angles are very acute – at its foot a bridge is thrown across the river, which brings the passenger very near the beach. This path has altogether a Swiss-like, Alpine appearance.

On the highest part of the Peak, which is the name of the western hill, the renewal of hostilities has again tenanted a signal-house, which was erected during the late war, with a lieutenant and two attendants. Frequently we see signals, of the precise meaning of which we are properly kept ignorant, made from this cabin in the air, for so it appears to a spectator below, or like an eagle's nest perched upon a rock. Ah! How happy would the world be, if the skill and industry of the human race, which are capable of such wonderful effects, were uniformly directed to purposes of reciprocal benefit and affection! In fine weather, the signal-house is often the boundary of a ride, or a walk, and the lovers of landscape beauty are richly rewarded for the labour of the ascent, by the vast panorama that from this point spreads its ample circle around them. Sea and land unite in the picture – if any vessels are passing, here they must be seen; and the land part of the prospect is replete with all those soothing and charming images which a fertile and cultivated landscape always affords – lovely green fields, spotted with sheep – thick hedges, breathing fragrance, and variegated with innumerable flowers – trees of every height and size – hills of different shape and magnitude – orchards, gardens, and copses – large stacks of hay and corn – a multitude of habitations, most of them a pure white, which contrasts so beautifully with the azure above, and the green below; and, in the distance, the neat spires of Otterton and Sidbury churches, which, peeping through the foliage, finish the prospect, by elevating the mind of the spectator to a better world. The contemplation of the heavens and the earth; a survey of the richness, the beauty, and variety of nature, is always favourable to devotion. In cities men are hurried out of themselves by the din of business, and the glare of dissipation. Confident in their numbers, they forget the natural helplessness of man. Every thing around them being artificial, refers them to human power and wisdom; but solitude, and the contemplation of natural objects, elevates them to the power and wisdom of God.

For the indulgence of that occasional retirement from the world which has always been the delight of the wise and the virtuous, and which is so friendly to both mental and bodily health, the immediate vicinity of Sidmouth is perfectly calculated – it abounds with sequestered and yet perfectly safe walks, which may dispute the palm of beauty with any part of the island; while to those of a contrary disposition, the beach, which is the grand public mall, the shed, and the billiard room, afford full scope for gossiping, lounging, and play.

The bathing at Sidmouth is commodious and reasonable; eight machines are employed; and a warm sea-bath has been erected for complaints which require that kind of immersion. There are two good inns in the town, the London and the New Inn; that called the London Inn is the largest, and contains the assembly and card-rooms – the assembly-room is larger and better fitted up than the rooms used for similar purposes at any of the places upon this coast – but when large parties meet, they feel very sensibly the want of a master of the ceremonies – this is particularly the case with such of the visitants as have no previous acquaintance with any of the stated frequenters of the rooms. Numerous as the lodging-houses now are, there are frequently not enow to accommodate the company in the height of the season. Some years ago a small theatre was erected here – an itinerant company were the performers, but the building, now converted into habitations for poor people, is a proof of the success they met with. Over the billiard-room is a room appropriated to the purpose of reading the public papers. The market-house is a convenient modern erection, and, particularly on Saturdays, is well supplied with provisions.

The supply of fish is by no means so regular or great as the proximity of the place to the great 'store-house of the deep' might lead one to expect; but sometimes mackerel and whiting are caught in prodigious quantities. It is a curious and entertaining sight to see the former of these species of fish when first brought on shore – the extreme brilliancy of their hues, and the varying appearances which the agonies of death occasion, cannot fail to strike the most cursory observer. One naturally hopes that most of these are muscular motions, and attended with little or no pain to the expiring animal.

None of the creatures, such millions of which are hourly giving up their lives to sustain ours, seem to die so soon or so easily as fish – humanity dwells with pleasure on such a circumstance, and imperiously commands those whose office it is to take away the lives of animals, to do it with utmost speed and tenderness – with the wretches who can deliberately doom these innocent beings to a painful dissolution in order to increase the flavour of their flesh, and pamper, with a new stimulus, a jaded appetite, humanity disclaims all connection – she leaves them to the retribution which cruelty must somewhere expect to meet with, and registers their names with the refuse of their species, the mere *Heliogabeli* and *Apicii* of mankind.

Opposite the eastern gate of the Fort field, so denominated from a little fort, with a flag-staff, and mounted with four pieces of cannon, which command the beach and the bay, stands the church, which is dedicated to St Giles. Nothing particular distinguishes this fabric; it is supposed to be about four hundred years old; its tower is a neat specimen of unornamented architecture; the date over the principal entrance, which is evidently a more recent work than the rest of the building, is 1680.

Many are the tomb-stones which crowd the churchyard – several, as may be easily be supposed, belong to invalids who, seeking too late the balmy breezes of Sidmouth, here dropped their earthly tabernacles. The handsomest of these mortuary erections commemorates a very amiable man, with whom I had the happiness of being acquainted; after lingering about a year, this respectable physician, for that was this profession, proved, in his own case, the inanity of all medical assistance. An oval compartment in the front of the tomb bears this inscription:

M.S.

Of Robert Halls, M.D.

Who died the 10th day of February, 1801

Aged 33.

At the remembrance of they worth Friendship drops a tear.

At the north entrance of the town there is another place of worship; it belongs to that body of Protestant dissenters commonly called Presbyterians; it is a small neat place, and in general is well attended. It was formed into a chapel about seventy years ago; previous to that time the meeting-house was nearly where the theatre now stands.

A place which still bears the name of Chapel-yard, and nearer the beach than the present church, seems to prove, either that there was once a third religious edifice, or that the present church was erected in the room of one which, in remoter times, occupied this spot. Sidmouth is a place of great antiquity; and geographers tell us, had once a considerable port, which has been so choked up with sand as to become unapproachable by anything but boats, and very small vessels. This is evidently inaccurate; no sand has destroyed its harbour, nor is it probable that it ever possessed one of any magnitude. Most likely, between the curing western cliff, and those rocks which stretch in a southern direction from one which, having survived its brethren, still rears its naked head, and bears the buffeting of the waves, there was a sort of natural basin, in which the comparatively small vessels of former days might ride in safety. Some of them might even discharge their cargoes with infinitely less risk than coals are now landed from a Brig upon the beach.

Tradition reports great things of the fishery which was once carried on at Sidmouth, and there is no doubt but it greatly surpassed any thing that is attempted now. Pool and Topsham are now the great depots of the Newfoundland trade, but not fifty years ago the principal inhabitants of Sidmouth were masters and owners of ships in that important but hazardous employ. All this is now over; the race of fishermen is almost extinct; and those of the inhabitants who do not live upon their estates, are supported, directly or indirectly, by the annual appearance of visitors which ill health, dissipation, or a love of rambling bring amongst them.

In the rocks and lanes of Sidmouth the naturalist may find many materials for study and amusement. Botany may cull its plants, and the Fossilist collect may of the curious internal productions of the earth. Beautiful Pholens are here to be met with, and the stones of the cliffs many of them abound with *echin marin*, petrified coral, and other similar productions. The *cornu Ammonis* is to be found here of all sizes; a friend of mine in the town has got a very fine one, in the common rounded form, of an embellished metallic appearance, and about 18 inches in diameter, which he found in the cliffs near Portland.

In the little basins worn by the waves in the rocks 'elegant corallines abound; and not infrequently that singular production of nature, the animal flower, commonly called the sea anemone.'

Sidmouth lies at a convenient distance for excursions from several other places – it is 10 miles from Exmouth, 15 from Exeter, 9 from Honiton, 15 from Axminster, 16 from Lyme, and 10 from Seaton. The neighbouring parish of Branscombe is a completely romantic spot; the lofty cliffs which defend it from the sea are paralleled, at a small distance, by a range of inland hills, which are ornamented with orchards, hanging woods, and enclosures, covered with grass or grain; between these hills winds a valley or rich pasturage, and a stream which, sometimes concealed, and sometimes in open view, after a multitude of sinuosities, falls into the common receptacle, the ocean. About the middle of this peaceful *Tempé* stands Branscombe church, the tinkling bell of which, when its sound floats through the vale, suggests the idea of some lone convent, that at stated periods calls the scattered inhabitants of an Alpine village to their plain unostentatious devotions. Salcombe and its little church repeats this picture, but upon a smaller scale, with fewer inhabitants, and less ornamental appendages. The parsonage house of Salcombe, lying snug under a hill, has a peculiarly neat and comfortable appearance. In such places as these Religion does not rear her 'mitred front', but where her dictates are obeyed with sincerity, her plain unornamented rites are infinitely more worthy the Divine acceptance, than the pomp of royal chapels, and the parade of cathedral services, where the heart of the worshipper does not make a part of the oblation.

This my dear friend, is a sketch of the place, and its immediate neighbourhood, in which I now reside. In my public services I am able still to engage: for this, I trust I am unfeignedly thankful, and, upon a deliberate review of my lot, I can adopt the declaration with which this letter will close: this I am sure will give you, as my real friend, true satisfaction: hoping that ere long you will be an eye-witness of what I have endeavoured to delineate, I once more subscribe myself your sincere and affectionate friend. E.B.

MRS PARRY PRICE
of
CHESTER, 1805

The front at Exmouth, *c*.1855

Berkshire Record Office, D/EEg/Z1. See Todd Gray, 'The Travels of Mrs Parry Price through Devon in 1805', *Transactions of the Devonshire Association* (vol. 128, 1996), 65–89.

Mrs Price, a widow and grandmother, was in East Devon on the return leg of her journey to a christening in Plymouth. She travelled with a female servant whom she referred to as 'Jones'. Mrs Price resided in Stanley Place in Chester. The Misses Lees that she met may have been Mary, Sarah and Thomasine Leigh of Salcombe Regis.

Friday June 21. Went to Mr Hunter's [in Exeter] to breakfast, Lord & Lady Graves came in about 12 o'clock, his Lordship said he should dine at the Mess but her Ladyship would take a family dinner with Mrs Hunter. He conversed in the most affable entertaining manner for about an hour, & then went away; Lady Graves stood talking in a window with Mrs Hunter in a low voice after he was gone. I took up a book that I wished to read before I went entitled 'Fashion displayed' which is a very sensible production & justified upon it. Mrs Hunter went out of the room without my observing it; & her Ladyship took up another book & read soon after Mrs Hunter returned & left the room, being in haste to prepare for my leaving for Exmouth, having taken a place in the coach to go there & was to set out between 4 & 5 o'clock that evening. Accordingly I returned when I had done by business & found Lady Graves & Mrs Hunter looking over a piece of worsted work, which was begun, & the pattern traced out, but would be a most tedious piece to finish, which I told her Ladyship & that I knew some easier & pleasanter stitches to work, upon which she desired I would show her one upon that canvas. Which I accordingly did & she was so much delighted with it, that she begged I would come with her & his Lordship to a shop to choose the worsteds & canvas for her but we were so long there that I began to fear I should not be in time for the coach & Mrs Hunter had shown such a fright least I should tell them I was going in it that I determined for her sake not to do it if I could avoid it & I had taken leave of her before I went with them; & they would bring me to the Inn & when we got in sight of it Lady Graves saw a Gentleman's Postchair at the door & asked me if it was mine, which I told her it was not, & luckily the Coach did not come to the door until they were gone. Before we parted his Lordship said when I was tired of my excursions to the sea, & chose to take my rest he hoped they should see me at Bishops Court, her Ladyship also behaved to me in the most friendly & obliging manner & made me lead upon her arm all the way we walked & they both shaked hands with me in a friendly manner when we parted. Soon afterwards a very good roomy coach came to the door in which were two genteel well dressed ladies, a charming boy who appeared to be a Gentleman's Son both by his dress & manners & an elderly man who looked like a tradesman. They went with us about half way, told us all the gentlemen's seats as we passed of which there were a great number. One of which I remember was Sir Alexander Hamilton's & then got out to go to their respective places of residence & there only remained the young Gentleman & a schoolgirl who came with us part of the way to Exmouth. The boy was very polite &

chatty, & put me in mind of my dear grandson. He told me his name was Turguan & he lived in a capital house upon Beacon Hill in Exmouth, was coming home from Exeter School for the Holidays, that he had brought a Guinea Pig, 3 Angola Rabbits with him which went in a wooden box pierced with holes on the top of the coach & seemed very anxious to get them there alive. I told him I had never seen an Angola rabbit, & that I should like to see one; he said he would show them to me when he got home & when we arrived at his father's house, he & his lady, who appeared very genteel people, came to the door to meet him & two servants, one of whom took his coat & the other his box, which as soon as he had kissed his parents he ordered to bring back again to the coach (for I did get out) to show to me, his parents went into the parlour, & he took leave of me in a very polite manner.

Saturday June 22nd. I still continued at the Globe Hotel, where we had put up & I slept, finding everything there very commodious & comfortable, I first called at Dr Moore's, who had taken a very pretty house in Parker Place for three months but they were unfortunately gone out a walking before I got there. I then took a stroll by myself towards Beacon Hill in hopes of meeting with my young friend, who had promised to walk with me but did not choose to force myself upon his mother & therefore would not go to the house. But I met with another nice boy about his age walking upon the beach who proved to be an acquaintance of Master Turguan, told him I was a stranger to the place, & begged he would show me to one pretty walk, he said he thought everybody ought to be civil to strangers, & that he would walk with me, which he accordingly did & showed me a very pretty walk by the seaside when we parted I offered him a shilling to buy him some cakes, or marbles, which he at first refused, but afterwards took. At 5 o'clock the Doctor, Mrs Moore & their children called upon me & asked me to a walking with them but as I had but just dined & was tired with my morning's walk, I declined it.

Sunday June the 23rd. Went to Exmouth chapel which is large & commodious & heard an excellent sermon – text 3rd 6 Revelations & 21 verse – 'to him that overcometh will I grant to sit with me on my Throne even as I also overcame & am set down with my Father in his Throne'. There was no divine service in the evening, & I drank tea, walked under & over Beacon Hill, & drank tea & supped with Mrs Moore, who played & sung for me & lent me a volume of Dr Downman's work to read. I also called on Mrs Moore after church in the morning when several people visited her & amongst the rest a

Mr & Miss Lee, who I afterwards met on the beach, when they invited me to their lodgings, lent me a sermon book & gave me a note to a Mr [John] Swete desiring he would permit me to see his place, & drive through his grounds on my road to Lord Lisbon's to Lord Courtenay's where I purposed going the next day. Exmouth, Sunday evening June 23rd in continuation.

Monday June the 24th went with Mrs Moore in a postchaise to the seaside, got into a small boat with one only man to tow it & the chaise & horses put into another, to cross the Passage over the River Exe. A pleasant voyage, got into the chaise again & drove through very narrow lanes...[at Dawlish] Mrs Moore & I took a most delightful walk after they were gone by the seaside, where there is a seat, & a smooth walk, & a large piece of rock, separated from the main body by the waves of the sea which appears at Exmouth like a ship turning the corner of a point of land, & I could not believe until I came near it that it was not one. When we returned the water was gone off the road, but the wind was high & I dreaded crossing over the Exe in so small a boat, but thank God we got very safe tho' we had only one Man to row us, by going up the River a little higher in the boat than we needed otherwise to have done & we arrived at Exmouth between 7 & 8 o'clock.

Tuesday June the 25th. At the Globe Hotel all day writing my journal & reading Dr Hugh Downman's Poems, took a walk on the beach in the evening with Jones.

Wednesday the 26th. Called on Mrs Lee, took a walk with her to see a house lately inhabited by Lord Ormand, which he took for three months after his marriage & brought his Lady there from London; it is an exceeding good lodging house with a beautiful little garden & the borders are edged round with the scallop shells, such as are made are of in Wales, to put oysters & cockles on for the table. They were pierced through & fastened to a narrow piece of wood, well tarred to preserve it & fixed at the edge of the border & had a beautiful effect. There was also an alcove at the end of the walk ornamented with them & a most charming view of the sea from it, & of Powderham Lord Courtenay's house & grounds, with the beautiful Belvedere above it, all which you see very distinctly. In the evening read one of Dr Downman's plays called *Editha, or the siege of Exeter*, afterwards walked on that charming walk under Beacon Hill to the last gate alone being about a mile & half; as I returned met the 2 Miss Lees, & extended my walk with them to the terrace near Ormond Place, took leave of Mrs Moore, & returned to the Hotel.

Thursday June 27th. Left Exmouth in a chaise, stopped to take a lunching at Ottery St May, a very rainy morning or meant to have got out to have seen Lord Rolle's [house of Bicton] which lies directly on the road between Exmouth & Ottery but saw the house which is a new brick one, not quite finished from the road, also the Park, Deer, Greenhouse & some part of the pleasure ground with 4 statues of a shepherd & shepherdess & drove under a curious arch of stone-work in a rustic style, over which there is a walk in his pleasure ground, which commands a view of the road for a considerable distance; also past his lodge, the pillars at each end of the gate are built of brick & ornamented with stone in the rustic style of the archway we came under & there is an obelisk erected in the centre of 4 lanes, which is built of brick terminated with a stone point, & four medallions of stone placed so as to be read from the road with inscriptions telling you which way each lane leads by way of finger-post, & is the handsomest & best I ever saw. The roads were as usual very hilly & many of them so narrow that 2 carriages could not pass & cut so deep in the grounds & the hedgerows so high that the bows of them joined together & form an arch so that we seemed to be travelling through groves of trees, which was very pleasant but in the winter time or in the dark the Postilion told me, they found those deep roads both inconvenient & dangerous but this only happens in the private roads. The public roads are in general sufficiently broad for two carriages to pass each other. The distance from Exmouth to Honiton is eighteen miles & were between 3 & 4 hours in driving it tho' I had a very good pair of horses & driver. I got to Honiton time enough to dress for dinner, which I was glad of as Mr Lott had company to dine with them, which were a Mr, Mrs & Miss Gidley, & a Captain Manly, Dr Robinson also came in soon after the cloth was taken away. Mrs Gidley is a very remarkably handsome woman, has 10 children, & looks so young, that her daughter appears more like her sister. Mr Gidley has also a good face, but a large person & Miss G. is well looking but not so handsome as her parents. Capt. Manley has a very Manly handsome face; with an uncommonly sweet countenance; in the evening Mr Leigh of Crampton came in; & I played at whist with him, Mr Lott & Mr Gidley. They all stayed supper & until near half past 12 o'clock when they took their departure to my great joy as I was tired & sleepy.

Friday June the 28th. a Mr Peers came in soon after breakfast, also a Captain Baytun of the 6th dragoon. Mr Peers is a very genteel handsome man & agreeable in conversation. He told me some quaint words of the Devonshire dialect: *jillim* for dust; *much adrowd* for dirt & *maze* for mad. Walked with Mrs Lott to a lace shop & to Tracey

House [in Awliscombe]; caught in the rain, so wet that we were obliged to change our clothes. Tracey House a pretty & convenient one, with a large & very productive garden & a most beautiful situation. The lands forming a very fine amphitheatre to the front of the house to a great extent & the river Otter, winding & meandering in a most charming manner in the middle of the vale in full view of the house. After tea we took a walk to the end of the town of Honiton, which consists of one broad handsome street, flagged on each side but the houses in general small & low. However, Mr Lott's [house] & some few others at the ends of the Town, are very good ones & have very convenient pretty gardens, are mostly white, & one or two of them stand in shrubberies & make a very genteel appearance, as you enter the town from Exmouth. On our return we met with Captain Baynton, who came with us home, played at whist, & supped with us.

Saturday June 29th. Col. Kingston called just as we were setting out for Sidmouth. Mr Lott drove me in his gig, & Mr Peers & Mrs Lott in another; went over Tenn hill, a most beautiful prospect from it, but a most terrible hill to drive up & down both on all the roughness of the road, the various turnings & the steep road when you got upon it. Drove also through Sidford & Sidbury. Saw at a distance Woodbine hill [which is the home of] Admiral Sir Thomas Graves knight of the Bath who fought under Lord Nelson at the battle of Copenhagen in consequence of which he got his title, also saw General Simcoe, ie Woolford Lodge, likewise [the home of] Admiral Richard Graves, Ambarg Foot Coll. Kington (who is married to the Marchioness of Clanicade) advised me before I set out to get out when I came down the hill & I determined also to get out when I went up it, tho' my party would have had me remain in the gig & I afterwards repented that I had not, as I believe I might have done it very safely & I was much fired with the walk. When I got to the descent of the hill I also got out much sooner that I need to have done & as Mr Lott's servant rode a very spirited hose I was afraid of his coming near him & he went down the hill with the carriages. When they went quite out of sight & hearing, to my great surprise & shock there came out of a field into the road I was walking a roaring bull & a young bullock which terrified me beyond description but as I saw them first at a considerable distance, took up two stones & hid myself as well as I could behind a tree for the road was cut so deep & the hedges so thick I could not get through them into a field, where I stood ready to die with fright when they went past me & soon after Mr Lott's servant came back in search of me, or I don't know what I should have done, as I was afraid before he came to move either backwards or forwards for I should see something again to alarm me. However, thank God I got safely down to my party, & had a very pleasant drive until we got into Sidmouth when we met with a man on a loaded cart, which when we were endeavouring to pass it, his horse ran back & was very near occasioning and being overturned but the goodness of Providence preserved us from it tho' we were in a most perilous situation.

We stopped at the London Inn & I went to see Mrs Perkins, she was not at home & I passed a boarding house, turned in & asked their rates. Then went to a walk on the shore where I saw a most beautiful thatch cottage enclosed in a court & a drive up to it, with a veranda in the front which was to be let. I went in & found it belonged to a Coll. Anderson, who was gone from home for some months; & they asked eighty guineas a week for it, & had left it with all the greenhouse plants in the bow windows & furnished in the first of expense & elegance but there was only one large room in it, which was the drawing upstairs, & that was the whole length of the house which I believe might be about 25 feet long. I then went upon the walk, which is the most delightful one I ever saw & is called the Marine Pavilion, in imitation of the Prince's at Brighton, with a large covered shed & benches to sit upon. From whence you see to the eastward the Island of Portland & the coast of Dorset by *Abbotbary*. To the westward the bays of Budleigh Salterton, Exmouth, Dawlish, Teignmouth & you also see Berryhead & Torbay. Off Teignmouth are two curious rocks called the Parson & Clerk. NB in my opinion Sidmouth is superior to Exmouth, as the sands in the latter smells very disagreeably & at Sidmouth there's none at all, but a fine pebbly beach. The drive home was very pleasant until we came to descend the hill when the breech-band broke & I got out & Mrs Lott was so obliging to give me her place in the other gig. Mr Peers supped with us.

Saturday the 30th. Went to Honiton church, a very handsome one built about 4 hundred years ago. From thence we went to Dr Honywood who had done the duty with great credit to himself & is a remarkable handsome man. His grounds are very pretty & laid out with great taste. Went we left his house I went into the churchyard in order to read the inscriptions on the monuments & gravestones, but found none at all out of the common style. However, as it was a very hot day, & we had determined to attend evening service & if we returned back to Honiton, which is 3 quarters of a mile from the church & a steep hill up to it I begged Mrs Lott to return home as she intended doing, & permit me to remain in the church yard until she came back which was accordingly done; & I walked round the church yard, reading the inscription & sitting very comfortably upon a grave stone until the church doors were opened, when I walked round the church saw some handsome monuments, & a piece of fine Gothic woodwork, painted like grey & white marble & gilt in some places which is a modern work presented by Sir John Honeywood, member for Honiton, & brother to the Doctor, which separates the chancel & communion table from the other part of the church & has a very pretty effect. The country people call it a screen & not very improperly as you cannot see that past it is placed before distinctly through it but there are 3 beautiful Open Gothic doors in it which are always left open for the clergyman & congregation to walk through from the different aisles of the church. When we returned from church we called on Mrs Buckworth, Mrs Lott's mother, who is a handsome genteel woman, lives in a pretty house, has a good garden, & behaved very politely to me, but was prevented by indisposition from visiting me at Mr Lotts, which she apologised for. We then went home to dinner, & in the evening Mr & Miss Pearse came to us, & a band of Marie belonging to a regiment played near the house which was very pleasant.

Monday July the 1rst. Set out about 2 o'clock in the afternoon in the Mercury, a long coach that holds six, but there was only two gentlemen & a boy about fifteen who was dressed as a Mid-Shipman, & was the son of one of them, & the other was his friend, & they were going down to Plymouth with the youth to take him to his ship, which they told me was the *Courageaux*, & that he had never been at sea; I thought of my son, as it was the ship he first went to sea in; I felt interested for the boy & anxious to serve him; & said if he remained any time in Dock; that I would recommend him to a friend of mine that lived there & who I was sure on my request would invite him to his house & pay him every polite attention but the father, who was a very respectable well-looking man about fifty, said he should not leave him until the ship sailed, seems sensibly affected at the thoughts of parting with his son & I sincerely pitied him; knowing how much I had suffered on a similar occasion. Soon after we got into the coach they said they expected another gentleman, who was a man of fortune, & came with them down from London, & that they meant to take postchaises from Exeter to Plymouth but the journey being so long & travelling so expensive they had determined to lessen the expense to come in the coach from London to Exeter, where they meant to stay two or three days to rest & amuse the boy before they took him to Plymouth. The other gentleman overtook us before we got far &

seemed a very pleasant cheerful man & told us some entertaining anecdotes. We arrived at Exeter about half past five & went to a different Inn so I saw no more of them when I had refreshed & cleaned myself from the dust. I went to a stationer's to buy some books Mr Honeywood had recommended to me. From thence to the Southernhay Walk, where there was a band of music playing & from thence to the Northernhay Walk where there was a still better. As I came back to the Inn I met Mr Hunter who begged I would come immediately to his house for Mrs Hunter was at home. I told him I meant to come there at 7 o'clock for tea, but I had dined. Accordingly I attended Mrs Hunter's tea table, & was happy to find her alone & after tea walked with her to call upon Mrs Thewles, & found the General & his lady *tete-an-tete*, we sat some time with them, & I then returned with Mrs Hunter to supper & stayed so late that I did not get to bed until between 12 & one o'clock.

Tuesday July 2nd. & at a quarter after four I was called to get up to go in the coach to Wells & we got into it precisely at quarter after five without any breakfast nor were we permitted to get away when we reached Cullompton, which is 30 miles from Exeter. However I had luckily procured some strawberries, oranges & hard biscuits at Exeter to eat on the road. On which I made an excellent meal & there was a gentleman who was a Swiss in the coach who had brought a bottle a cherry brandy & a small cap which he offered his Lady & Me to taste & we both took a little of it & I thought it did me a great deal of good. His name is Houch, he has been a merchant & acquired, as I afterwards heard, a large fortune, has a house both at Exeter & Exmouth for the bathing season & they were only going two stages to visit Mrs Houch's sister. Mrs Houch is a genteel pleasant woman, & has seen a great deal of the world, I found her a very [word missing] companion & was sorry to lose her soon...

An Anonymous Former Schoolboy *at* Exeter, 1816

Louisa Terrace, Exmouth, *c.*1855

Anonymous, *Recollections of a Ramble, during the summer of 1816, in a letter to a friend* (London, 1817), 140–144.

This tour took place during the month of June and the writer's motive was to travel to Exeter to relive his school days and visited Exmouth to seek his former instructor who had retired there. He came to Exmouth via Dawlish.

...On a cliff immediately in front of us, was seen situated the town of Exmouth, rising on the summit of the hill, enriched with luxuriant scenery around, and commanding a fine view of the sea. Dismissing the carriage, I was in a few minutes ferried over the stream, and by a very short walk, soon found myself safely lodged in the town.

I need scarcely explain to you the motives that brought me to this place; you are aware, I was not influenced by its local situation, however enchanting, or its grand coast-view, however striking, though it possessed much to interest the coldest lover of nature. My wish was to visit the instructor of my youth, to shake him once more by the hand in later life, and thus renew the pleasurable recollections of my boyish days. You may smile, but I know you cannot disapprove the idea. I had long amused myself with such a hope, and being now at length so near accomplishment, I was all anxiety for its being realized. He had here retired from public life, to spend the remainder of it in the exercise of a well-stored mind, and a refined taste. When a boy, I had every cause to prize Mr B–'s valuable qualities. I hurried through the town, and knocked at the door; it was not long ere I obtained an entrance. I was ushered into the room, for some moments we surveyed each other, but it required no introduction, a hearty shake of the hand soon dissipated every doubt, and assured me of a welcome.

It is impossible to describe to you, my Friend, the pleasures I experienced that evening; every little incident of early life brought afresh to my recollection, each little freak at school, and every minor occurrence, that had died in my memory, but for such a collision and meeting, rose again in rapid view to my mind.

> Busy meddling memory,
> In quick succession muster'd up
> The past endearments of each
> Tender hour.

With them I seemed to feel myself again the school-boy.

It was not the least gratifying to hear the event and disposal in life of those, I once congregated with, and had been in close youthful fellowship; one had risen to high distinction in his profession; another to an eminent station in the church, whilst each seemed not to have thrown away the well-enforced instructions of the adviser of their youth; – in all it was evident that education was the crucible of life, the refining fire that separated the dross from the varied mass of their youthful minds. Now then, did the thought of having been the successful instrument in the prosecution of such a cause, seem to form in him the most exhilarating considerations, especially too as there had been others like myself, who had been equally disposed to renew the sympathies and recollections of past years.

I had once parted from my master without regret, I now found I was taking leave, perhaps for ever, of a much valued friend; this feeling, as it was just, seemed to be cordially participated, and with a chastised satisfaction, I bid him farewell, with the warmest interchange of good wishes.

Leaving the town, I took the road which passes along the left bank of the Exe, which soon became deep and shady, whilst the thick hedge-rows of stately elms, suffered the eye to have but a contracted view. The climate was soft and luxurious, and the country was so exceedingly fertile, as to afford every thing in which the farmer can glory. Numerous cottage-residences shot up their comfortable roofs in the midst of these cultivated spots. The view across the water exhibited the opposite bank, as it lay strikingly adorned with its richly varied and interesting scenery. Mamhead, the beautiful seat of Lord Lisburne, stood in a commanding situation, and the dark woods of Powderham swept even to the very edge of the stream. I passed through Topsham, still, as ever, a dirty and insignificant town, in which there was nothing claiming attention, but the bustle of ship building, and from being situated on an arm of the Exe, many vessels make it their rendezvous, for the city of Exeter…

MRS HARRIET MUNDY
of
SOUTH ORMSBY, LINCOLNSHIRE, 1819

Boats on the beach at Sidmouth, 1837

Lincolnshire Archives Office, MM10/32

On 15 July Mrs Mundy, accompanied by her husband Charles and their two children, Harriet and Sophy, began her travels from Weymouth along the south coast of Dorset, Devon and Cornwall to Land's End and then returned to Weymouth on 18 August via Bodmin, Callington, Clovelly, Lynton, Dunster, Taunton and Dorchester. She estimated that they travelled some 730 miles.

Wednesday, June 16th 1819

A journal kept by Mrs Charles Mundy during a tour which her husband Mr C: Mundy, and their two little girls, Harriet aged 11 & Sophy 9 years, commenced from Weymouth travelling in a Barrow-chette with the servants in a gig, and with their own horses...We afterwards went forward to Axminster, the distance 5 miles & the road the greater part of the way through a country richly embellished with cultivation, hedge row trees, pretty villas & neat white cottages which leave a pleasant impression on the traveller's mind of the taste and comfort of the inhabitants. The height of the hedges in some parts interrupt the views which cannot but be regretted, but the luxuriant [sic] of their growth & the great variety of plants & flowers which adorn them strike one who like myself is only accustomed to a simple quick hedge. At Axminster we saw the Carpet Manufactory, the immediation of the Turkey is brought to the highest perfection, the whole of the work is done by Women, they told us they came as Children into the Manufactory and went through the various gradations of preparing the Materials till they were capable of working at the frames. They seemed very comfortable & it is the first Manufactory I have seen which is perfectly clean and free from all unpleasant smells. We went into the Church. The pulpit & reading desk are most beautiful from the fine carving which ornaments them; our drive from hence to Honiton is certainly the finest for prospect which we have yet seen and the most extensive & fertile that can well be imagined. I had heard of the extreme beauty of the view for the two last miles into Honiton & [the] report had not at all exaggerated this drive. The hills are truly tremendous but the reward to the admirer of prospect is amble on reaching the summit. We dined at the Golden Lion at *Hennington,* Webbers, & found it remarkably comfortable. I visited the Lace Workers opposite & made a trifling purchase, the sprigs which are put into the lace imitate the Brussels are all made here. We proceeded to Sidmouth & for some miles the prospect continues quite as beautiful as it was on the other side of the town. On getting near Sidmouth, we were obliged to leave the main road from its being under repair & mistaking the way found ourselves in some narrow lanes which were extremely awkward for the carriage & in on place dangerous. We however reached the London Inn without accident about 10 o'clock & our Children not tired & this day having been a most delightful one.

Thursday 17th. We walked to the beach a short distance from the inn. The cliffs are fine & their red colour add much to the richness of the scenery. The shore is covered with pebbles, the sands bad for walking. There is a promenade above the beach & the houses fronting the sea appear good. The coast is bold & the rich verdure & cultivated inland view to which so much hedge row timber greatly contributes pleased me exceedingly and gives this place a great superiority as far as beauty is concerned to any we have yet seen on the coast. There are two public libraries in the row of houses fronting the sea. At one of them I purchased some prints and some specimens. From hence we proceeded by appointment to call upon Mr & Mrs Steward who reside in one of the villas here & they accompanied us to Miss Wright's most elegant cottage. It appears the most complete of any in the place, both with in & without. She has adorned it with every elegant luxury & the its [sic] style of architecture gives it the name of Cottage. The interior has excellent & handsome rooms commanding delightful sea views & the shady walks in the shrubberies were delightfully cool this hot day. After taking our leave of Miss Wright & her friend, who were both extremely obliging, we proceeded with Mr & Mrs Steward to Lord LeDespencer's Cottage which is in fact a large house from the size & number of rooms but I thought it gloomy & tho certainly very beautiful I should not like to reside there more than a couple of months in the hot weather, we afterwards walked over two or three more in the same style tho smaller & passed through many delightfully shady lanes & saw many most pleasing views. After dinner at the Inn we walked on the shale towards a singular piece of rock which stands along in the sea. It appears to have been gradually separated from the shore by the incroachments of the sea. We returned by the shale to tea & by the number of people we met walking this appears to be the fashionable promenade of the place.

Friday the 18th. After breakfast we walked to the top of *Salcomb* hill, which is as nearly perpendicular as a hill can be which is ascended at all by horses or carriages. I should be very unwilling to go up it with either, the prospects at each point where we halted to take breath became much more interesting, & when quite at the top we could extend our eyes over an eminent prospect of sea & land. To the West after casting the sight down the pretty valley in which Sidmouth is situated at the foot of this hill, the whole coast is delightfully varied by rising cliffs & on the verge of the sea many picturesque caverns can be seen. The promontory which from Torbay is distinctly seen & also Beer Head. We walked on this lofty terrace, to the verge of the Hill which forms the descent on the eastern side, to the village of Salcombe & here there is another small but very pretty valley & bay terminating it to the sea. The church & village at the upper end is exceedingly pleasing in it situation following the park we got into a lane & seeing some sheepshearers in an Orchard on our right we went to them & Mr C.M. talked to them about their modes of farming and we found them very civil. Gradually descending the hill we returned to dinner at the Inn, passing in our road a pretty small place inhabited by Sir George Armitage & another near it by Mr Ram. This walk took us from 11 o'clock till past two & could not have been much less than ten miles. The little girls with us & not tired. We were glad of some luncheon & after it, went to the Marble works & ordered two chimney pieces for [?]Barton to be sent there. Then dined again, strolled out into the lanes & were not sorry to retire, after this day of much pleasure but a good deal of exercise.

Saturday the 19th. We left Sidmouth at 8 o'clock in the morning & sending the carriage with the luggage to the top of Peek Hill, we followed on foot. The walk is delightful through the pretty lanes nearly half way up the Hill, & then the extensive prospect looking across the valley in which Sidmouth stands, and the opposite hill of Salcombe is both very rich & very well diversified. At the top of the hill we got into the carriages & proceeded on our road to Exmouth. The scenery the whole way is beautiful & the road romantic, winding through narrow lanes the hedges abounding with wild flowers, privet & holly, & in many parts it appears as if cut through the rock & the trees in the hedges arching across give that elegance & dressed appearance that one is tempted to fancy the drive is through some ornamented pleasure ground enriched with the views of gentlemen's seats in some parts & in others the agreeable variety of a wild uncultivated heath bounded with the sea & rocky shore. Exmouth appears an excellent town...

MISS WYNDHAM PORTMAN *of* SALISBURY, 1820

Budleigh Salterton, 1842

Wiltshire Record Office, 865/572/37–8. See also Christine North, 'Miss Portman's Cornish Diary, 1820', *Journal of the Royal Institution of Cornwall* (NS II, Vol. I, Part 3, 1993), 269–76.

Miss Portman, an elderly maiden lady, travelled from Salisbury to Cornwall accompanied by her friend Miss Phillippa Grove. She returned through East Devon.

...September 1, Monday

Rode to Budleigh Salterton, a pretty little bathing place, across the heath (from whence fine sea view from Berry Hill to Portland) to St John's in the Wilderness, in the parish of Withycombe [Raleigh], said to be the oldest church in England. After dinner went on the sea.

September 2, Saturday

In the morning went on the sea, in evening rode to Lympstone.

September 3, Sunday

Evening – rode on donkeys thro' Lympstone, & returned by the river.

September 4, Monday

Left Exmouth, passed thro' Budleigh, on left is Bicton House, Lord Rolles', the chapel, garden and house are now near the public road, which has lately been turned to avoid hills, thro' *Collaton* [Colaton Raleigh], where there is a curious Fir Tree, thro' Newton Poppleford, cross river Otter, ascend long hill, very narrow road cut thro' the rocks, descend gradually to Sidmouth, a pretty place & beautiful country around it. From thence ascended a hill 2 miles long & continued a fine flat road 5 miles on left is Shute House, Sir William Pole's, on right *Bere* & Seaton & fine distant view; thro' Colyford, on right is Mr Hallet's, pass over Axe Bridge, which parts the counties of Devonshire & Dorset. The beauties of the former we left with regret, to pass over a dreary cold country to Lyme, a melancholy looking town, where we dined & then went to Bridport to sleep.

September 5, Tuesday

Dined at Blandford, & returned home to Sarum, delighted with our excursion, & without any difficulties.

Richard Franklen
1822

Glamorgan Record Office, D/D Cl/1/14

Franklen was on a visit through Scotland and England and travelled with a male companion. The diary may be a fair copy of the original tour. Franklen is unusual in his noting the factory at Ottery St Mary and in his disapproval of the George at Axminster.

Thursday April 18th

We left Exeter in a chaise for Honiton and in our way at Ottery St Mary saw the woollen manufactory of Misses Ball & Fowd in which they employ from 2 to 300 persons principally women & children, the whole is worked by a water wheel of 18 horsepower, the wool goes through about 10 processes before it is fit for spinning, they send the greater part of their wool to *Kiddeminster* for the Carpet Weavers, we likewise noticed some coarse clothes which are sent to China where they are very finely covered. At Ottery the church seems a large building, and the town to have been of more importance formerly than now. From hence we went to Axminster where we dined at the most villainous Inn any two unfortunate fellows ever entered called the George, and proceeded to Bridport…

Henry Fitzherbert Stroud
of
London, 1825

Plymouth & West Devon Record Office, 551/1a

Stroud, a trustee of the Countess of Huntingdon's Connexion, was on a journey from London via Cheltenham to Cornwall. He had hoped to further the work of the Connexion in the West Country by opening chapels: Edwin Welch, 'The Diary of H.F. Stroud, 1825 and 1826', *Devon & Cornwall Notes & Queries* (XXXIII, Part VI, Spring 1976), 223–4. Mr Welch had intended to publish the diary.

Tuesday 6th [September]

Left Dorchester per Mail at 11 o'clock. Arrived at Exeter at 6 o'clock, put up at the New London Inn – passed through the following places – Bridport, Charmouth, Axminster, Honiton. Some fine country between Axminster and Honiton. Day fine & no dust. Performed the journey very agreeably with the exception of suffering some measurement from the effects of my bowel attack. Which occasioned me a good deal of suffering yesterday evening in consequence of not being able to retire from the company of old friends. I desire however to be thankful for the measure of health and strength afforded me & pray that I may have grace to emanate it entirely to the service of that gracious Lord from whence I derive it…

THOMAS POUGHER RUSSELL
of
GLOUCESTER, 1837

Entrance to Knowle Cottage, Sidmouth, 1823

Westcountry Studies Library, typescript, MS WES/1837/RHS/1–9.

Russell was a Gloucester banker who came to Sidmouth for four weeks in August and September of 1837. He left on 10 August and travelled through Newport and Bristol. See S.H. Jeyes, *The Russells of Birmingham* (London, 1911).

...on reaching Honiton we went on immediately for Sidmouth – the road continued very hilly & through a dreary though tolerably well cultivated country – were surprised to find the harvest much more backward here than in Somersetshire where it was chiefly cut & beginning to be carried, & the crops there seemed to be heavy & well ripened. Arrived at Sidmouth about 2 o'clock & went to the York Hotel & then went in search of lodgings & found great difficulty in procuring such as we all liked. After going about from place to place we fixed on some as being the best we could find but not at all such as were altogether desirable. We then went to the Hotel to dinner & while there heard of a house to be had, which we went to see & liked very much & were induced to give up those we had first taken & pay the week rather than not make the exchange. The house we took was on York Terrace, larger than we wanted but very pleasantly situated on the beach & very clean & commodious – here we immediately took up our abode.

The appearance of the place pleased us much, a fine open sea with high rocks enclosing the bay on every side – hills thickly spotted with handsome houses & surrounded by thick rich woods – the town not large but clean, a fine esplanade in front of the houses on the beach which is pebbly but without sands.

Saturday 12th August. Our maid Tedstill joined us this morning having come by coach to Exeter & thence hence & we were occupied most of the morning in making domestic arrangements & afterwards walked on the beach & took a survey of the place with which we were pleased. It seems however to have lost its attractions as a fashionable place for there is little company on the walks & there appears to be no gaiety going forward, but of this we shall judge better by & by.

Sunday 13. Went this morning to the Unitarian chapel where we found a very small congregation – the minister is Mr Gibson who gave us an excellent sermon both morning & afternoon, in the evening we took a pleasant walk & were delighted with the appearance of the country. So many pleasant houses & grounds, with beautiful lanes & walks in all directions.

Monday 14. Went this morning to Knowle Cottage, a beautiful place belonging to Mr Fish about a mile from the town, shown to strangers every Monday. It is quite in the Gothic style. You enter a long gallery & there are numerous rooms on each side, all fitted quite as much as convenience will admit with tables of all sizes & shapes covered with ornamental china, jewellery & knick-knacks of all description in the greatest profusion & beauty, a surprising collection of tasteful articles of all kinds arranged with the greatest art, china of every sort, clocks & watches on elegant stands – paintings & miniatures – in short everything that fancy can imagine is collected without regard to expense. The grounds are nicely arranged with many foreign animals in the park & many rare plants in the conservatory & plantations. There was a great concourse of visitors who were admitted through the gates a few at a time – see the printed description. In the afternoon we went [on] a beautiful walk through the fields & lanes into the Exmouth road & ascended a very high hill from which was a splendid view of Sidmouth & the neighbouring hills with which it is surrounded & a fine expanse of sea on the other side.

16. The weather has been very hot the last two days so that we have not done much beyond strolling about the beach & shady lanes. Went yesterday to see the Infant school where there are about 60 children who went through their drilling remarkably well, repeating the books of the old & new testament & spelling all of them as they went on, the same by the countries of the four quarters of the globe, all the kings of England and other repetitions which showed great pains to have been taken with great success.

17. The weather being mild & pleasant, we took a boat, went out upon the sea, the sailors took with them their mackerel lines & when we got out about ½ a mile they began to fish. They bait the lines with a strip of the skin of the mackerel cut off near the tail in the shape & size of a small fish so that when in the water it looks like a sprat. This bait is put on the hook & a few yards of fine line at the end of which is a lead weight & then follows a long line of twine fastened at the end to the boat. They know by the feel when there is a fish caught & soon began to haul them out & there were seldom many minutes without doing so on one side or the other – we caught between two & three dozen & after sailing about for two hours made for land & got on shore after a very pleasant sail – in the afternoon it became very foggy indeed. We have most days fogs hanging over the rocks, more so it is said this year than common.

19. We had thick fog this morning with rain but about midday it cleared up & in the afternoon we hired two donkeys, one for Willie & one for the ladies & went to Salcombe [Regis], a small village about 1½ mile off. To get to which we had to ascend almost all the distance a very high hill on one side of the town. On arriving near the top we had a most beautiful view of the distant cliffs & sea with the valley & surrounding country immediately below extremely rich & the town itself lying deep in the valley below sheltered on all sides by high cliffs clothed with verdant fields & thick woods & abundantly

interspersed with habitations comprising handsome seats & rural cottages, forming altogether a most picturesque & interesting landscape – they were busy in their cornfields gathering in the harvest which we were surprised to find more backward that Somersetshire or even what we saw the beginning of our journey – we could not but be struck however with the luxuriance of the vegetation, in the trees & hedges especially – the shady lands are innumerable & the gardens seem extremely luxuriant – on the top of the hill we found an extensive common covered with gorse & beautiful heath – went along a level road till we came to the village of Salcombe [Regis] down in a glen & a church down in the bottom – the mountain air on the top of the hill was quite refreshing – after enjoying it for some time the evening coming on we returned down the hill looking again with delight on the beautiful prospect.

20. Foggy unpleasant weather – ill with lumbago – could not go to chapel Mrs R & the girls with Willy went & were much pleased with Mr Gibson's sermons morning & afternoon – but sorry to have see so small a congregation.

21. Foggy & rainy weather this morning – cleared up mid day went to call on Mr Heinequin (Rev. N.S. Heineken) a Unitarian minister who we recollected lived here with his daughter – he had been invited to Gloucester on Mr Brook leaving but declined leaving this place – he was at home & received me kindly – walked out this afternoon away from the sea in the sheltered lanes which are so frequent here.

23^d August. Exchanged visits today & yesterday with Mr Heinequin (Rev N.S. Heineken), a Unitarian minister who is residing here & with Mr Gibson the regular minister in this place – the former is a very intelligent pleasant man living here for the benefit of his young daughters health – the latter more reserved but must be a worthy conscientious man having given up preferment to some amount in the church from having become an Unitarian – Mr H had been invited to Gloucester on the resignation of Mr Brook but declined leaving this place – owing to the unfavourable state of the weather we could not make several excursions we had in view – being foggy and rainy we went about the neighbourhood however & found delightful lanes & fields on every side interspersed with handsome country houses in all directions – on one ramble we came to a gardeners where all was luxuriant & plentiful – fruit & gooseberries still hanging on the trees went along the *Lime* Road one evening & found the same picturesque scenery – Salcombe hill on one side & the vale of Sidmouth on the other with the little river Sid below Mr Lusada, a

Jew, is one of the largest landowners in this neighbourhood – he lives in a large handsome house near the town – his uncle left him it is said a few years since £30000 pr annum – a great part of the houses in the town belong to him – He & Mr Coteaterris who lives near him married two sisters close to the esplanade is the house where the Duke of Kent died belonging to Genl Bagnes – embedded in trees with a beautiful verdant lawn before it.

26. We were obliged to call in medical advice to little Willy this morning – his bowels have been disordered from the first day he came here & he was now so unwell that we thought it necessary to have advice – Mr Gibson recommended a Mr Jeffrey whom we sent to & he said complaints of that sort were very common he prescribed of course & sent the physic we had the greatest difficulty to make him take it & sent over to the D^r who came & assisted & at last it was taken.

27. Willey better today – a most beautiful day – heard two sermons from Mr Gibson & walked out in the evening enjoying the delightful neighbourhood of the town.

28. This morning being tolerably fine & Willey much better we went an excursion to <u>Budleigh Salterton</u> about 7 miles off – a very nice bathing place – fine view of the sea from several terraces along which were a great number of apparently good lodging houses as well as in other parts of the town which is small but neat, high cliffs near it on which there seems to be fine walks for breathing pure sea air – after seeing all worthy of attention we returned in the fly we had hired for the trip – the roads very bad most of the way along narrow lanes where for considerable distance two carriages could not pass – passed through the poor village of Otterton & also Budleigh saw Bicton Park – Lord Rolles at a distance – at Otterton a grove of large Horse chestnut trees under which markets & fairs are held – got home about 3 when it began to rain & continued all the evening – a great deal of orcharding along the road but chiefly old ill-shapen trees – in many places the corn not yet cut.

29. Raining all day – windy south east – no fishermen out.

30. Very fine walked a long way on the beach under the cliffs in some places quite overhanging & very lofty a great depth of strong loamy soil – no shells or curious stones or sea weed found on the shores.

31. Very uncertain weather – my niece Patty arrived this afternoon having come in the Exquisite Coach to Taunton & in the mail from there – she has never been at the sea before was of course much delighted – though the weather very gloomy she did not see it to

advantage Mr & Mrs Smith who live near this place & whom we had seen at Chapel called on us this morning but we were all out walking on the beach.

Sept[r] 3. Unsettled weather, nothing new in our daily occupations – went on bathing, walking &c – intended to return at the end of the month but willing to give Patty more time here we have determined to stay another week – she was unwell today so that we could not go out in a boat as we intended nor pay a visit to Mr Fish's cottage – a steam boat came in from Dartmouth with a number of passengers to see Mr F[ish']s cottage but they arrived too late & were obliged to return without seeing it – went to the Promenade in the assembly rooms this evening – Mr Jeffrey our doctor went with us & was very attentive & procured partners for the girls – about 60 people there – about ten had tea & went away about eleven – stormy night with much rain – met Mr Reynolds & Mr Saunders of Gloucester – who are come to stay here.

Sept[r] 4. Called this morning on Mr Smith – they have a very pretty house & grounds on the Lyme road where he lives like a comfortable English Gent – the views are very pleasing – the garden very gay & well laid out – Mr. S. was gone out a shooting.

Sept[r] 6. Went out in a boat this morning sea rather rough so that the ladies were under some alarm & did not go far from the shore – the boatmen showed us sea kale growing on the rocks & said it was excellent eating in the spring – there used to be much smuggling along the coast but none now since there so many stations belonging to the custom house along the shore these stations must be a great expense to the country all owing to the prohibiting duties which ought to be done away with.

Sept[r] 7. Went this morning to Exeter in a fly with Mr Reynolds & Mr Saunders – 15 miles – I wanted to see John Lombard who had been long settled in that city as French master – on arrival I found him out with difficulty & he was very glad to see me – it is about twenty years since we had met I should not have known him nor would he probably have recognised me – his voice however is not altered & it recalled many lost recollections to both of us – he is very well established here & is laying by a good sum every year in hopes of retiring in the course of a year or two – he goes every year to see his mother near Caen – he took me about to see the cathedral & other objects of curiosity especially two new markets which are built upon a splendid scale – it is a fine city very large & handsome – being Friday it was fast day so John gave me a meagre dinner two sorts of fish, fruit &c – we had a great deal of talk about old times about France & Ardennes & our old acquaintance there most of whom are gone off the stage – John wondered we should ever have left Ardennes where we had everything we could desire & were so respected – after enjoying a few hours chat with him returned to the inn & set out on our return home where we arrived between 6 & 7 & Mr Reynolds & Mr Saunders drank tea with us.

Septr 11. Last two days have been rough & today it blows a gale from S.W. so that we cannot go to see Knowle cottage again as we intended – it has also stopped both bathing & walking out yesterday we went out to Chapel twice Mr Saunders went with us, he is a decided Unitarian we proposed going to Lyme tomorrow but it does not seem likely that the weather will permit.

12. About midday it began to blow hard & continued quite an equinoctial gale all the day & night so that we were glad to have a fire & keep snug to the house – all the boats were drawn up on the terrace & the bathing machines too for which they have a moveable crane – called on Mr Gibson this morning with Mr Saunders, to take leave of Mr G. Mr S dined with us, Mr Reynolds being gone to Exmouth – storm very violent & continued through the night.

14. Weather more moderate – preparing for departure tomorrow – walking on the Beach every spare minute, bathed this morning for the last time – no boats out, fish do not bite soon after a storm – we were told we ought to have seen *Branscomb* 5 miles off – remarkably romantic – also *Beer* a resort of smugglers formerly & now seem to be a race of that sort.

15. Tedstill & Patty set off this morning in the Coach for Taunton to meet the Exquisite coach from Exeter they started at 7 o'clock & we set out about 9 for the same place, the weather fine after rainy night about 3 miles off at the top of the hill had a beautiful view of the valley & surrounding hills in which lies Sidmouth with the sea beyond – this was covered by a thick fog as we went to Sidmouth – another magnificent view about 3 miles from Taunton on the top of *Blackdon* Hill – changed horses at Honiton & got to Taunton between 11 & 12...

Walter White *of* London, 1855

Otterton church, 1842

Walter White, *A Londoner's Walk to the Land's End and a Trip to the Scilly Isles* (1855), 75–103.

White had been a cabinet-maker in Reading and New York before 1850. A second career followed when he became employed in the library of the Royal Society some eleven years before his Westcountry tour and in 1861 White became assistant secretary before becoming librarian. His other publications include *A month in Yorkshire* (1861) and *Eastern*

England from the Thames to the Humber (1865). White was forty-four years old when he visited East Devon and died in 1893.

...Holme Bush is in Devonshire; and you have not to go far from it, pursuing the same path, and through a short lane, before you emerge on a scene, one of the most charming approaches to the loveliest of the southern counties that could well be imagined. The hills here rise to a height of about five hundred feet, in huge, extended masses of chalk and greensand resting on lias and red marl, a formation more than usually liable to disturbances from the weather; for after abundant rains the two upper deposits, loosened by the percolation of water, slide away from the lower two by whole acres at a time; sinking here into hollows and pits, there a ridge leaning inwards, yonder a shelf like a great step, and all so broken up with steep banks, hummocks, and knolls, as to form a very chaos. Imagine all this, when, after the lapse of years, the perpendicular wall behind is faced with foliage; when the rugged slope reaching down to the shore is covered with copsewood; when the hillocky shelf midway is carpeted with the softest turf, its deformities beautified or concealed by a luxuriant vegetation, and you will have an idea of the undercliff that stretches nearly the whole distance of six miles from Lyme to the mouth of the Axe. The ground is further diversified by little clumps and thickets: here a single thorn, close and rounded as if clipped with shears; there a straggling group interwoven with formidable brambles, yet so sprinkled with wild roses and honeysuckle, so festooned with the slender arms of the wild clematis and other creepers, as at a short distance to resemble bowers such as we read of in fairy tale or poet's song. And here you may wander at will: up and down, and in and out among the grassy knolls and flower thickets; now shut into a lovely nook; now taking a fresh survey from the top of some little hill; now threading your way among foxgloves so tall as to bring their "dappled bells" to a level with your eye; now doubling a dense bed of thistles, nettles, or gorse, cumberers of the soil in other places, but here playing an effective though subordinate part in the general luxuriance. Yonder a gray, old, ivy-coated turret projects from the screen of wood on the cliff above; coming nearer, you find it to be a buttress of limestone, left standing when the chalk fell away; and beyond it are more of the gray crags and red gravel peeping out from the abounding foliage. How the birds flit in and out of the woods and bushes, as though conscious that here they dwell in security, on inaccessible heights or in impervious thickets. Why do not the birds migrate hither from all parts of the kingdom? Here grim winter loses most of his terrors. The whole place lies half asleep in the sunshine; and every hundred yards or so you feel inclined to lie down on the soft slopes of turf and give yourself up to indolent repose. And why not? A holiday ramble should be enjoyment, not taskwork. Recreation comes by quiet as well as by exercise; so feast your eyes on the romantic scene and its teeming verdure; or on the sea spread out there on the left, so deeply blue, that you doubt if even the Mediterranean can be bluer. Often as I have read Milton's *Il Penseroso*, never seemed it so sweet and spiritual as on that sunshiny afternoon, loitering there "in glimmering bowers and glades," with nothing to disturb. Save the fluttering of the birds, the chance bleating of a sheep, and the hum of bees, the silence was unbroken. And I was there alone, for the momentary glimpse of a hat and bonnet moving behind the bushes in the distance could hardly be called an intrusion.

By-and-by a wall, which shuts off the lower slope on the left, slants across, and you way is stopped; but coming out from among the bushes you see a narrow archway in the barrier, and there runs the path between a wall and a bank, completely barricaded in places by long overhanging grasses and creepers, and brambles that pluck off your cap as you pass. But there are gaps which you may get through from time to time, and look back on the cliffs and out upon the sea. An unseen rill makes a pleasant noise tumbling among the rocks; and if you go down to the beach by the path that turns off at the old lime-kiln, you will see the pretty little cascade in its lower leap; or, continuing onwards, you perceive that while the cliffs recede the path descends, till it falls into one of those amphitheatre-like hollows so frequent along the coast, with space enough for a cottage, an orchard, and a little field. Pause here for a few minutes and look round on the wooded heights, and the foreground falling away to the pebbly shore. While crossing the field to the stile opposite, a man who was digging told me I could go no farther along the undercliff, the path soon disappeared, everything was let to grow just as it liked, no one could get through the tangle nor go round it. There was Pinney, he said, and there Whitelands, pointing to the two sides of the amphitheatre; strangers came as far as here, then they either went back, or turned up a lane on the right, which led to another, and that to another, then across the "barton" of a farm, and on again to Dowlands and the great landslip. I was incredulous as to the impossibility of finding the way along the undercliff, notwithstanding the rustic's earnest assurance that I should be all night in getting to Axmouth, and kept on: I could take to the lanes in case of failure.

True enough the path soon disappeared, and brambles and briars had it all their own way; and who would grudge to Nature a little space for running riot in a land where she has to submit to so many restraints? It was, however, possible to circumvent the thorny barriers, though not without labour and rough scrambling: exertion well recompensed by the sight of wild solitudes and rich, hanging woods. After a couple of miles I came to another break, and wishing my first view of the landslip to be from above, I there turned up a lane on the right, crossed a "barton," as the walled farm-yard is named, passed the old-fashioned farm-house of Dowlands, and taking the first lane on the left, found myself presently looking down on the undercliff, about two miles beyond the opening where I had diverged. Here the view is even more picturesque than that which I have endeavoured to describe, the cliffs are higher, the ups and downs greater, some of the sunken masses are mountain ranges in miniature, others rise bold as an acropolis with rugged walls of chalk. Whatever of sternness there may have been is changed into beauty by the thick-blossoming elder and graceful ash, rooted apparently where most needed to make up a picture. Before descending I went a short distance farther to the west, to the edge of the famous landslip. Though prepared for the sight, it took me completely by surprise. You see a huge chasm, in which two or three of our London squares might be placed, with room to spare, formed by the sinking of the solid earth to a hundred and fifty feet below its former level. Fields and hedges, patches of wood, and an orchard, all went down together; the surface in some places remaining unchanged, except a little tilting up on one side, and the woods are still green and the orchard bears fruit; but here and there a lifeless trunk, stretching its withered branches aloft, remains to testify of the catastrophe. Two cottages which went down at the same time have since been rebuilt, and now stand snugly among the trees. But as a contrast to the verdure the greater part of the chasm is as bare as the desert; nothing but gravel and clay, on which the seasons have not as yet had time to sow grass, fern, or lichen. The lofty cliffs exhibit a variety of colours, ashen gray, rich red, yellow, and brown, which are repeated and strangely intermingled in the heaps of débris at their base, and wherever the bottom is exposed. Indeed, so fresh are the surfaces, that you might suppose the slip had occurred but a few days before, and your idea of the immediate effect of such a convulsion becomes more distinct that it could be were the precipices covered with vegetation. This is seen still more strikingly at the eastern end, where the subsidence having been less regular than elsewhere, large masses of gravel are left in the form of cones, cubes, gables, cylinders, standing in the strangest confusion, leaning this way and that way; some prostrate, others perpendicular, with the circle of turn still green and flourishing on their top, and presenting such an intermingling of warm and cool colours as is seldom witnessed. And what adds to the singularity of the scene is the bluff left between the chasm and the sea; though somewhat disturbed when the sinking took place, it remained standing, and now serves to mark the original level.

All this happened in 1839, a year with a very wet summer. Cracks had been observed running parallel with the edge of the cliffs, but no great mischief was apprehended. On the 24th of December the folk at Dowlands heard strange underground grumblings, and noises of heaving and crushing, as though the old earth were getting uneasy, yet not such as to spoil their anticipations of the coming holiday. However, before sunrise on Christmas-day, the noises recommenced, the cracks widened, and a few of the coast-guard passing the spot, saw to their amazement the fields and pastures with which they had long been familiar begin to sink down, at times with a sudden slip, then slowly; here portions dropping through all at once, there others protruded upwards. Now the falling tract heaved as if rocked from below; now a shudder seemed to pass through it, and the adjoining ground trembled. And so the disturbance went on until forty acres, comprehending a space nearly a mile in length and three hundred feet in width, had descended to their present level, and realized to the astonished neighbourhood some of the phenomena of an earthquake, The direction of the chasm is east and west, separated from the sea by an isolated mass about half a mile wide in some places, which was pushed forwards and thrown out of the perpendicular by the shock; and ridges, banks, and shallows were heaved up along the shore by the tremendous pressure.

I returned to the spot where the field-path strikes the edge of the cliff, and descended by the rough, narrow cart-road, which from thence winds down to the bottom. Then on to the east, until the whole range as far as the break where I had struck inland was in view, so as to leave no part of the undercliff unseen, after which I turned my face once more to the west. The view of the great chasm from below was not less impressive than from above; and to wander about the confused masses at the extremity, to creep in and out of the caves, or climb some of the little tables of turf on the tops of the pyramids, was by no means uninteresting exercise, especially as you may learn a lesson in geology at the same time. It is here, while looking up to the perpendicular walls, that you become aware of the tremendous nature of the subsidence; and you begin to fancy that perhaps it may be repeated before you can get away.

One charm of all the undercliff is the total absence of guides and retailers of information. A guide, indeed, is not wanted; for while you have the sea on the right or left, according as you are journeying east or west, and the high cliffs on the other hand, you cannot fail of arriving in time at either extremity. At Dowlands, however, if you are seen, a sixpenny admission-fee will be sometimes demanded; but as no trespass is committed the reason why is not obvious. No one came near me in all my stay.

By a path which zigzags up the gravelly steep I got to the top of the cliff once more, made my way to the flagstaff in the rear of Culverhole Point, from whence there is a rapid descent over the hill to the valley of the Axe. You come out upon the road a few yards above the ferry, and may cross at once, unless you wish to go and look at the fantastic gargoyles on the church at Axmouth, a small village about a mile higher up the river. At all events, it is worthwhile walking down to the little pier at the mouth of the stream for the fine view there obtained of the whole sweep of the bay, the variegated cliffs, and away up the valley. The narrow outfall of the Axe, encroached upon by the immense bed of shingle which stretches all across the bay, is often shifting; and after a strong gale the current flows through the obstruction with difficulty. Crossing the ferry, you land on the loose slope of shingle, and trudge across it to the beaten walk, which serves as a parade for the little village of Seaton, standing among the trees on the right. Most of the level land here at the mouth of the valley has been reclaimed from what was once the estuary of the Axe.

Axmouth is one of the stations of the survey made in 1837, by authority of the British Association, to determine the difference of level between the Bristol and the British channels; and with the further object of establishing a fixed mark by which any subsequent elevation or depression of the land might be detected. The line runs from Bridgwater up the Parret to Ilminster, reaching its highest point, 280 feet, at Chard, and passing from thence by Axminster, terminates at the mouth of the Axe. The mark is a copper bolt let into a block of granite, weighing more than a ton, and may be seen on the grounds of Mr Hallett, who furnished the block at his own cost. Two other blocks were given by the corporation of Bridgwater, one of which is fixed on Wick Rocks, near that town, the other at East Quantocks Head. A copper bolt, as an additional mark, is inserted in the wall of Axmouth church, and a second in the wall of Uphill church, on the west of the Mendips; and in the whole number future geologists will have data for solving one of the most interesting problems their science affords.

Telford was once employed to make a survey nearly on the same line for a ship canal, by which vessels were to pass from one channel to the other safe from the tedious and dangerous navigation round the Land's End.

Right onward lies the road; but if you wish to keep the sea in view get over the stile on the left, when you come to White Cliff, and climb the path to its summit, where the chalk, for fifty feet or more downwards, is mantled with ivy, green and vigorous, though exposed to the spray and winds of the Channel. It is a sign of something genial in the Devonshire climate. About a mile farther the flinty path descends suddenly to Beer, a village nestled in the mouth of a glen, opening on a little cove, with just room enough for a few fishing-boats to lie snugly at anchor. Behind, the road winds down the hill, and a stream that comes brawling through the glen shoots over into the waters of the cove with a noisy plunge; and altogether the place has enough of the romantic about it to make you pause more than once on the descent to look at it. The avocations of the inhabitants are of a very opposite nature, for while the men catch fish and perhaps smuggle a little – if true to what was their reputation – the women make lace. You may see the wives sitting on the door-steps with their pillows on their knees as you pass. The village was all astir as I walked through, in consequence of the "Women's Club" celebrating their anniversary. Garlands were hung out at the windows, and the band of music, which had paraded the narrow street, was keeping up a storm of sound in a field behind the houses.

No sooner down than you have to mount again: Beer Head, with its two tower-like masses of chalk, is the next point – a grand companion to White Cliff; but not to be reached without some rough walking. From thence, looking westward, you see the range extending at the same height for miles beyond where the white bluffs come to an end, and are succeeded by others of a rich, dark red colour. And now you may proceed along the cliffs again, and above the undercliff at Southdown, till you descend once more by a slope so steep that steps are cut in the turf to Branscombe Mouth, a hollow about half a mile wide, where three valleys open to the sea. The beach is loose and pebbly, in keeping with the rest of the coast; but calcedonies are to be found on it by those who know how to seek them. I searched, but failed; most likely from want of the requisite knowledge. A small stream meanders from each valley through the hollow, and creeps across the sands to the sea, near the coast-guard station, under the opposite cliff.

The village of Branscombe, which comprises a few scattered groups of houses, lies about a mile inland, and is encircled, as you will see while walking up the lane towards it, by a strange assemblage of hills. At the *Masons' Arms*, a public-house in the largest of these townlets, I found quarters for the night, comfortable enough, although the hostess thought fit to apologise for the rustic nature of the accommodation: people came there for refreshment during the day, but rarely stopped all night. The mutton-chops, however, and the bread and butter were excellent, the tea was refreshing, the bed scrupulously clean, and what more can wayfarer want? Then, you may have a talk with the host over a glass of cider, and hear all the gossip of the neighbourhood, and if you will, something about the redoubtable Jack Rattenbury, who was once chief of the smugglers at Beer.

About half-way between Branscombe and Beer is a remarkable quarry by the side of the road, where those who take pleasure in subterranean explorations may gratify their wishes. Having missed it by coming along the cliffs, I walked back to the place early the next morning. The nearest way, a little more than a mile, is by a path across the fields; but if you wish to commence an acquaintance with Devonshire lanes, keep the road. On the right, opposite to a large limestone quarry, is a narrow recess, that might be taken for a little dell overhung with trees, and at the end of it a low flat arch fringed with hart's-tongue – the entrance to the quarry. It is a gloomy passage hewn out of the solid rock, just wide enough for the trucks on which the stone is drawn out, turning soon to the left beyond the reach of daylight, and continuing onwards for five hundred yards into the bowels of the hill, with branches running off in all directions. Should the miners be at work within, one of them will answer your shout, and come with his candle, to serve as guide. But though he will show you the huge masses that bear up the superincumbent roof, and the holes where smugglers, as is said, used to conceal their unlicensed merchandise, the passages are so damp and dreary that to penetrate them is somewhat of a penance. Some people like such adventures. I don't: and after groping my way in till empty space was undistinguishable from solid rock, I was glad to return to the sunshine outside. The stone dug from the quarry is good for building purposes, as it hardens by exposure, as may be seen in many cottage walls in the neighbourhood; but it is less worked now than formerly, and the adventurous visitor must not reckon on always finding a guide to attend his summons.

Whatever political economists may say in favour of parallelograms, one sees when walking about this dear old England of ours that the boundaries of her counties were not drawn by mere arbitrary expediency. They who first made the divisions were truer to nature than we, and drew the lines of demarcation around the shires by a principle which, as may still be seen after the lapse of a thousand years, seldom misled. Strange as it may seem that crossing a stream but a few feet wide should introduce you to different landscape, different dialect and habits, it is nevertheless a fact, and to the traveller an interesting one. Why leave home if we are always to see the same sights and hear the same sounds? If a Devonshire peasant pronounce Sir as though spelt *Sur*, and with complete indifference to the value of pronouns says, "Hur's a-going' along o'we," and brings peculiar local words, not understood elsewhere, to aid his utterance, we have only to remember that he but repeats a few surviving sounds from the old Anglo-Saxon speech, and we shall hardly regret he speaks not with the tongue of Middlesex. "The smallest difference," says a philosopher, "acquires value of constancy;" and the homely dialect which connects us by a living link with the dead past is a valuable illustration of self-perpetuating phenomena.

You will not have been many hours in Devonshire before becoming aware of more than ordinary differences: you have entered a distinct part of the island. The distance in a direct line from Lyme Regis to the bottom of Bridgwater Bay is not more than thirty-four miles; the country beyond has thus somewhat the character of a peninsula. Of this, which comprehends nearly five thousand square miles, not more than about one hundred are level; all the rest is uneven and hilly, and such as presents striking contrasts. Rocky and desolate wastes, wild table-lands rising high in the interior, are cut up on their outskirts by glens and gorges teeming in their sheltered depths with the vegetation denied above. These, expanding into wooded valleys and broad fruitful vales branching in all directions, are watered by the thirty-four rivers of the county, along the courses of which the scenery varies, from the romantic and picturesque to the sylvan and pastoral. There are spots of beauty even in the dreariest moors; and then the lanes! which seem to be deep grooves left between the cultivated fields for Nature to frolic in. The climate, too, so soft and genial, that along the southern shores the rigours of winter are almost unknown; and plants that must be tenderly nursed in other places grow and flourish in the open air. Many who go to foreign lands find less to interest them than is to be seen in Devonshire.

From Branscombe again westwards. The road runs along a pleasant valley which has been likened to some of the rural scenes of Switzerland. When you come to the church – an ancient edifice dedicated to St. Winifred – turn off by the path on the left through the churchyard, up the wooded hill beyond, where the ascent is so steep as to render the cool shade of the trees doubly welcome. You will need to pause at times for breath; but once on the top the cliffs are not far off, and there the breeze from the sea blows with invigorating freshness. The height is more than three hundred feet: you can see the Heytor Rocks on Dartmoor, which seems a sullen mountain mass some distance inland, and ahead are the magnificent red cliffs of Sidmouth – the glory of this part of the coast. Here and there an old limekiln has the appearance of an old fort ruined by long service, yet still looking forth across the sea; and in places below the small banks of undercliff are turned to account by cultivation, with potato-plots and little fields close to the water's edge. Snug sites these for a cottage residence; secure against all intrusion from the surly north.

Three miles of this, and you look down on Weston Mouth, another glen, where another brook tumbles into the sea near another coast-guard station. You must descend cautiously, for the path is precipitous; and when you are on the shingle, Dunscombe Cliff, which shuts in the western side of the Mouth, assumes a gigantic elevation. It is more than three hundred and fifty feet high. A path winds up in the rear leading to Salcombe Down, by which you may get to Sidmouth, three miles farther; or, should the tide be out, along the beach. I chose the latter route, wishing to see the crimson cliffs from below as well as above. Their structure is interesting, the prevailing colour being chequered by veins and patches of gray and yellow, with here and there a stray lump of chalk in which flints are imbedded. In some places threads of water perpetually trickling down have worn deep channels in the hardened clay; a little farther, and you see the effect of copious springs; the cliff is washed into deep gullies, and lumps of all sizes come sliding down the saturated slopes, multiplying the heaps below, and running across the beach in red slimy streams. The process of waste is going on before your eyes, from small to great; but the greatest when the sea, dashing on the shore in its wrath, undermines the solid cliff, and with tongue of foam licks off the fallen masses by thousands of tons. The demolition that takes place all round our coasts every year is almost incredible to those who have paid no attention to the subject. At one point the accumulation of large flints washed out of the clay made a barrier not easily passed; and the whole line of beach is pebbles, walking on which will try your patience. The Chesil Bank would soon disappear were the advance of pebbles from the west to be checked; but as pebbles constitute nearly the whole shore for a hundred miles or more, you see that without a geological disturbance the immense supply must still go on. I picked up a fine specimen of red jasper, a pocket-pebble, and carried away a small crystalline lump of sulphate of lime from the face of the cliff, where it was kept in a state of moisture by percolation from the clay behind. The substance was tender enough to be cut with a knife, and the minute thread-like crystals of which it was composed could be easily separated one from the other. But as it dried, the lump became hard as limestone. If the walking be toilsome, there are many things to observe that will make you forget it: one is the mouth of the Sid, which, instead of being an open mouth, is dammed up so as to form a pool by the pebbles, and through these it oozes away timidly to the sea.

Sidmouth has its fashionable quarter, and some of the pretentious artifices which watering-places usually invent for the amusement of visitors, while in the older streets, within a stone's throw, you may see houses roofed with unsophisticated thatch. The chief signs of life outside the esplanade are a few coal ships discharging cargo, a few boats, and the bathing-machines, with the row of capstans by which they are hauled up from the water; but turn your back to the sea, and round from right to left, the view is one not be left unnoticed. High Peake, the cliff on the west, is a magnificent object. But the walk from Branscombe will have provoked an appetite for breakfast, and you will find wherewith to satisfy it on reasonable terms at the *Commercial Inn.*

High walls again, as you go up the hill on leaving the town; but at length the view opens, and you see the vale of Sid, the town a mixture of red and gray, the houses in the rear straggling away to the fields, Salcombe Down opposite, cut in two by a white stripe of road, and the hills around more or less flat-topped. Within the woods that darken the hollows are pleasant nooks well know to visitors; and yonder is Sidford, where "the merry monarch" as he is called, after his hurried flight from Lyme, hid in a chimney, to escape the party in pursuit. The royal fugitive had to learn that there were worse hiding-places than within the crooked arms of an oak. But chief, the red cliffs attract your eye; the bright green runners of plants and grasses hanging from the summits and shooting from the crevices, in beautiful contrast with the deep rich colour full against the sun.

In the neighbourhood of Sidmouth you may see an instance of what is often taught by the learned in such matters – that the fertility of surface depends more on the underlying rock than on climate. The vale is less sheltered from the north than Lyme, yet having a soil composed of red marl and sandstone, occasionally mixed with gravel and greensand from the adjacent hills, it is much more fertile, as is evident to the eye. Lyme rests on the lias: hence the throwing out of rain, landslips, and a damp soil.

The shaggy crown of High Peake is one of those places which print themselves, so to speak, on the memory, and remain prominent among the reminiscences of the Devonshire coast. The ground falls so rapidly inwards that you can see across the country for miles, away to a brown moorland range in the north-west. By steep, yet pleasant paths, you descend to Ladram Bay; now with scant room between the tall wheat and the edge of the cliff; now beating a fresh track across a field newly sown with turnips; now again on the open turf. At times the path appears to end against a bank with no visible outlet; but on coming up you find it has made a sharp turn to the right or left, and there will be a little stile of the most rustic construction barring the narrow passage through the hedge. In some places the way lies through such curious nooks and corners, that you will not find it without a little searching, and occasionally not at all; in which case there is nothing for it but to advance as best you can – the nearer the edge of the cliffs the less chance of losing the way.

Ladram Bay, three miles from Sidmouth, presents a strange assemblage of rock and island, cavern and promontory, some of the projecting masses arched or tunnelled, and the red shadow of the cliffs quivering in the glistening water below, where it rolls from the arches and plays among the rocks. The dottings of white and gray seen on the crags are colonies of birds, which seem to lead a pleasant life on their sunny perch, or floating with outstretched wing, as though conscious of appearing beautiful by contrast with the green sea and the dark-hued precipice. Less fortunate in winter, they then become targets for the shots of adventurous sportsmen, who row into the bay and fire up at them from the boats. The cliffs here exhibit the several strata in well-marked horizontal bands; and if you are a botanist, the rare plants growing from the clefts will soon be transferred to your specimen-book.

Farther down, and there is the little coast-guard station, so happily situated, that whether it be rural or marine would be a nice question.

While the man on duty, a hale old fellow, was directing me how to find the way through the lanes to Otterton, I could not but be struck by the difference between his instructions and those of a rustic. Your genuine peasant seldom succeeds in communicating topographical information; he omits the points most essential to the stranger, and exemplifies unconsciously the difference between education and the want of it. Yet have patience with him, and you shall find a substratum of shrewd common sense under that uncultivated exterior. And what endurance equals his toiling on from year to year for nine shillings a week.

Otterton is a thorough Devonshire village – thatched cottages built of "cob," a material much used in all the southern part of the county. It is composed the red gravelly earth mixed with straw, moistened, and trodden down to form the walls, one layer being left to harden before another is put on. When of the requisite height the two sides are trimmed smooth with a hayknife, and the outer surface is generally rough-cast. A cottage of four rooms and the etceteras can be built for 50*l*. From eighteen inches to two feet is the usual thickness; but three feet is not at all uncommon in old walls, and a strange appearance they have, with their small deep-set windows. The floors are made of lime and ashes, which in time become almost as hard as stone. Sometimes these cottages are whitewashed; most are, however, left of their natural colour, and you may see a village completely red from one end to the other; and pretty enough they look, with their little flower-gardens in front, and honeysuckle and roses climbing to the thatch. But prettiest of all when you come upon a single cottage at the bend of a lane, where a spring bubbles out of the bank, or on the edge of a grassy opening; then the weatherworn thatch, the red walls, the glimmer of the casement, the thin curling smoke, all seen amidst the surrounding verdure, is a picture for the eye to dwell on. There is, however, another side to the picture: cob walls, when neglected, lose patches from the surface, the children grub holes, and the dwelling looks squalid and miserable. But when the neglect has passed into decay, and the cottage becomes a ruin, then all is picturesque again, as you will discover by numerous examples.

The main street of Otterton was gay with flags and garlanded fir-trees, remains of a celebration held the day before. The "Women's Club" had brought in their year's product of lace – the factor was there on his annual visit to receive the delicate tissue – accounts were squared and balances paid – the women, serenaded by a band of music, drank tea under the tall, spreading chestnuts at the end of the street, and the village generally took part in the holiday. "It does 'em good to have a little sport once a year," said the landlord of the *King's Arms*, which I drank my glass of cider; which is hardly to be doubted, only rural sport is too apt to degenerate into grossness. I asked him if it were possible for a man to become intoxicated on cider, as it seemed to me a sufficient quantity could hardly be swallowed to produce the effect. "It takes a smartish drop to do that," he answered; "but if you'll come in here in the evenin' you'll see some of the labourers swaller eight or nine quarts, and go away rolling drunk." Eight or nine quarts! How is it possible to force the bibulous appetite to such an extreme and on thin, hard cider, too, sour enough to make a stranger shudder. The sweet cider sold in London is but little esteemed in Devonshire, the native palate not being satisfied without a smack of the opposite flavour.

At the end of the village you cross the Otter, a small lively stream, winding through meadows and between the red scarped hills to the sea, some four miles distant. The footpath running along its margin tempted me; but for the moment the object which led me away from the coast had greater attraction – it was to see the house where Raleigh was born. If you have time, it is possible to get a sight of Bicton Gardens, about half a mile away to the right, said to be an exquisite specimen of horticultural art; there are, however, some things which the passing traveller must make up his mind to forego, unless he wish to carry home none but tessellated reminiscences.

Less than two miles farther and you come to Budleigh, a pretty village, enlivened by the noise of a swift-flowing brook, where one in search of health or quiet might find a peaceful sojourn. To see the lace-makers sitting at their doors, with pillow on knee, and plying their task with nimble fingers, was like going back a hundred years to a scene of homely industry. Turning off by a lane on the left, near the church, another mile brings you to *Hays* Barton – Raleigh's birthplace. It is a solitary farm-house – once the manor-house – built in the picturesque style of four hundred years ago, with gabled wings and portico, thatched roof, small mullioned windows, and a heavy oaken door thickly studded with iron nails, standing at the end of a garden, partly concealed by a few old trees that rise from among the herbs and flowers. At one side of the barton, in front, is a modern brick barn; but there are two or three sheds and stables built of cob on the other side, which keep up the olden character. The whole scene, shut in by low swelling hills and lines of tall hedges, is eminently rural; and how much more so in Raleigh's day. Just the place for a happy childhood.

I knocked at the door: it was opened by a good-humoured-looking damsel, who, to my inquiry as to whether it was true as I had read, that strangers were permitted to see the interior of the house, answered, "No it isn't. We used to show it, but had to give up; people hindered our time so; and now they stand and look at it as long as they like, and then go away again." This was said with a smile, as if not meant seriously; and as she stood still at the half-opened door, seeming in no hurry to retire, we had a chat for some twenty minutes. I might sit under the porch for an hour if I pleased and look at the beehives and the old trees, and at the upper window on the left – *the* window of *the* room. There Raleigh was born. They had a book in the house containing his life and writings, but did not like it so well as *Uncle Tom's Cabin*.

Did the gallant adventurer ever think of the quiet homestead in the days of his courtly prosperity? He could not have helped reverting to the hours of boyhood, when adversity overtook him; when he lay stricken with fever on the coast of Guiana, or during his long and weary imprisonment in the Tower. Was he thinking of the woods around Hays Barton when he wrote his *Country's Recreations*, and with a pen sobered by experience drew so true a contrast between the "anxious sighs and untimely tears" of courts, and the silent groves, downs, meads, and gliding fountains, which he tenderly apostrophises? Did recollections of innocent youth come back upon him when, in his after years of sorrow, he said:

"Give me my Scallopshell of Quiet;
My Staff of Faith to walk upon;
My Scrip of Joy, immortal Diet;
My Bottle of Salvation;
My Gown of Glory, Hope's true gage,
And thus I'll take my Pilgrimage."

To me, musing under the rustling leaves, while the scent of hay filled the air, there was a touching moral in the great man's history. Here the glad beginning; and far away, within the shadow of the court, its heroic ending. Whatever his faults, he deserved better than to lose his head by the executioner's axe, at the behest too of a king foolish enough to imagine that by tearing a leaf from the Journal of the Commons he could deprive the nation he misruled of their rights and liberties.

I returned to Budleigh, and from there made my way back to the coast by the road, nearly three miles, leading to Budleigh Salterton. This is a village watering-place with a growing reputation, and not undeservedly; for it stands in a valley so narrow and well sheltered that myrtles grow in the open air all the year round, and like its namesake in the interior, it has a sprightly brook running by the side of the road, crossed by numerous light bridges to the trim gardens in front of the houses. A place of cheerful aspect. From an eminence on the beach the Otter is seen, its vivacity left behind, creeping ingloriously through a marshy flat to the sea, where a long reef stretches out at one side of its mouth. The coal merchants here, wiser in their generation than some elsewhere, have laid a tramway across the pebbly shore, along which the laden trucks are hauled from the vessel.

As usual, a cliff sided hill on the west, and still of a red colour – West Down Beacon. Seats are placed at short intervals on the long sloping ascent; and from the top you can get a view of the three miles of cliffs which you may have missed by the visit to *Hays* Barton; and in the other direction, down to Torbay and Berry Head. To an unaccustomed eye there is something surprising in the successive headlands, each stretching farther and farther to seawards, that to walk to their extremity seems an endless task, so different from what it appears on the map, and you can scarcely help fancying that the last will take you far into the sunny regions of the south. Pacing the coast mile by mile for days together, you find England to be not so small a country after all.

The path skirts the edge of the Beacon Cliff for some distance, and drops down to the small out-of-the-way village of Littleham, from whence to Exmouth by lane and highway is nearly three miles. About half-way down the descent on which the town is built you come to a broad terrace on the right, the Beacon-walks, with a grand hotel and rows of aristocratic-looking houses behind, and in front a shrubbery sloping away to the long sea-wall beneath, where trees, grass-plats, and winding paths make up a pleasant lounging place. Before you spreads the estuary of the Exe, narrowed by encroaching tongues, islands, and a wild waste of sand on the opposite short. That dark rugged point beyond Dawlish is the Parson and Clerk; there is Starcross, there the woods of Powderham; there, some ten miles up the valley, the towers of Exeter stand up massy against the clear evening sky; there the Haldon Moors, seeming a distant mountain range, black and barren, shut in the view of the green cultivated country. Pleasure-boats glide here and there over the calm waters; larger vessels steer lazily in or out of the sea-channels, and while you look, a rushing streamer of steam bursts into view on the other side, and the swift roar of a train comes faintly across from the South Devon Railway. There is something impressive in the view, though nothing like to beautiful as some you have seen and are yet to see; and it is not easy to see why Exmouth should have become famous. Its immediate neighbourhood is prosaic enough to delight an inhabitant of Cambridgeshire; a visitor, however, able to explore, may find a few pleasant walks – to *Withecomb*, Orcomb Point, and to the sanctuary of St. John in the Wilderness – a picturesque little ruin. You might see this by coming directly across the country from *Hays* Barton to Exmouth instead of going down to Budleigh Salterton.

The ferry here is of considerable width; while crossing, you see that the "bight," as the estuary is named within the shoals, has all the appearance of a lake; – rough enough in windy weather to frighten timid folk. You are landed on the Warren, the wild waste of sand before mentioned, which juts out two miles from the main shore; and a dreary expanse it is when seen as I saw it, in the gloom of twilight...

ELIHU BURRITT
of
BIRMINGHAM, 1864

Photograph of Elihu Burritt, *c.*1868

Elihu Burritt, *A Walk from London to Land's End and Back* (1868), 137–49.

Mr Burritt, an American from Connecticut who was apparently residing in Birmingham, made this journey during the American Civil War 'originally to see and note the agricultural system, aspects and industries of Great Britain and to collect information that might be useful to American farmers'. While visiting Honiton Burritt commented on the effect of the American war on lace making in Devon. He had visited Exeter on 20 February 1863 to give a lecture on 'The Benevolent Associations of the Day'. Burritt's book was a sequel to *A Walk from London to John O'Groats* (1864). Other publications included *Ten-minute talks on all sorts of topics* (1873) and *A journal of a visit to Skibbereen and its neighbourhood* (1847). Burritt had first visited England in 1846, was 54 years old on this journey through East Devon and died in 1879.

...Soon I crossed the boundary of Dorset into rich and picturesque Devonshire, the most remarkable county in England for several salient characteristics. Not the least of these is the circumstance of its having a northern, eastern, southern and western sea-coast, without being an island. Passed through Axminster, famous for giving an everlasting name to the carpets of royal palaces and mansions of nobility and gentry. The first specimen of this luxurious fabric was made here in 1755, by a Mr Whitty, who received the medal of the Society of Arts for his taste and skill in the production of an article which has come to such wide celebrity. It was manufactured here for eighty years, when, in 1835, the establishment was closed, and the business transferred to Wilton. Axminster is a little sedate, but not sleepy town, though it looks like one pensioned off and living on the annuity of an ancient reputation. It is pleasantly situated on a rising ground overlooking the valley of the Axe, a quiet little river sauntering leisurely through a rich and meandering savannah, with its green vest well studded with butter-cup buttons.

About half way to Honiton I passed along the rim of a vale of wonderful beauty, presenting the peculiar characteristics of Devonshire in bold relief. And these are many and strikingly variegated. In the first place, the soil itself is a vivid peculiarity of the county. It might be called the precipitate of red sandstone held in solution by the Flood. Nothing could contrast more vividly with the soil and scenery of Wiltshire. There white fields, interspersed with crops red and green, were the striking feature. In Devon, fields as red as brick dust, alternate with the green mosaic that covers hill and valley. When a strip of this soil is ploughed, harrowed, rolled and moistened by dew or rain, it takes a deeper red, like varnished mahogany. Put a dozen strips of this background among fifty patches of wheat, oats, barley, beans and white clover, and you have a picture spread out before you which you will see nowhere else in England. Then in no other county do you see such unique figures in the great Axminster carpet of verdure. Euclid himself, with square and compass, could not parcel out such queer allotments. They baffle geometry altogether. It affords no measurements nor dimensions applicable to these odd morsels of land. In some sections you will not find a rectangular field in a mile; neither square, nor parallelogram, nor triangle, nor any shape belonging to circles or their segments. If the hedge had followed the path of a snake bewildered with excitement, it could hardly be more irregular. Now when you look off diagonally from the rim of one of these grand, great amphitheatres, you see a mosaic work of extraordinary variety and vividness. The valley you look down upon, as you descend into Honiton from the north, is one of the most beautiful in England. Right in the centre of it apparently arises Dumpdon, a remarkable hill panelled to the crown with these infinitely-varied patches of verdure and red soil. The name seems to suggest a down 'dumped' bolt upright in the middle of the great valley.

I had diverged a dozen miles from my direct course to see Honiton, where the fine and costly lace which bears its name is manufactured. It is a pleasant and comfortable town, mostly built on one long street. A note of introduction admitted me to the oldest and largest lace establishment, which has supplied royalty, nobility, gentry, and the rich and fashionable world generally with these fine white blossoms of the needle for half a century. It is indeed an exquisite fabric, perhaps the finest ever wrought for the adornment of human grace and beauty. Queens have worn it with pride at the bridal altar, and on the coronation days of their grandeur and glory. Still, it is the handiwork of 'fingers weary and worn', of women hungry, lean and thinly clad; of women working on the clay floors of low, damp cottages, whose coarse, patched garments show their poverty all the more vividly against the slowly-wrought tissues of the beautiful fabric they bend over from day to day. How little do the brides of princes and nobles and the prima donnas of fashion and luxury think of the domestic history of the delicate foliage and vine-work of their flounces, mantelets, collars, cuffs, and caps!

To begin with, the thread is a marvel for fineness and strength. The finest costs about £4 or nearly $20 a pound; the next quality, £3. The lace flounces of Queen Victoria cost about £40, measuring about eight yards. A flounce of six-and-a-half yards had just been completed for a titled lady at the cost of £20. The venerable proprietress of the establishment showed me a great number of specimens of the art in different articles, all wrought with the greatest delicacy of design and execution. As some of my fair American readers, who appreciate as highly as any other ladies in the world 'loves' of lace veils and caps, may be curious to know the prices of such articles at the factory, before they are loaded with duties, the following rates may give them a little information:

	£	s	d		$	¢
A Vandyke	4	5	0	=	20	40
A Veil	2	5	0	=	10	80
A Pair of Sleeves	1	7	0	=	6	48
A Collar	0	10	0	=	2	52

I do not give the factory prices of these articles to stir up any discontent in the minds of American ladies at the difference they have to pay for the elegancies at Stewart's or Lord's. If the profits and duties charged upon them bring them up to nearly double the figures given here, the additional cost, doubtless, enhances their intrinsic value in the estimation of the fair purchasers.

I wished much to see how this delicate fabric was wrought, and by what kind of fingers and in what kind of houses. So the proprietress of the warehouse sent one of her assistants with me to a small cottage on a back street, where three women were at work on a floor of cement spread upon the natural earth. It was a small apartment, hardly high enough for a man to stand upright with his hat on, which he never ought to do in such a presence. I felt impelled to lower mine with unusual reverence at the sight. Two of the women, occupants of the cottage, were sisters between sixty and seventy years of age. The third was a neighbour who had dropped in with her working pillow, and was plying her needle with her bonnet on; just as in the olden time neighbours in New England would make a morning call, taking their spinning wheels with them. I sat down on a stool and had a long talk with them on their art and occupation. The eldest of the sisters wore spectacles and a long, still, solemn face, which seldom took on the sunshine of a smile in the course of the conversation. She had worked on lace for more than fifty years. She had wrought on the wedding-dresses of three generations of queens, – Adelaide, Victoria and Alice. She worked the royal arms, with the lion and the unicorn, and the motto, put up before the window of the sales' depot – an exquisite specimen of taste and art. The business was now very much depressed. She could hardly earn *a penny an hour*. Many of the young women had been obliged to abandon it altogether, and seek service as common house servants, scrubbing floors, and handling pots and kettles with fingers that had worked white tissue of flowers and foliage which queens were proud to wear on their coronation days. She had heard of some of the causes that made the trade so low; but she had understood them dimly. She did not read the newspapers; but she had heard of the war in America. They had told her it was something about exchange that hindered the sale of lace. Poor woman! I looked into her still and solemn face, at her worn, lean fingers, as she spoke of these things in such a subdued and unmurmuring tone. She little knew the long-reaching and ruinous sweep of war, the infinite ramification of its destructive issues. She had not vigour of mental vision to see, though she felt it to the core of her hungry wants, how the invisible sirocco of war blows with unabated breath over the widest oceans and continents, and blights the humble industries of the poor in distant lands.

The process of lace-working is exceedingly interesting, requiring the nicest judgment of the eye and a finger-skill of the greatest felicity. Although it is wrought in clay-floored cottages, and in the one room that serves as parlour, kitchen, cellar, and sometimes sleeping apartment, the lace, worked in the most elaborate and varied patterns, is delivered at the sales room as pure and unsullied as the thread at its giving out. It is wrought on round, plump cushions, or pillows, and as fast as the figure progresses, it is covered with a thin belt, or veil of oiled silk, so that only a very narrow slip or space is exposed at one time to any subtle dust, or accidental touch of the finger. Of course, Honiton lace is all wrought by hand, and has to compete with a very elegant article made by machinery in Nottingham, and other towns that manufacture it in vast quantities for the markets of the world. In face of such almost overpowering competition, this slowly-worked fabric of the fingers struggles to hold its own. It still 'rules' as the most perfect and durable, as well as the most elegant embroidery of bridal dresses of princesses and ladies of high nobility and fashion. It is a pity, when they are so proud to wear it, that the *artistes* who clothe them with such flower-work should be so poorly paid. Somehow or other, this inequality between the wearer and the maker is the widest and worst in articles of luxury. Diamond-diggers, and pearl-divers, and ermine-hunters, have always had a harder time of it than even the Honiton lace-workers. The blunt-fingered men who follow the plough and wield the sickle fare better.

After a long talk with the lace-workers, I left them with a little more sunny expression on their faces than they showed at the beginning. Whether a shilling an hour dropped into their hands for the information they gave me, or the words of cheer I dropped into their ears at parting, of both together, produced the change, it was doubtless as pleasant to one party as the other.

I now faced directly southward, and walked down a beautiful valley to Ottery St Mary, a most unique and acute-angular town. Indeed, the streets make a very maze of angles, if that term may be applied to any other lines than circles. Here is one of the most beautiful churches in the kingdom, internally. It is really a *bijou* of a cathedral, worth a long journey to see. Still it is better to see it without expectation; to come upon it accidentally as I did, without knowing beforehand of such an edifice in an out-of-the-way village like Ottery. The interior embellishment is as full an illustration of what modern taste, art and wealth can effect, as anything you will find in England outside the Temple Church in London. It has a long and interesting history, including a century or two when it was the appendage of the hierarchy of Normandy, and belonged to the Church of Rouen. Oliver, the Cathedral-bruiser, smote its monumental statuary and interior sculpture with some bad blows in his day, and it has run the gauntlet of five hundred years of peril and difficulty. But it has come up out of the ashes of its former self, a very phoenix of broad and beautiful plumage. In this quiet, antique little town the poet Coleridge was born; and thanks to the spirit of his verse, as well as to the large means and munificence of the Coleridge family, the church in which he was baptised has been renovated and embellished to such admiration.

Friday, June 17th. – Went on to Bicton, the celebrated residence of Lady Rolle. This lady is a remarkable woman, without equal or like in England, in one vigorous, well-developed individuality of will and genius. She is a female rival of Alexander the Great. If Virgil has lived in her day, he might have been tempted to substitute *Arbores dominamque cano* for his famous introductory line, *Arma virumque cano*. The world that the Grecian conqueror subjugated was a small affair in space compared with the two hemispheres which this English lady has taken by the hair of the head and bound to her chair of state. It seems to have been her ambition for nearly half a century to do what was never done before by man or woman, in filling her great park and gardens with a collection of threes and shrubs that should be to them what the British Museum is to the relics of antiquity and the literature of all ages. And whoever has travelled in different countries and climates and vistas her *arboretum*, will admit that she has realised that ambition to the full. Let the most scientific and enthusiastic of American arboriculturists travel from the Rio Grande to the St Lawrence, and from the Atlantic to the Pacific sea-board, and he will find here at Bicton more varieties of American trees and shrubs than he named and noted on the Western Continent. When he has seen the pines of California, of the Rocky Mountains, of Michigan, Canada and Maine, and heard the solemn sough and murmur of their branches in the forest breeze, he will indulge the self-complacent sentiment that no one can tell or show him anything new in the race of *conifers*. He may boast that he has seen twenty, perhaps even fifty kinds of that tree in his explorations. Let such a man visit Bicton and run down its tree-road and read its record after this rate:

Pine two hundred varieties
Oak two hundred nearly
Willow three hundred
Elm one hundred and twenty
Ash sixty
Poplar thirty
Maple twenty
Hickory fifteen
Thorn one hundred and sixty
Bramble forty-six
Holly twenty-six

The whole number of varieties of trees and shrubs in this wonderful collection is nearly *three thousand*. Now take any one country or continent, and select a specimen of every distinct variety of tree and shrub to be found within its area, and then place the whole side by side with the Bicton arboretum, and the disparity will indicate the unparalleled assiduity, effort, taste, genius and pecuniary means brought to bear upon this British Museum of nearly every wooded trunk, branch and bush that fans its foliage in the breath of heaven. To make climates, and soils and genial surroundings for these productions of all the zones, so that they shall be at home and thrive as in their native lands, requires an insight into their habits and wants, and a genius to cater to them, which must rank with the inspiration of the artist as well as the science of the savant. This genius, science, and devotion in the gardener of Lady Rolle, Mr James Barnes, work out her taste, mind and will to their best conceptions and conclusions. He gave me a most cordial reception, and took me through all the glass-roofed conservatories, and plant and flower houses, then over the park ground, and showed me all the striking features of the establishment.

The park is very extensive, most pleasantly undulated, and presenting the happiest variety of surface for picturesque embellishments and views. It is well studded with fine old English oak, beech, elm, chestnut, sycamore, and thorn. One striking feature is a long avenue of *auricaria imbricata,* to use the ugly Latin name given to a South American pine, which would lose all its comeliness and value if it were as common as white birch with us. Here it is esteemed among the rarest of the pine tribe, so that an avenue lined with it for a long distance is a sight peculiar to Bicton. It is a very porcupine among trees; the trunk and branches being tiled with ear-shaped scales, pushing out their outer ends, as a hen ruffles her feathers, and looking very rough and shabby. There is an artificial lake with its blue bosom broached with islets studded with trees and shrubbery, which flower and breathe – and blush at their faces in the water. Aquatic birds of every form and plumage swim about on their shadows, mingling these with the reflections of the blossoms drooping to the silvery mirror from overhead. This lake is not a wide and shallow pool, but deep enough to float the *Great Eastern* at the lower end, if it does not draw more than 40 feet without its ballast.

There is another pond forty feet above the level of this lake, beautifully formed and ornamented, and mirroring another group of interesting features. Of these, nothing I ever saw in the same department of art and ingenuity equals a Swiss cottage, designed and made by a rustic, unlettered artist among the common labourers employed at the establishment. I doubt if anything of the kind ever produced in Switzerland could approach this unique specimen of architecture. It is an infinitesimal cathedral in shape, wrought in the most graceful gothic, out of trunks, branches and leaf-stems of young trees of every species known to this country. The rural architect embroidered and painted the interior and external walls of the little edifices with these little split segments of green wood with the T on them, with a delicacy of design and execution truly wonderful. If the small bits had been globules of various colours on an artist's easel, and he had taken them up with an artist's pencil, he could have hardly painted more pleasant pictures, inside and out. What is very remarkable, he could not read nor write his own name. He signed the receipt, on being paid for his work, with a cross as his mark. Yet, among other pictures he embroidered with barked bits of wood, were the arms of the Rolle family, with the usual show of wild animals and scrolls and allegories and hierglyphics that characterise a Norman heraldry. The most delicate lines and tints were drawn by the artist with the ligneous colours on the point of his penknife. Then, unlettered as he was, and unable to write his own name, he wrote on the scroll of the arms, in beautifully formed letters, the motto of the family – *NEC POPULO, NEC REGI, SED UTROQUE* – a most excellent motto, by the way, the best I ever saw interpreting devices of British heraldry: 'Not for People, not for King, but for both'. T

The flooring of this miniature palace was more unique and extraordinary still. To say that the apartments were paved with ivory would not come up to the actual fact, in the eccentricity of the achievement. The whole space is paved with the knee-bones of sheep, with the half joints uppermost, making a delicately-sculptured surface of great beauty. They are fitted together so compactly that 400 of them only make a square foot. Now as there are 190 square feet of flooring to the cottage, it required 76,000 sheepshanks to pave it with these fluted and scrolled joints of ovine ivory.

North of the park is a great pine plantation, with carriage drives diverging in different directions, and lined and overarched with foliage and flowers that were never seen in England when Thomson wrote his 'Seasons'. I mean the aerial blossoms and the leaves of glistening green which the American rhododendron gives to the shrubberies of this country. I doubt if Thomson ever saw this garden queen of beauty, or dreamed of such tinting as suffuses the cheek of its summer glory. *Nine miles* of this Juno-shrub among flowering plants line the drives through this great plantation; and when in bloom they both perfume and illumine the quiet pathways among the tall pines, whose protecting shade and shield prolong the blossoming, holding out their broad palms against the unfriendly winds.

Bicton House is almost as distinguished for its aviary as for its arboretum. Birds of every imaginable feather and family are housed here in kingly and queenly state, and watched and tended with the greatest care. A drawing-room orangery, designed entirely by Lady Rolle herself, is the most characteristic feature of the mansion. It is far more graceful and picturesque than the one at Chatsworth. The trees do not stand in tubs or pots, but in squares of soil, enclosed with marble slabs, and divided by aisles beautifully paved with mosaic work. On festive occasions, this parlour orange-grove is hung with coloured lamps at night, which light up the scenery with a glory all its own, making the yellow and luscious fruit look like 'apples of gold in pictures of silver'.

Having taken me over the grounds and showed me the most interesting features of Bicton. Mr Barnes set me on the road to Exeter, and I continued my walks toward that city, well pleased with my short visit at an establishment well worth a long journey to see. I think it must be but little known, even by reputation, to American travellers, as I know of none of them who have alluded to it in their descriptions of English localities and sceneries. For many miles my way passed over one of those wide, cold, waste lands which occupy, in their aggregate, such remarkable spaces of this otherwise highly-cultivated country. It is called *Blackheath Hill*, and its abandoned barren looks all the most poverty-stricken and desolate from its fertile and picturesque surroundings. But then these surroundings are brought out in more vivid grace and beauty to the eye.by the contrast. Indeed, these heath and waste places in England seem to stand as way-marks by which to measure the improvements which centuries of art, industry, and wealth, have made upon all the rest of the country.

Exeter, taking it all in all – location, scenery and history – is hardly surpassed by any city in England…

H.G.
of
London, 1866

H.G., *A Traveller's Notes in Scotland, Belgium, Devonshire, The Channel Islands, The Mediterranean, France, Somersetshire, Cornwall, The Scilly Islands, Wilts and Dorsetshire in 1866* (1867), 146.

The author, unidentified except by his initials, noted in the preface that 'A very serious illness, resulting from over-work and anxiety, having necessitated a continuous change of air and scene for several months, these notes were made for the amusement of relatives and friends at home, to whom it would have been difficult, or rather impossible, otherwise to have conveyed a succinct narration of my travels. They are now published, almost word for word, from my pencillins by the way, without the smallest pretension to literary merit.'.

[15 October]...and then started [from Exeter] by train for Salisbury. It was a lovely afternoon, and the aspect of the country very beautiful; though when you have been over part of Devonshire, and the adjoining counties, you have seen all – alternate hills and dales, in the most verdant dress that nature can deck herself in, and pretty looking villages studded about at short intervals.

I got very tired of the monotony, however, before we reached the Yeovil Junction...

The Reverend Alfred Guy L'Estrange c.1872

Forde Abbey, *c.*1872

A.G. L'Estrange, *From the Thames to the Tamar: a summer on the south coast* (1873), 246–64.

The Reverend Alfred Guy L'Estrange was on a tour of southern England. His motives for writing the book, he claimed, were to publicise English tourism and to draw attention to ancient monuments in the hope they would be preserved. He was aged about forty when he visited East Devon. L'Estrange also wrote *Yachting round the West of*

England, History of English Humour and *The Literary Life of the Rev. William Harness*.

...Winding for nearly two miles up a steep hill which commanded magnificent coast views towards the west, we came to the toll-gate which separates Dorset from Devon. The road now passes over high ground for several miles, and is prettily edged on either side with a wide margin of fern and gorse, and soon a fine view opened over the rich vale which stretches northward from Colyford. Thence we descended through a beautiful Devonshire lane with high banks and overhanging trees. Then we crossed the Axe, a small river flowing through a level pasture plain, and passing Colyford arrived at Seaton.

Seaton is a picturesquely situated watering-place, with very indifferent accommodation. We made a pleasant expedition from it to *Ford* Abbey, passing through a richly wooded country, abounding in orchards and overlooked by many ancient earth entrenchments, which crown the line of hills on either side of the Axe. This may be accounted for as the Axe formed the boundary of the Damnonii and Morini. Musbury lies four miles from Seaton. An entrenchment overlooks the village, and twelve earthworks are visible from it. Some suppose that, this was the scene of the battle of Brunanburg, in which Athelstan defeated a combined army of Danes, Scotch and Irish.

In the little church of Musbury is a fine stone monument of the Drake family, the colours and gilding on which are still in excellent preservation. Three pair of figures, as large as life, are kneeling as if in three pews; each knight is represented as fully armed in steel and gold, with large ruffles and closely cropped hair. At the side of each kneels a lady, also with a very large ruffle, and a long gold-laced bodice. Open prayer-books, with verses from the psalms, are before each figure. They formed three generations; the first, John Drake, dating 1558, the second, Bernard his son, and the third, John his grandson, dating 1624. The story is told that this Bernard Drake had some misunderstanding with the great Sir Francis, in Queen Elizabeth's time, about their coat of arms, and that he waxed so wroth that he boxed the Admiral's ears in Court. About a mile distant, in a farm homestead, are the remains of the extensive mansion this family once occupied. The building evidently formed two quadrangles, but one wing and the chapel are all that are standing. The outside of the latter is grand with many dim windows and the large old kitchen remains, with its broad hearth and oaken beams. The old farmer – a silvery-haired man – rose to greet us as we entered, seemed to take great pride in the ancient hall, and told us that many a goodly marriage had been solemnized there. His son said that, among the foundations of the buildings, they found a large number of bottles stamped with the name of the master of the house. John Churchill, the great Duke of Marlborough, and a Prince of the Empire, was born in this mansion, at which his mother, who belonged to the Drake family, was on a visit. The Dragon and Hand, the Drake crests, are visible over the chapel door.

About two miles further on at another farm, are the traces, I can hardly say ruins, of Newenham Abbey – for the little that remained five years ago, an east window and some arches, became infirm for want of repairs, and have been blown down. A stone carving – two heads under a hood – has been preserved, owing, probably, to the strangeness of the conceit. In digging in the neighbouring orchard, pavements were found at a depth of ten feet, and in some places encaustic tiles. This abbey was founded by Reginald de Mohun, who, with his descendants, reposed in the aisles and chancel of this noble church. It was colonized from Beaulieu in Hampshire, whence the future abbot, monks and lay brethren marched in solemn procession across Dorsetshire to take possession of their new abode.

Axminster, a mile further, is a small clean town, and we halted there for luncheon. There was little of antiquarian interest to detain us; the 'castle', which stood near the market-place, has been burnt down. The name of the town is derived from the Minster, which Athelstan built here for seven priests to pray for the souls of the slain.

To *Ford* Abbey was a farther seven miles, although we were told it was but five. We passed on the road two ancient buildings, now farm-houses, but showing by their stone quoins and mullions that they were once manorial residences. Further on, we entered very narrow roads, and passed over steep hills, coming at last in sight of our destination, a grand mass of buildings lying in a hollow; the old monks preferred low ground, because of the superior richness of the soil, and the Cistercians always chose remote and solitary places. Stephen Harding, abbot of Citeaux, founded the order of Les Citeaux – the Cistercians or white monks.

This abbey is one of the most beautiful and remarkable instances of restoration, and I may say, of preservation, which can be found in England. Such a perfect condition of things can only exist when a stately building has been constantly passing through the hands of wealthy and careful owners. The entrance hall, which formed the refectory, built by Chard, the last abbot, in 1528, is magnificent in size and decoration. It is panelled with oak, has a carved and gilt ceiling, and is fifty-five feet long by twenty-eight feet high. The cloisters once paced by pale-robed monks, are now formed into a corridor, bright with banks of flowers and crimson hangings, and the decorated arches are glazed to protect the walk from the weather. How changed the times! The chapel, originally the chapter-house, which adjoins the cloisters, is the oldest and least interesting part of the building. It is said to date from the time of Stephen, but it has been little cared for, except so far as making some late and inharmonious alterations in its architecture. The dormitory presents a picture of what existed in early days, of what we now seen in Roman Catholic countries, and are generally called upon to tax our imagination to re-construct from the crumbling stones of ruined convents. Here is the long corridor lighted by its narrow windows, and on the opposite side the row of doors which entered into the monks' cells, now used as servants' apartments.

One reason why the building is in such perfect condition is that, during the rebellion, it was the property of the Attorney General of the Commonwealth, Edmund Prideaux. He afterwards employed Inigo Jones to alter and decorate it. The finest portion of the work thus accomplished is shown in the artistic arrangement and splendid carving of the grand staircase and saloon – as the drawing-room in these large buildings is called. The staircase is of great width, and cases of carved flowers and fruit stand on the massive oaken balustrade, surrounding a central trophy of exulting Cupids. The saloon is adorned with rich panelling, and tapestries representing the cartoons of Raphael; it is fifty feet in length and twenty-eight in height. Jeremy Bentham rented this Abbey for three years, and here wrote some of his remarkable works.

We left for Budleigh Salterton, by the old Beer road, as the new one was, fortunately, not yet finished. At first we passed by several newly built villas with bright parterres, showing that the neighbourhood is at length becoming known and appreciated. Towards Beer Head we began a very steep ascent by a lane embowered in wild flowers of unusually deep hues. Here aromatic masses of capitate mint, knop weed with large purple blossoms, quaint yellow spikes of toad-flax, and sheets of scarlet poppies brightened our narrow road. On cresting the hill, we walked to the summit of the head to obtain the wide view from Portland to the Start, for which this point is celebrated; but it was veiled from out sight. It was a dreamy day – a dead calm – and a haze hung over the water, and seemed to fuse the two elements together. Nothing was visible but a single fishing-boat, with sails full set, lying asleep in the drowsy mist. Passing on, we descended into the ravine in which the old fishing village is situated. The small houses, with their thatched roofs, appeared clean and comfortable, notwithstanding their age; the doors were generally open, and at them sat many a neat housewife and child, plying their lace-work with twinkling fingers. The rapidity with which they produced the beautiful designs for which Honiton is celebrated, was quite marvellous, and they seemed to work almost mechanically – often looking away at people passing in the road. Yet, there on the cushion was the delicate fabric, with its flowers and leaves, as true as if made by fairy spells. It takes a year and a half to learn the art, and we were sorry to hear that the poorer inhabitants often apprenticed their children to it when they were only eight years old, and before they had received any proper education.

On our descending to the little beach, the view was remarkable. On one side rose the lofty Beer Head – a huge tower of chalk; on the other, the cliffs extended like the façade of a long, many-gabled building, ending in an archway leading to caverns in the rock.

Returning up the village, we turned westward to visit the quarries, which are said to have been worked from very ancient times. The entrance to them is romantic, beneath an archway of rock in the side of a hill, festooned and overshadowed with wild foliage. A cloud hung at the mouth of the cavern, owing no doubt to the different temperature of the outer air, and I was told that in frosty weather the steam could be seen rising up to the top of the hill, and that if then felt at warm within as it was in summer cold. Candles were not provided and we entered the opening. The light was very insufficient, but we groped our way onwards, sometimes knocking our heads against the low roof. Drip, drip, the path was rendered very wet for walking by the water which was constantly falling through the rock. It seems to undergo a process of filtration, and is so pure that it is collected in one place in a stone for the use of the neighbouring cottagers. At length we found ourselves in a vast cavern about fifty feet in breadth, supported in the centre by pillars some eight or ten feet square. A great difference was observable between the ancient and modern part of the quarry. In the former, the rood was as smooth and the sides as cleanly squared as if they were for the ceiling and walls of a drawing-room; in one place a kind of dome had been hollowed out, having four symmetrical arches, and resembling the interior of a cathedral crypt; but in the quarrying, which had been carried on since the invention of gunpowder, the rock was jagged and uneven, pieces having been blown out wherever they could be most easily and cheaply obtained. The old excavations were interesting, as the stone for Exeter Cathedral was hewn out of them, and the amount of labour employed must have been immense. 'Time was not object to people then,' our guide quaintly remarked, pointing to the neatness of the work. But although the stone is free-stone, and well adapted for carving, these quarries, which were formerly so highly esteemed and industriously worked, now only furnish occupation to one man. It is surprising that the large blocks can be, in any way, removed along such rough roads from the inner recesses. The Bath stone, which is very similar, costs much less, and has supplanted the earlier and more durable material.

This cavern, so intricate in its windings, and so convenient to the sea, could not be overlooked in the days of smuggling, and became a favourite resort of Jack Rattenbury, the 'Rob Roy of the West'. It was for the same reason a frequent place of search for the preventive officers, who were accustomed to sound and probe it with iron bores. But Jack hid his kegs so deeply, and heaped such a quantity of stones and rubbish over them, that their exertions were in vain. The place can now be seen where they were secreted, and the marks of the rafters he placed over them in the wall of the cave. One Sunday morning, it is said, some person informed the Coast Guard authorities of the real whereabouts of his store, and immediately after dinner the officer repaired there with his men; but the smugglers had stolen a march on them, and just before their arrival had managed to remove fifty kegs from the hiding place.

Rattenbury died some twenty-five years since – a very old man. He did not leave much money, for although he sometimes did a good stroke of business, he generally laid out his gains in purchasing new craft and entering upon fresh enterprises in which he often failed, and lost his boats. Many anecdotes are told in the neighbourhood about his ingenuity, his fortunes, and mishaps. On one occasion when a preventative officer had followed him, and discovered one of his hiding places, he seized the unhappy emissary of justice and bound him hand and foot, until all the merchandise was removed. Upon another adventure we find him surprised, and his contraband stores seized, and he coastguard men somewhat exhausted by the chase, wanting to buy a goose he had that they might celebrate their success by a good dinner. But I would not let them have it,' observed Jack, 'for I knew what its stuffing was made of – point lace.' Rattenbury's son, who at one time 'did a little himself,' is still living, an old man, in Beer. (close to Beer lies Branscombe, a little village where the Queen's lace wedding dress was made. On an old tomb here to a father and son dated 1658 there is a fanciful simile –

> The wine that in these earthen vessels lay
> The hand of Death has lately drawn away,
> And as a present sent it up on high,
> Whilst here the vessels with the lace doth lie.')

Pursuing our way towards Sidmouth, we turned into a very picturesque road between wide margins of indigenous foliage, where hazel, heath, gorse, and fern were sweetly intermingled and confused. Here also the folks'-glove began to appear, for we were approaching the fairies' land. Fine trees afforded at intervals a grateful shade, and now and then we obtained views over the rich and undulating country. Passing through an isolated toll-gate, the keeper of which told us 'that she was a lone woman, obliged to keep a lace school for company, and get the biggest girl to sleep with her,' we soon perceived that we were approaching Sidmouth, and entered it by a line of bright villas ensconced among luxuriant evergreens.

There are few traces of the past in this town, which is in every sense modern, if we except the old church, lately restored, and much indebted to the Earl of Buckinghamshire for the East window, and other gifts. The West window was erected by Her Majesty, as the inscription testifies, in memory of her father, with an allusion to his charitable disposition. The central design represents Christ blessing little children, and the compartments exhibit eight acts of mercy. The sun was setting during our visit, and the rays of light falling through the stained glass produced a very rich effect. There is also a memorial window here to Mr Fish, who lived in the neighbourhood, but never attended the church. He was a very eccentric man and seldom went out, but kept up handsome gardens, aviaries, a menagerie of rare animals, and in the 'cottage' a collection of minerals and bric-a-brac, to all of which the public were admitted once a week. At his death he bequeathed the property to his solicitor, and passing through several hands it is now in the possession of Mr Thornton, who kindly throws it open to visitors, and has made it one of the attractions of the place. Here are fountains, ferneries, camellia and orchid houses, pineries, orangeries and graperies – a supply of fruit being obtained from the last for every month in the year except April.

Few places in England can rival Sidmouth in variety of scenery, in combinations of cliff and sea and wooded valley. The esplanade exhibits the beauties of Nature and Art, the beach below it those of

Nature alone; and although we set a high value on golden tresses and little shoes, we must not be forgetful of the treasures of old Nature's domain. Here is a rich harvest thrown up by each succeeding tide; here are shells, agates, jaspers, and petrified wood. The yield of the coast gradually changes as we advance westward. At Hastings, Brighton, Worthing, and Bognor we have the landscape agate with its trees of moss and lakes of chalcedony; at Weymouth and Portland petrified wood becomes more common, but it is so soft that it cannot be polished. Here the wood becomes as hard as flint, and the moss agate is rarely found, while at Dawlish and Teignmouth madrepores make their appearance, and the other kinds are very uncommon.

Compensation is the great law of Nature. We cannot have lovely scenery and freedom from railway trains without some drawback, and the sufferers in the present case are the carriage horses, of which I am happy to say there are very few. On leaving for Budleigh Salterton we began to ascend Peak Hill, 'too much for man or beast' as the people say. At its foot we passed Woolbrooke Glen, very narrow and shaded by large elms. In the centre of it, on a smooth lawn by a purling rivulet, stands a low one-storied house with a pretty veranda. Here the Duke of Kent, who came to Sidmouth for his health, died, and here the Queen spent some of her earliest days.

It was hard collar work up the hill; there had been rain in the night, and the road was almost as rough as the bed of a torrent. More than once we halted to give the horses breath. Our toils were at length rewarded on the summit, by one of the most magnificent views in England, or perhaps in any country. It extended from the glistening cliffs of Portland Isle on the east, to Torbay, and the south-western 'Start'. The rich tree-studded country towards the Exe stretched immediately beneath us, and inland rose Dartmoor with its three peaks – the double head of Heytor being very clearly defined. As we ascended, our attention was attracted by a group of country boys, who, holding stones larger than bricks in their hands, presented a somewhat formidable appearance. We were reassured, however, on being told that they were only playing the game of 'duck', a very peaceful Devonshire amusement. A boulder is put up in a convenient position, a small stone is placed upon it, and the object of the competitors is to knock off this stone by throwing at if from a certain distance. The stones they were going to cast seemed to be very heavy, and the game must have required considerable strength.

The road became deep cut towards Otterton. Sometimes the rock rose on either side of us to a height of nearly twenty feet, and then passing through a well-planted country we arrived at Budleigh –

rightly named after its 'buddle' or rivulet, for a stream of some size runs through the village, and crosses the high road. Near this is Bicton, Lady Rolle's residence, with its deer parks, fountains and aviaries. Her ladyship keeps up old-fashioned state, and cheers up the neighbourhood by dashing along in a coach and four with postilions and bells.

Two miles further on brought us to Budleigh Salterton, our destination. It is a sort of miniature Sidmouth, but far more quiet. There seems to be something soporific in the air of the place. A stream like that of Lethe wanders through the street down to the sea, and the houses are reached by little bridges over it. Many of the places are to let, and notices are put up in the neighbouring fields that eligible building sites can be obtained, but there seems to be no purchaser. All is quiet, and perhaps there is something soothing and alluring in this tranquillity. People feel so calm and sleepy that they often drop off in the day-time:

> In the afternoon they came into a land
> In which it seemed always afternoon,
> All round the coast the languid air did swoon,
> Breathing like one that hath a weary dream.

The place is so primitive that, when there is no starlight the inhabitants go about the dark carrying lanterns; and I may mention as a characteristic circumstance that, before we left, a quack doctor drove into the town, knocked at all the doors, presented his card, and told the people that they 'looked bilious'. The Wesleyan chapel here is interesting, as having been built by Lackington, the celebrated bookseller, of whom mention will be made at Kingsbridge.

One of our drives about the neighbourhood was to St John's in the Wilderness and Hayes Barton. Commencing by the hill on the west of Budleigh, between fragrant honeysuckle hedges, we gradually mounted to a higher and barer district, brilliant with red heather and golden-gorse, until, a magnificent view opened before us over the rich lowland around Exmouth. We then sank into the embrace of dark oaks and silver birch-trees until we entered a woodland region, and drew up at a lonely sanctuary once known as St Michael's, then as St John the Baptist's, and finally, owing to its remote situation, as St John's in the Wilderness. It was once the mother church of the neighbourhood, but, to judge from its size, the population must have been always small. It is still and silent now as the grave-stones around it, as the yews and lignums which grow beside it, and, as service has ceased to be performed her, it will no doubt soon lapse into ruin.

May the soil of Devon lie light on the man who loved her shores, and looked from them into 'the Far, the Bright, the Unattained!' The golden islands still glow beneath the sun, but the hand that gathered their treasures is no more!

Returning by another road, we passed over Black Hill – a heathy moor – and descended near Hayes Barton, now a farm and homestead, in which Raleigh was born. It is in the cottage style, and very picturesque with its thatched roof, Elizabethan gables, white walls, and carved oak beams. The porch has a room over it, and the massive studded hall-door bespeaks ancient strength and solidity. The house is said to be exactly in the form in which it was in Raleigh's days. It is in the shape of the letter E, and although one of the wings fell down a short time since, it was rebuilt with all its former characteristics. The room in which Raleigh was born is still shown; it is partly in the roof, and the upper story of the house exhibits the strong wooden frame-work on which buildings were then erected. In the dining-room the wide hearth remains, and the housekeeper told us that a lady, who had lately visited the place, said that her family had been connected with the Raleighs, and that she possessed a picture in which Sir Walter was represented as sitting by that very hearth, 'smoking his first pipe', while a servant was coming in at the door with a glass of water, afraid that he would set himself on fire'. The house is large, and evidently belonged to a man of some importance at that time.

A mile further on, we visited Budleigh Church, which Raleigh attended. His pew remains close in front of the reading-desk, with his arms carved upon the end of it, and, beside it, in the aisle, is a slab in memory of Joan, his wife [sic], beneath which his head also is said to be buried. The old carvings on the pews of this church are very elaborate; many of them seem to represent the coat of arms or physiognomy of the occupier, and some his calling. In one place a cook can be unmistakably recognised by her holding a sheep by its tail, and having a trussed chicken hanging beside her. All kinds of objects are represented, from a pair of scissors to one of the high-castled ships of ancient days. From this point we returned back, being within three miles of home.

But, perhaps, our most enjoyable excursion was to Ladram Bay, situated half way between Sidmouth and Salterton. We again passed peaceful little Otterton, to which its central square, shaded with dense horse-chestnuts, gives an almost Continental appearance. Beneath ruins the silver Otter, circling around its ruddy rocks, and above stands a relic of the ancient priory founded soon after the Conquest, and belonging to the Abbey of Mount St Michael in Normandy. The building, which is now an alms-house and school, came afterwards into the possession of the Dukes, a wealthy family, who lived in this neighbourhood from the days of Edward III to 1741. Their crest, a griffin and wreath, still remains over the entrance.

Few places can vie with Ladram in scenic effect. Stand on the Flagstaff Point, and gaze upon the panorama, the boldness of form, the brightness of colour. Gigantic pillars of red sandstone rise around from the blue wave, whose soft, but ceaseless action has carved passages and archways in every direction. Beyond High Peak, which towers to a height of 500 feet, and commands a view far and wide, is an interval in the cliff, and the white houses of Sidmouth appear nestling down along the coast. Then the red rock begins to yield to white towards Beer Head, and along their warm lower slopes are grown some of the earliest potatoes which reach the London market. On the other side of our position lies Ladram Bay, hollowed out of the sandstone, and the light can be seen through a cavern which pierces through to the River Otter. A bright beach of small round stones lies beneath the cliffs, and here a jovial picnic is being held, while the margin of the tide is sprinkled with white-footed nymphs and goddesses. The sea is gradually washing away the shore. The coast-guardsman told me that he could remember when, seven years since, one of the masses, now completely isolated, was connected with the land, and had a garden upon it. The islet rocks are not generally names, but the two most remarkable are called King George's Head and Lad Rock. On the Flagstaff Point, I observed a quantity of hare's-foot trefoil covering the rock with its soft, furry blossoms. It is a rare plant in most parts of England.

Our road from Budleigh to Exmouth was as beautiful a four miles' drive as blue pines and crimson heath could make it, and, on gaining the little town, we alighted, and sat down for some time in the shade of the ornamental plantation made by Lord Rolle, which commands a lovely view of the water and the hills beyond. The Imperial Hotel, with its gay parterre, formed a pleasant foreground to the prospect.

Exmouth is a clean town, containing some good houses, and, although still a quiet abode, is not that dull old-fashioned place which it seems to have been in [the Reverend Richard] Polwhele's time, who records that, 'It boasts no public rooms or assemblies, save one card assembly in an inconvenient apartment at one of the inns. The company meet at half-past five, and break up at ten; they play at shilling whist and two penny quadrille. We have very few young people here and no diversions; no belle dames amusing to the unmarried, but some belle dames unamusing to the married'.

At Exmouth there is a ferry across the river to Starcross, but, although it is much used, some persons consider it not safe; and as we also wished to visit Exeter, we continued our road in that direction along the left banks of the Exe, passing Lympstone and some pretty villas towards Nutwell Court, Sir T. Drake's, where there are some mementos of the great navigator.

The river, as far as Topsham, forms a fine sheet of water, and formerly large vessels could reach Exeter with the tide...

John Denison Champlin, junior *of* The United States, 1884

Champlin and Company on the Road

John Denison Champlin, *Chronicle of the Coach: Charing Cross to Ilfracombe* (1886), 176–96.

Champlin travelled from London in the 'famous American four-in-hand-in Britain coach'. He set out from London with a number of companions who were given nicknames, including Oxford, Saxon, Maecenas, The M.P., Antiquo and the Countess Hibernia, while he called himself 'the Chronicler'. They were in East Devon from the 17th to 18th of June. Champlin was 50 years old on this visit to East Devon and died in 1915. His other publications include *The young folks' cyclopedia of common things* (1916).

...After passing the great estates of Lord Bridport, we diverged from the main road, and driving by Leigh House, a handsome Elizabethan mansion on a hill-side, turned into the stately avenue leading to *Ford* Abbey, the seat of Herbert Evans, Esq., formerly a Cistercian convent, founded about the twelfth century by Adelicia, daughter of Baldwin de Brioniis. Henry VIII gave the house and its demesnes to Sir Richard Pollard, whence it passed through several hands to the Gwynn family, who held it until 1847, when it was sold to the present owner. Mr. Evans was absent, but Major Bonden being recognized by those in charge as a friend of the family, we were given the freedom of the house, which we greatly enjoyed, wandering around the beautiful grounds and exploring the many apartments and devious passages of the old pile. It has an extended front, opening on a well-trimmed lawn and terrace, consisting partly of the old abbey walls and partly of modern work ascribed to Inigo Jones, with a fine entrance through a square tower in the centre. At the east end is a round chapel of the twelfth century, and at the other a great hall or refectory of the sixteenth century, fifty-five feet long and twenty-eight high, with wainscoted walls and panelled ceiling painted and gilded, with four great Tudor windows on one side and an immense fireplace on the other. On the outer wall of the latter part are the initials of the last abbot, Thomas Chard, and the date 1528, together with several crests of arms, including that of Henry VIII. In the ancient chapel, formerly the chapter-house, which was undergoing repairs, we noticed some tombs of the Prideaux and the arms of the several families who have occupied the abbey. The great saloon in the second story is hung with copies of the tapestries from Raphael's Cartoons, and contains some excellent specimens of old furniture. From the roof, which is covered with heavy sheets of lead, we had a most charming view of the surrounding grounds – fine meadows, groves, fish-ponds, and the river Axe – with a glimpses of the hills beyond.

Seven miles further brought us to Axminster, where we were comfortably provided for at the George Inn. An irregularly built town on the little river Axe, it derives its name partly from that stream and partly from the minster founded there by King Athelstane in the tenth century in memory of seven earls slain near by in a battle with the Danes. It is said to have been an important place in the time of the Saxons and was again of some consequence in the last century when the famous carpets, still called after its name, were manufactured there. But Axminster carpets are no longer made at Axminster, and the town is now an uninteresting example of the places which, for convenience' sake, may be classed under "once were." Its only business appears to be the manufacture of toothbrushes, which the proprietor informed us were largely exported to the United States, a fact certainly in their favor. We wandered around the silent streets and visited the ancient church, which shows traces of many styles of architecture from the Norman upward, but we could get up little interest in the place, even the offer, for the paltry consideration of three guineas, of an exhaustive treatise on the great battle with the Danes failing to arouse our enthusiasm. So we sought the "George," and devoted ourselves for an hour or two to discussing the good dinner which the landlady of that hostel had provided for us.

The inquiries which we made concerning the carpet manufacture elicited little that was new. We were informed that the business was started there in 1755, by one Thomas Whitty, who, two years afterward, was given a premium of £25 by the "Society for the Encouragement of Arts, Manufactures, and Commerce" for a carpet made on the principle of Turkey carpets, but which was adjudged to "excel them in pattern, colour, and workmanship." The peculiarity of the Axminster carpets was that they were made in one piece, of any size or pattern, and of any shape. They were woven in large perpendicular looms, worked by women, five or more on the same piece, who were guided by a printed pattern before them, and having the colored threads ready on needles, which they used singly, as the pattern required. The nature of the stitch permitted it to be cut, which gave the fabric the softness of velvet, the pile being at the same time higher than in ordinary carpets. As all the work was done by the fingers, the progress was necessarily slow and the cost in proportion. An Axminster carpet made in the early part of this century for the Sultan of Turkey was seventy-four by twenty-two feet in size and cost more than £1,000.

Hand-made Axminsters are still manufactured at Wilton, England, and at Tourgoing, France. They are very beautiful, being rich in color and heavy in pile, but they are too costly to suit the purses of ordinary mortals, some of the French patterns selling as high as two hundred francs the yard. The ordinary Axminster carpet of commerce is machine-made by the chenille process, thus differing from the Wilton carpet, which is woven on the Jacquard loom. The chief seats of manufacture are Glasgow in Scotland, and the United States.

We left the George at sharp ten o'clock on Tuesday morning, with pleasant anticipations of a superb coaching day, which fortunately were not to be dispelled. The party, recruited by accessions to its full number again, was in the best of spirits, the newcomers, under the combined influence of the bracing air and the infectious jollity of the veterans, adding no little to the measure of enjoyment. Even the horses caught the spirit of the occasion, and started off at a pace which gave good evidence that they appreciated the importance of making the most of the morning hours.

After passing the railway station – one of the neatest we had seen, with well-kept flower-beds around it – we crossed the Axe and then the Yarty, and with *Clocombe* [Cloakham] Lodge in sight on the hill-side at the right, with a background of pretty woods, wound our way through green valleys and over sharp hills, now and then catching a glimpse of the sea, the British Channel being only about seven miles away. Thence on by Coryton Park and around Shute Hill, along the great highway to Exeter, which in many places follows the Roman military road, through pretty hamlets of thatched cottages overrun with roses and occasionally with wisteria vines, we came into a country of smaller and better cultivated fields, where the arable land bore a larger proportion to the grass land, and where more cattle than sheep were seen. But though we passed many evidences of civilization, we saw few of the civilizers. Besides a few men at work in the fields or cracking stones by the roadside and an occasional donkey-cart in charge of the customary boy or old woman, we had little evidence that the country was inhabited. The scarcity of pleasure carriages on the route was a surprise and the subject of comment to the Americans of the party, who expressed the opinion that such excellent roads would not go unused in their country.

At Wilmington, a hamlet of a few thatched houses, a little group of people were gathered by the roadside, admiring a beautiful May-wreath, set upright by its staff in a grassy knoll. It was a very tasteful emblem, about three feet wide by four feet high, made of cut flowers, with the letters V[ictoria]R[egina] on the top, a mark of loyalty in this little Devon village which, strange to say, elicited no comment from Maecenas. It had been carried, we were informed, in a procession of the Friendly Society the day before.

A steep hill appearing before us, we were all glad to dismount and try a walk once more; and it proved to be one of the longest and pleasantest tramps of the whole journey. The road, so hard and smooth that our footsteps raised but little dust, was shaded by oaks and limes and shut in on each side by beautiful hedges, through which were caught glimpses of the valleys and cultivated lands below. The grass by the roadside was the greenest that Old England can produce, and the wild flowers seemed more plentiful and in greater variety that we had seen before. Though a mere catalogue has little interest for the ordinary reader, the Chronicler cannot refrain from noting a few of the treasure of Wilmington Hill, giving their names in the order of their finding, without regard to affinities: Ragged-robin (*Lychnis flos-cuculi*), Purple Orchis (*Orchis mascula*), Wild Strawberry, Dove's-foot (*Geranium molle*), Stichwort (*Stellaria hollostea*), Lady's-smock (*Cardamine pratensis*), Bluebell (*Campanula rotundifolia*), Campion (*Lychnis divica*), Meadowsweet (*Spiraea ulmaria*), Forget-me-not (*Myostis arvensis*) Buttercup, Daisy (*Bellis perennis*), Crosswort (*Galium cruciatum*), Purple Vetch, Red Vetch, Yellow Vetch, Speedwell (*Veronica chamœdrys*), Bad-man's Oatmeal, Celandine, Foxglove, Dandelion, Pennywort.

What a delightful air of homeness and homeliness there is in this simple list of wild flowers, common to every lane and hedgerow in England. The names smack of the very soil and people, and bear within themselves many a bit of folk-lore, many a suggestion of the past and its history as interesting to those who can read them as the record which the geologist translates from the fossil. The modest little Lady's-smock, for instance, which, notwithstanding Shakespeare, who sings:

> When daisies pied, and violets blue,
> And lady-smocks all silver-white,
> And cuckoos buds of yellow hue,
> Do paint the meadows with delight.

Is not silver-white, but the most delicate lilac, is one of the several flower names which the Virgin's – Our Lady's – name is directly connected. How it came to bear this honoured title and why it was chosen with other simple flowers, like Lady's-grass, Lady's-slipper, and Lady's-mantle, to wear a semi-sacred character, the Chronicler has not time to discuss, beyond suggesting that it may have arisen in the twelfth or thirteenth century with the growth of Mariolatry in the Church. To the New Englander this little flower has another and a scarcely less sacred significance, for from it was named the ship which bore the Pilgrim Fathers to the 'stern and rock-bound coast'. Lady's smock is the Mayflower of Old England, and in some counties is called wholly by that name. It is also designated in other places

Cuckoo-flower, Cuckoo's-bread, Cuckoo-spit, Bread-and-milk, Meadow-cress, and Meadow-bittercress, for the names of plants and flowers seem to differ as much in different parts of the kingdom as do the dialects of the people. The exquisite little blue Speedwell, from which another of the Pilgrim ships derived its name, is called differently God's-eye, Angels'-eye, Birds'-eye, Blue-eyes, Blue-stars, Blewort, and several other less significant names. Ragged-robin, too, who plants his tattered finery under every hedge, masquerades in different localities as Wandering Willie, Wild William, Crow-flower, Crow-soap, Cuckoo-flower, Meadow-pink, and March Gilliflower; and our common Ox-eye Daisy, which, despite John Burroughs (who is so unpatriotic as to call it rank and coarse), has a beauty of its own, passes in its various British homes as the Big, Bull, Dog, Horse, Ox-eye, Moon and Midsummer Daisy, the Horse Gowan and Large White Gowan, the Moon-flower and Moon-penny, and the White Bothew and White Goldes.

So profusely has Dame Nature scattered her treasures throughout England, that the American visitor is at first inclined to the belief that the wild flowers of the mother country surpass those of his home; but a careful investigation and comparison will soon convince him that he is in error. As others have pointed out, we have in the United States not only a greater number of varieties but far more beautiful varieties than exist in the British Isles, but, like all things rich and rate, they are not produced in such abundance. They are, too, more modest and retiring, seeking the shade of the woods to escape our more fervent skies, while their English cousins are forced by the lack of sunshine into the open fields and roadsides. With us only the plainer varieties of field flowers, like the Ox-eye Daisy, the Dandelion, and the Buttercup, are as prolific as the English wild flowers which, in their seasons, really carpet the meadows with their respective colors.

Though Wilmington Hill was long, many rests by the way brought the different groups into which the party had divided to the summit as fresh as when they started, and all were sorry to find the coach awaiting and a level road in advance. In remounting, Oxford managed to secure a seat upon the box beside the driver, whither he had been seen to cast many a longing eye during the morning. This proved to be but the entering wedge of his desires, for Jackson had scarcely got his horses thoroughly in hand before Oxford had possession of the reins. Though he belonged to a 'coaching family' it speedily became evident that he was not quite as much at home on the box as his accomplished brother-in-law, Major Bonden. Jackson, a veteran

Jehu, soon began to venture suggestions as to the proper management of 'osses', which gradually grew into a regular course of instruction. This was at first *sotto voce,* so that those sitting behind caught only an occasional sentence, such as:

'Reins between your fingers – so'

'That nigh wheeler wants watchin.'

'Need the brake 'ere.'

As he warmed with his subject he became oblivious of all around him and talked quite loquaciously.

'Keep your leaders jus' so the whiffletrees 'ill dangle goin' down 'ill, and keep on the nigh side o' the road. Touch up that hoff leader. He's a lawyer.'

'Oh-ho! Cos a lawyer 'as to be paid as he goes. Jus' so with that 'oss. If he don't get tickled now an' then, he'll 'ang back.'

'Oh! I see.'

'Did you ever see a 'oss step like that 'ere off wheeler? Jus' watch 'er tracks – all four of 'em in a straight line. Yet – would you b'leeve it? – that mare took second premium at the Wolver'ampton Fair. All right, too. She a'nt none the worse for it.'

'Nigh side, sir, if you please. If you go left on the road you're sure to get right, you know.'

'Yes. You've heard the old rhyme, haven't you?'

'Wot rhyme, sir?'

The law of the road is a paradox quite,
In riding or driving alone;
If you go to the left you are sure to go right,
If you go to the right you go wrong.

'Oh-ho! That's good, sir. Would ye mind writing that down for me?'

'Certainly not. Remind me of it to-night.'

'They say the Hamericans always drive to right. Is that so?'

'I've heard so.'

'Queer people.' And with this oracular remark Jackson relapsed into silence for the space of a minute as if needing time to meditate on the moral obliquity of a race so barbarous as to persist in passing to the right on the road when the left offers so many advantages. But he could not long forego the opportunity to talk, and he was soon venting his opinions again as loquaciously as ever.

'That nigh leader and this 'ere mare 'll outtravel any two 'osses I ever knew. Thirty miles a day, week in and week out, and won't turn a hair. W'y, them 'osses went on the great drive.'

'What great drive?'

'Oh-ho! Didn't you never 'ear o' the drive from Brighton to Inverness, two years ago? W'y, it was in all the newspapers, and there was a book made about it. This wery coach! Eight hundred miles and over in seven weeks! And them two 'osses on the team! Yes, sir, and they're good for another one.'

An exclamation from one of the ladies diverted the attention of the party from horse-training to a magnificent scene which was gradually unfolding before us. We had reached the declivity of the hill bounding the valley of the Otter on the west, and spread out before us, like a gigantic panorama, lay the beautiful Vale of Honiton, with green meadows and sunny slopes, one of the richest of the celebrated dairy districts of Devonshire, and consequently of England. On the undulating ground, above the Otter, rose the church towers and roofs of Honiton, against a background of steep hills with wooded slopes and picturesquely broken summits. All were unanimous that it well deserved its reputation as being one of the fine views of Britain.

A short half hour took us down the long hill and past pleasant farms into Honiton, where we stopped to water the horses at the Dolphin. While some of the party walked on through the town and others searched for photographs, The M.P. and the Chronicler interviewed the landlady and tested the quality of her brewage, greatly to their satisfaction. She volunteered the information that there is little to interest the antiquary in Honiton, excepting the old church, on a hill about half a mile from the town, which dates from the fourteenth century. The modern aspect of the dwellings and shops on the main street is due to disastrous fires in the last century, which swept away the old buildings.

Of course, we asked about the famous Honiton lace, which has made the name of this old town a household word throughout the civilized world. We were told that but little is now made by hand, the invention by Heathcote in 1809 of a machine capable of producing an exact imitation of pillow lace having given a death-blow to the industry. The art is said to have been introduced by Flemings, who took refuge in England during the persecution in the Low Countries by the Duke of Alva, though there are some reasons for thinking that the newcomers only gave an impetus to an already established industry by the introduction of the fine thread, then spun almost exclusively in their country. However this may be, the manufacture appears to have been in a flourishing condition in the reign of James I. [Thomas] Westcote, writing of Honiton in 1630 says: 'Here is made abundance of bone lace, a pretty toy now greatly in request.' One of the early patterns is shown in the initial letter at the head of this chapter, copied from the tomb of Lady Doddridge in Exeter Cathedral, who died in 1614.

Honiton lace long preserved its Flemish character, its great reputation being due to its sprigs, which, as in Brussels lace, were made separately. They were at first worked in with the pillow, but were afterwards appliqué or sewn on. The net, says Mrs [Bury] Pallizer in her 'History of Lace', was very beautiful and regular but very expensive. It was made of the finest thread produced from Antwerp, the market price of which, in 1790, was £70 per pound. * * * The lace-worker often received eighteen shillings a yard for the workmanship alone of a piece of this elaborate net, measuring scarce two inches in width. * * * A Honiton veil would often cost a hundred guineas.'

Queen Victoria made an attempt to revive the industry by ordering her wedding-dress made of Honiton lace. Only with the greatest difficulty could the necessary number of workers be obtained, and none of them from Honiton, the dress being made at the little village of Beer and its environs. It was composed entirely of Honiton sprigs, connected on the pillow by open-work stitches, and cost £1,000.

In walking through the town we made some interesting additions to our list of inn sings, noting, among the beasts, a Black Lion, a Golden Lion, a White Hart, a Red Cow, and a Lamb; and among others, the Three Tuns, Crown and Sceptre, Fountain, Anchor, and Chopping Knife. Beyond Honiton, we passed a Turk's Head by the roadside, and hard by many neat yellow-washed cottages with moss-grown roofs and now and then with ferns sprouting from the thatch. Our route took us across the railway and down the beautiful valley of the Otter, through rich meadows dotted with cattle, with many a fine house on the hills-sides behind. Luncheon-time brought us to the hamlet of Fairmile, a veritable Arcadia, on a little affluent of the Otter.

The luncheon-place on the Test near Romsey had been pronounced the ideal one, but it was acknowledged by all that this exceeded it. Bare description can do it scant justice; it needs the pencil of an artist. But no one had come to fill Bleistift's place, and the Chronicler is therefore reduced to his own resources to depict a scene which must forever live in his memory.

The table was spread in the greenest of meadows beside a babbling trout stream, that flowed over glistening pebbles between banks pied with daisies, buttercups, and tufts of yellow iris. At our right the stream lost itself in clumps of alders that concealed a road leading to a manor house, at the base of wooded hills in the distance. At our left it was spanned by a moss-grown stone bridge of a single arch, over the parapet of which was visible an ivy-covered chapel, with cottages hard by. In front, across the brook, was a cottage embowered in rhododendrons, and surrounded by trees, among which the coppery foliage of a large purple beech was conspicuous. Behind us, beyond a hedge, the ground gradually rose in a slope, on which were ploughed fields with men at work. Save the babble of the brook, the hum of bees, and the twitter of birds, scarce a sound broke the stillness of the scene. We could even hear the voices of the men talking on the hillside behind us.

'Hark!' exclaimed Maecenas, looking upward, 'There's a lark!'

'There are two,' said The M.P., quietly.

'Three! Four! Five!' cried several of the ladies in a breath.

A flood of melody came down from the clouds. We could just see the five songsters soaring in the sunlight far above us, looking so small – such mere specks against the sky – that we could but wonder how their song could reach us at all. But every note was clear and distinct, reaching our ears even after the tiny specks had faded away in the azure vault. After hearing five larks at once, it is easier to appreciate Izaak Walton's feelings when he heard the nightingales sing as he sat angling. 'Lord,' said he, 'what music hast thou provided for the saints in heaven, when thou affordest bad men such music on earth!' The song of the nightingale is certainly sweet, Good Izaak, sweeter perhaps to some ears than those of the skylark, but the Chronicler, if called to choose between the two, would feel it is his duty to express a preference for the week speck that 'at heaven's gate sings.'

And having thus expressed his opinion in regard to these noble British songsters, he feels moved to go a step further and to say that he knows of a bird which neither the Angler nor the bard of Avon ever listened to, a bird of his 'ain countree' – the American mockingbird – whose song is in every respect preferable to that of either lark or nightingale. It is sweeter, richer, mellower, more varied and more brilliant, of greater compass, more powerful and more prolonged than that of any songster in British woods. The Chronicler makes this assertion with a due sense of responsibility, in the full consciousness that he is incurring the enmity of all the romancers and poets of both past and present. But what is writ is writ, and he cannot unsay it.

The cup of delight of the lunchers at Fairmile was not yet full. As the voices of the larks died away, a cuckoo began to call its mate from the copper beeches over the brook, and a pair of wood-pigeons to purr in the willows by the roadside.

Maecenas could contain himself no longer. He clapped his hands in applause, and said:

'My friend, God is good to you! You have come three thousand miles to hear a lark sing, and you have heard what I never heard before – five larks singing at once, and cuckoos and wood pigeons thrown in!'

The Chronicler might have wept tears of you at this announcement, and probably ought to have done so: but while he was searching industriously for a clean pocket-handkerchief to do justice to the occasion, The M.P. announced that the champagne, which had been cooling under his supervision in the brook, was of the proper temperature for testing, and so the opportunity passed away forever. Laughter, not tears, is the proper accompaniment to the music of corks, especially at a coaching party; and so the Chronicler ceased his unavailing search, and joined heartily in gibing a poor unfortunate, who, in his haste to respond to the luncheon call, had spoiled his suit of light clothes, and injured the integrity of his fingers in crossing a tarred fence. Poor—! Sand and brook-water relieved the hands somewhat, but the tweeds were ruined forever.

While we were discussing the luncheon in our usual hearty manner, a trout fisherman passed down the stream, throwing his fly as he went. He wore high water-proof boots, and was fitted out with all the paraphernalia that the most inveterate angler could wish for. Tramping along with the air of an expert, he crossed from side to side to seize the most available places for casting his line, but with all his efforts caught nothing. The M.P., who is a veteran with the rod and reel, and has cast his fly into most of the best streams of England and Scotland, watched the proceedings for a few minutes with a disdainful air; but at least, unable to stand it any longer, he sprang to his feet with the exclamation:

'A tyro! A very tyro! There are plenty of trout there, but he'll never catch one. Come hither and I'll show you.'

Lighting our cigars, we strolled up to the old bridge, and finding a cosy nook beside it where we could peep through the willows, he pointed out trout after trout, some breaking water under the bank, some rising to catch the insects hovering over the surface in mid-stream, and others lying in quiet pools along the pebbly bottom. The water was so clear that we could easily see their gills open and close as they lay with heads up stream, breathing in the cool water.

'I should not want any better fishing,' said The M.P. 'It's good enough to satisfy even the author of 'I go a-Fishing,' and I know that he would be content with only the best. Look! Look at that fellow!

Three pounds at least! Ah! What is there more delightful than to watch the speckled beauties! One needs no other companionship. I have spent days at a time, from early light to dusk, all alone, beside a trout stream. What more does a man want?'

'To catch fish,' humbly suggested the Chronicler.

'That follows as a matter of course, if you know how. But you must not go threshing the water as if you were driving cattle, like yon fellow. Don't flatter yourself that trout are soulless, unreasoning creatures, ready to bite at anybody's hook. Instinct, do you call it? A trout reasons like a man, and if you expect to get the better of him you must meet him half way. Any respectable trout would rather be caught by an adept than by a bungler'.

'Halloo!', came a voice from down the road. 'Are you going to dream there all day long? We are off for Exeter.'

It was hard to part from pretty Fairmile; but the coach, like time, waits for no man, where the road is level, and we had to tear ourselves away.

Our route soon took us among the hills whence we caught a glimpse of Ottery St Mary, the birthplace of Coleridge, in the valley of the Otter at our left; and before long the roofs and spires of Exeter came into view...

The Coach

Evelyn Burnaby
of
Southampton, 1892

Axminster, from the Axe, 1859

Evelyn Burnaby, *A Ride from Land's End to John O'Groats* (1893), 11–12.

Evelyn Henry Villebois Burnaby rode with a companion from Southampton. Their horses were named Bonchurch and Punch. He wrote that the tour was inspired by the ride to the central Asian city of Khiva (now in Uzbekistan) of his brother Frederick, a well-known travel writer who died in the attempt to relieve Khartoum in 1885. Burnaby also wrote that he hoped it would be interesting to read and that it may 'help to fill up a few leisure moments for those who have visited the many lovely spots in which our island abounds'. He added that he hoped to gauge public opinion for the upcoming General Election and that bicycles made such tours 'a matter of everyday occurrence'. He also wrote *Memories of Famous Trials* (1907).

...From the lane we pushed on to Crewkerne, and thence over a range of hills, past the 'Wind Whistle' hostelry, where to the eastward and westward we were rewarded by a grand panoramic view. On the one side the wild moorland of Exmoor and the Quantocks renowned for famous runs with the red deer, loomed in the horizon; whilst on the other the cliffs of the English Channel between Seaton and Beer let in a view of the sea. Riding past the 'Tytherleigh Inn', we were arrested by the host, who insisted on our inspecting his symbolical signboard, and his original inscription. We rode on through Axminster, and were not sorry to arrive at the 'Dolphin' at Honiton, the quaint little Devonshire town nestling beneath the hills which environ it. They ministered to our comforts at the hotel, and next morning we started for a comparatively short ride to Exeter, which was crowded with all classes, as it was polling day in that usually sleepy old city...

CHARLES G. HARPER
of
LONDON, *c.*1892

"a loathly Cockney worm…who leaned against a seaworn capstan"

Charles G. Harper, *From Paddington to Penzance: The record of a summer tramp from London to the Land's End* (1893), 106–15.

Harper was about thirty years old when he visited East Devon and died in 1943. His publications included *The Brighton Road* and *The Great West Road.* He was aware of other travellers' accounts including Elihu Burritt ('that Yankee prig... a welter of cheap facts and interjectional essays in the obvious') and the 'horribly-informative' Walter White ('this dreadful tourist was used to sing and recite to the rustics whom he met.'). In contrast Harper wrote 'with what I take to be a care rather for personal impressions than for guide-book history'.

...To Ashe presently succeeds the straggling village of Axmouth, whence the sea is visible at the farther end of the marshy lands where the Axe struggles out into the Channel over a bed of shingle. Just above Haven Cliff the highroad is carried over the river by a bridge of three arches that gives access to Seaton.

Seaton is in process of rising, and to all who have witnessed the evolution of a seaside town from fishing village to "resort" – that is sufficient to say *Verb. sap. sat.* It possesses a terminal railway station on a branch line, and is the scene of Sunday "there and back" excursions from London in the summer season. On those occasions the place is crowded for a brief three hours or so, when trippers snatch a fearful joy. At other times Seaton is sluggish and dull, and really the bourgeois plastered buildings of the little town are an insult to the magnificent scenery on either hand.

Visitors there were a few on the beach – quiet folk mostly, and provincial of aspect, save indeed a loathly Cockney worm who had by some mischance missed his Margate, who leaned against a seaworn capstan, the sole representative of his particular stratum of civilisation – lonely, ineffable.

When the rain came down that had been impending all the forenoon, Seaton became doleful. There was nothing to do but take the next train to Exeter in search of a waterproof civilisation...

Seaton Bridge, *c.*1892, by Harper

Charles S. Brooks *of* The United States, *c.*1931

Ottery St Mary church, by Mary Seymour Brooks, *c.*1931

Charles S. Brooks, *English Spring* (New York, 1932), 74–82

Charles Stephen Brooks, an American, was accompanied by Mary Seymour Brooks, the book's illustrator and most likely also his wife, on a journey through the West Country. He showed that he had read Elihu Burritt's travel account. Brooks also wrote *Journey to Baghdad* (*c.*1927) and *An Italian Winter* (1933). He was 53 years old when he visited East Devon and died only a few years later.

...There was a public bus billed to Exeter, but I struck a bargain for a private motor that would give us on the way an hour at Ottery St Mary, where Samuel Taylor Coleridge was born. Nobody leaves Stratford out of his travels, and few of them omit Ambleside or Stoke Poges. Now and then a curious tourist finds himself at Winterslow on account of [William] Hazlitt. But we have never heard of any traveler, except Elihu Burritt, an American blacksmith of seventy years ago, who ever took the pains to read the signboards and turn aside to Ottery. If one is not a student of sorts he has never heard of this small town; and, with better information, he will know that Ottery is to Coleridge no more than the faint horizon of his youth and the mere cradle of his undeveloped fancy.

Coleridge was born at the vicarage of Ottery St Mary in the year 1772 and remained there until the end of his ninth year when, by the charity of a family friend, he was sent to the Charterhouse School in London for his education. Only a few anecdotes of his childhood are preserved in his writings. He was a devourer of fairy stories of the bloodier sort and, when their plots were hot within him, he walked about the graveyard near his father's house striking at nettles with a stick pretending that they were giants. He never joined in games, but always sat reading or in thought. He must have been a little old man even when in dresses; and later, at his school in London, when he was still of an age for jam and crumbs, he was already reading the Greek philosophers. His precocity matched that of [Thomas] Macaulay and [William] Hazlitt, of John Stuart Mill, who had read Herodotus in the original before he was eight. Not even the humor of his Charterhouse playfellow, Charles Lamb, could make Coleridge entirely human.

An occasional letter or poem of his mature years recalls his childhood in his father's vicarage – a plank that was a tiny bridge above a stream where willows bent across the margin, a release from study to launch in the pool a paper navy against the scarlet armada of October's drifting leaves, an old church tower whose bells were a poor man's only music.

But these visions, recalled from childhood, are seldom concerned with happiness or the playthings of a normal youth. Spectres haunt the graveyard and rub their gaunt noses on his window as he tries to sleep. There are nights of fever with 'armies of ugly things' bursting in upon him. There is a flight from punishment when he lies all night in the wet grass besides the River Otter. And darkness always waits breathless for the comfort of the dawn. Perhaps the lives of all great poets have begun in nightmare – in wild imaginings that have outstripped in growth their frail bodies, to be the ugly trumpeters of beauty's long procession that shall later pass before their eyes.

If Coleridge had possessed the ability to depict childhood as his friend, Charles Lamb, possessed it, Ottery would be a place of pilgrimage. For who is there who does not know the pattern of each room at pleasant Blakesmoor and wish that this village could be found upon the map? We have ourselves in vain scanned Hampshire. 'Every plank and panel of that house,' Lamb wrote, 'for me had magic in it...the cheerful store-room, in whose hot window-seat I used to sit and read Cowley, with the grass-plat before, and the hum and flappings of that one solitary wasp that ever haunted it about me – it is in mine ears now, as oft as summer returns...'

Coleridge's lonely hours of youth had fed themselves on sickly meditation. How different is Lamb's boyhood! 'The solitude of childhood,' he wrote, 'is not so much the mother of thought, as it is the feeder of love, and silence, and admiration.' But Coleridge, casting back upon his early days, wrote frigidly of Pierian springs, of zephyr-haunted brinks, of elfin tribes and of Solitude, the wood-nymph; and Ottery, in consequence of these chilly phrases, is a deserted shrine. Lamb carried forward his childhood with him into the reality of the nineteenth century, while Coleridge left his behind to keep stilted company with the ghosts that the French Revolution had killed forever.

When Coleridge left Ottery at the age of nine, he left it for life. At most he returned for one or two brief holidays, but they lent no magic to his pen. Later on our travels we shall pass through Nether Stowey and see the house of his mature years; and there we shall find Coleridge and reality, his pen dipped in no artificial Pierian spring.

We crossed the breezy hills from Lyme Regis, entered Ottery and halted at a book-shop.

'Perhaps,' I said, 'you will be good enough to direct us to the house of Coleridge.'

'Which Coleridge?' was the answer.

This was disconcerting, for I had forgotten there was more than one Coleridge whose birthplace was worthy of a visit.

'The poet, of course,' I replied. 'Who else is there?'

'Lord Coleridge lives at the top of the street,' the bookman answered. 'The vicarage where the poet lived has been pulled down these many years.'

I looked around the book-shop. I saw no edition of the poet's verse or any volume of his prose – nothing, not even a biography or any coloured postcard of his face. There was a riffraff of cheap novels of crime and excitement, a whole shelf of Oppenheim, of Fletcher and Edgar Wallace, a display of monogram notepaper, boxes of bouncing balls, children's dolls and folderol, London's evening journals and little plaster casts of Charlie Chaplin and his flat feet, priced at six-pence. It was evident that we were in the prophet's country.

'If we inquired at the church,' I asked, 'could any one tell us there the old vicarage once stood?'

'That's as it might be,' the bookman answered. 'But the sexton would be sure to know.'

A little girl had entered the shop and the merchant turned away to help her choose a rubber ball.

At the top of the town we came to St Mary's Church. It sets in an ample graveyard on the slope of a hill above the level of the near-by buildings in the High Street. Later in our travels farther west, we shall discover the hill-tops whose lonely church towers are solitary fingers pointing to the sky; but here, on this tamer edge of Devon, the hills are of easier slope and of a less extensive outlook. At Ottery St Mary's, as is proper in a parish churchyard, the view included only the houses of the town and their homely chimney-pots and windows. The evening bell blends with the sound of traffic on the cobbled streets.

I have remarked in another book how intimately an English village surrounds its graveyard and how children swing upon the sagging gate or pick daisies among the tombs. To any grandsire whose day has come, the transit is so short from his aspidistra in his window on the green to his lilac just beyond the graveyard wall. Death is so slight a change of lodging that he will still hear the children at their games. Something of this intimacy with the life hereafter is true of Ottery; but on a second view we saw near by the great house of the present Lord Coleridge and in such a presence no child surely would swing unembarrassed on the graveyard gate.

The name of Coleridge is on many headstones and but seldom without a title. Poorer stones of less important families across the path bend forward in obsequious gesture. Inasmuch as the poet's father was the half-paid vicar of the parish and the mere master of an undistinguished grammar school, with too little wealth to educate all of his sons except with outside help – inasmuch, moreover, as the poet died without wealth or title, I was confused by this grandeur of the Coleridge family. It seems, however, that a nephew of the poet married money and that the nephew's son achieved distinction in the law, to be made in time the Lord Chief Justice of England. Ottery

St Mary, therefore, in its present magnificence of wealth and social station, acknowledges Samuel Taylor Coleridge as merely collateral and a poor relation.

St Mary's is a lovely building of irregular and mixed types of architecture. Inside there is an amazing seventeenth-century clock which, although it seems to work on the theory that the world is flat with the obedient sun and starts revolving around it, does nevertheless contrive with tolerable accuracy to tell the hour of the day and the position of the moon. In the churchyard old stocks are set up for curious display. Adjoining the graveyard, in a plot of ground now covered with newer headstones, is the spot where the vicarage stood in which Coleridge was born. I could find no memorial of him in St Mary's. He died July 25 1834, and was buried in Highgate Churchyard of London. The trees, however, of the parish of his youth, were reciting his verses on this windy day of April of our present visit.

> All seasons shall be sweet to thee,
> Whether the summer clothe the general earth
> With greenness, or the redbreast sit and sing
> Betwixt the tufts of snow on the bare branch
> Of mossy apple-tree, while the nigh thatch
> Smokes in the sun-thaw; whether the eave-drops fall
> Heard only in the trances of the blast,
> Or if the secret ministry of frost
> Shall hang them up in silent icicles,
> Quietly shining up to the quiet moon.

Our Pickwickian industry finds another celebrity in Ottery – Joanna Southcott, once famous throughout England and now forgotten. This old fraud in petticoats was born near by in the year 1750, and has had her life recorded by [Sabine] Baring-Gould. She was a domestic servant in Exeter until her head was turned by the shrieks of a crazy preacher in a Methodist revival; whereupon she set herself up to be a prophet and a seer. In 1791 she was already 'beginning to see visions.' Later, being now famous and the leader of a sect of her own contrivance, she earned her living by the sale of 'passports to heaven' – six or seven thousand of them, mostly at a guinea each. Such a scheme was not entirely new, being somewhat a cousin to Roman indulgences, but she bettered the old dogma by taking all the profits for herself. St Peter had distributed them more generously outside the Vatican and out and had even built a mighty church with them.

In 1801 Joanna Southcott began to publish books of prophecy – partly in rhyme, which she asserted to her followers was the direct word of God to his inspired amanuensis. 'Once she declared,' writes Baring-Gould, 'that she had scratched the devil's face with her nails, and had even bitten off one of his fingers, and that his blood tasted sweet.'

Presently she announced that she was pregnant, by no one in particular it seems, and that her unborn son would be Shiloh, another saviour of the race. Gifts from the faithful came pouring in. 'One wealthy proselyte sent a cradle...another sent a pap-spoon...and that nothing might be lacking at this accouchement, laced caps, infant's napkins, bibs, mantles, some of white satin, pap-boats, caudle-cups arrived.' While Joanna was in this delicate state, certain physicians said 'a baby', while others called her figure dropsy. And it was in the midst of this uncertainty and excitement that the lady died.

But this was not the end. Joanna, it seems, had foretold her death to the friends who were gathered at her bedside and had assured them that she would be dead four days, at which time she would revive and be delivered of her son. It was but decency, therefore, that she was wrapped in warm blankets and that a hot-water bottle was placed against her chilly feet. The fourth day passed with unavailing watch, and then poor Joanna was laid away. This was in January, 1815.

Nor was this the end. The sect lived on, attending to all rumours that there was any disturbance of the graveyard sod; for her resurrection, although delayed, was still expected. In January, 1817, probably on or about the second anniversary of Joanna's death, a conclave of her church at Leeds inhibited those of the faith from going to their shops or business in order that they might be at hand and in a proper religious mood for the lady's somewhat dusty reappearance. In London her disciples assembled and made their way in a procession down the Strand, past Temple Bar, and to St Paul's Churchyard. They were decorated with white cockades and carried a huge trumpet that was larger than Gabriel's, although the purpose of both horns was quite the same. And here a leader arose and shouted out to the throng that Shiloh had come gain. The brazen trumpet sounded. The crowd shouted its welcome. But it was not Shiloh but a company of London bobbies that appeared. There is no law in England against new prophets, but it is a serious misdemeanour to obstruct traffic in the Strand.

Baring-Gould informs us that Joanna's sect lingered on for many years, still hoping for Joanna's resurrection and Shiloh's birth, but that gradually it fell from faith until at last only a few of her disciples were left.

We can ourselves add a postscript to his narrative.

In the winter of 1928, one hundred and thirteen years after Joanna's death, I passed a day at San Diego in Southern California, and went for lunch to the vast hotel that stands on Coronado Beach. As I crossed the paved circle where motors are left standing, I observed that one of these motors was wrapped about in a printed canvas, as if it advertised a circus or a patent medicine. I stopped to read what the canvas offered, wondering if it would tell me of bareback riders or of a cure for Bright's disease. It was a notice that Joanna Southcott was still expected to return to the glimpses of the moon, and that in the meantime a wicked world would do well to heed her warnings of the hell to come.

I walked all around the motor, read each sentence and then stopped.

'What is the price today,' I asked. 'of a passport into heaven?'

There was no response from inside the canvas, for the driver and his saintly crew had gone to lunch.

I pulled off a handbill from a package that was tied to the extra tire. It was a demand that the prophetic writings of this lady of Ottery St Mary, now deceased and waiting for her special trumpet, must be read by every one who wished to curry favor with St Peter – that, at last, there were portentous stirrings in an English graveyard.

California is the home of ecstasy and strange religions, of new churches that are built on novel heresies and those reborn on old. It was fitting, therefore, that Joanna Southcott should have lugged her poor old bones there for resurrection.

And now, having seen the best of Ottery St Mary, we climbed into our motor, where I fell asleep. Across my dreams there was a low whir and murmur until I awoke at the door of the Royal Clarence Hotel in Exeter. I stood shivering on the curb while our bags were pulled out. 'A double room with an open fire', I demanded from a young woman at the office wicket...

STANLEY R. BARON
of
ESHER, SURREY, 1933

"Red mud. Red earth. Red Devon..." Ploughing in Devon, 1938

Stanley R. Baron, *Westward Ho! From Cumbria to Cornwall* (1934), 198–200.

Baron worked at the *Daily Mail* and then afterwards on the *News Chronicle* where his boss instructed him to ride by bicycle from Bristol to the Land's End. Baron travelled with Reg Gammon 'who draws the pictures'. The reports were published daily.

...Bonny Beaminster, carefree Crewkerne...To get from one to the other the road flew up, ducked its head at the sight of a larger hill than ever, dodged through a hole in the middle, and then slipped down so fast that before I knew what had happened I was out of Dorset and into Somerset. The tunnel was constructed in 1851 by a resident 'of Beaminster, Gent.' A Gent he was...

I came to the Whistle, but a Wind there was none. A white inn overhung by trees, an infant playing 'Alice' with a looking-glass, a road that may have been built by the Romans, a house or two and a dog or two – there was my Windwhistle; and then the road swung down again to Axminster and Seaton, and just where it dipped I discovered on my right a red earth lane. Red earth! Red mud. Red DEVON!

In this excitable way, by associated notions, the imagination leapt. It was not, in literal fact, a Devonshire lane at all, and if ever a county council comes to tar it, and trim it, and tidy it, and gird it with kerbstones, and ruin it, the council will be Somerset's. But all the same, it belongs in spirit to Devon. It is the vanguard of the land of hollow lanes. On this day when I found it the earth of the surface was carried in a single sweeping curve to a point nearly 8 feet high on either side, and every inch of the banks thus formed was smothered with green and primrose-yellow. From the tops of the banks a couple of rows of saplings sprang toward the sky, but long before they reached it their arms were so entwined that, looking from the lane below, nothing of the sky, neither cloud, nor sun, nor blue, was visible.

So secluded from the world was this red earth lane that it seemed, by its own glowing colours, to provide for itself a particular character, a particular life and a particular atmosphere. The lighting of the lane was a subtle infusion of the reds, greens and yellows of its parts. Had the lane been flat one would still have loved it. Had it climbed, the fancy of the traveller would have climbed with it also, to a world of strange illusions, in which rabbits were kings and moles lord chancellors. Had it fallen – but it *did* fall, in a glorious curve, to the level lands north of the hill, and thither I followed it, until the lane, after twisting a little, became a broad, magnificent road, the grandest road in England, the road of the Roman legionaries – the road called Fosse Way! I wish I could tell you how I saw the Axe at evening, spreading and glowing in a valley overlooked by hills, how I climbed up again by lamp-lit gipsies' camps, all strung out as methodically as a village, and how the darkness came and ended in a great light – the light of Exeter. There was mud on my wheels that night. Red mud. Red earth. Red Devon...

"The land of hollow lanes", Devon, 1938

Illustration Sources

Title page, steel line engraving by W. Le Petit after T. Allom of Bicton, 1849
page 1, Lucy Toulmin Smith, *The Itinerary of John Leland* (1907), frontispiece
page 7, detail from map by John Speed of Devon, 1610
page 9, Westcountry Studies Library, SC29
page 11, Westcountry Studies Library, SC29
page 13, Westcountry Studies Library, SC29
page 16, detail from map by John Speed of Devon, 1610
page 18, portrait of William Stukeley, used by kind permission of Hartland Abbey Estate
page 21, engraving by William Stukeley, *Itinerarium Curiosum* (1776), 159
page 22, Westcountry Studies Library, SC1855
page 26, Westcountry Studies Library, SC436
page 30, Emily J. Climenson, *Passages from the Diaries of Mrs Philip Lybbe Powys* (1899), frontispiece
page 33, William Gilpin, *Observations on the Western Parts of England* (1808), 249
page 40, Westcountry Studies Library, SC1178
page 44, Westcountry Studies Library, SC1179
page 46, Westcountry Studies Library, SC435
page 52, Westcountry Studies Library, SC317
page 62, Westcountry Studies Library, SC2460
page 69, Westcountry Studies Library, SC1179
page 75, Richard Warner, *A Walk through the Western Counties of England* (Bath, 1800), 202
page 78, Richard Warner, *A Tour Through Cornwall in the Autumn of 1808* (Bath, 1809), 28
page 79, Martin Dunsford, *Miscellaneous Observations* (Tiverton, 1800), frontispiece
page 82, John Evans, *The Juvenile Tourist* (1816), frontispiece
page 93, John Evans, *The Juvenile Tourist* (1816), title page
page 94, Westcountry Studies Library, SC2462
page 110, Westcountry Studies Library, SC1084
page 119, Westcountry Studies Library, SC1084
page 122, Westcountry Studies Library, SC434
page 126, Westcountry Studies Library, SC310
page 130, Westcountry Studies Library, SC2553
page 137, Westcountry Studies Library, SC1849
page 154, A.G. L'Estrange, *From the Thames to the Tamar* (1873), 177
page 165, A.G. L'Estrange, *From the Thames to the Tamar* (1873), 177
page 177, John Denison Champlin, *Chronicle of the Coach* (1886), frontispiece

page 188, John Denison Champlin, *Chronicle of the Coach* (1886)
page 189, Westcountry Studies Library, SC38
page 191, Charles G. Harper, *From Paddington to Penzance* (1893) 107
page 192, Charles G. Harper, *From Paddington to Penzance* (1893), 106
page 193, Charles S. Brooks, English Spring (New York, 1932), 74
page 200, Alfred H. Shorter, *Set in Silver* (Exeter, 1938), 44 used by kind permission of Paternoster Publishing.
page 202 Alfred H. Shorter, *Set in Silver* (Exeter, 1938), 38 used by kind permission of Paternoster Publishing.

Index of Personal and Place Names

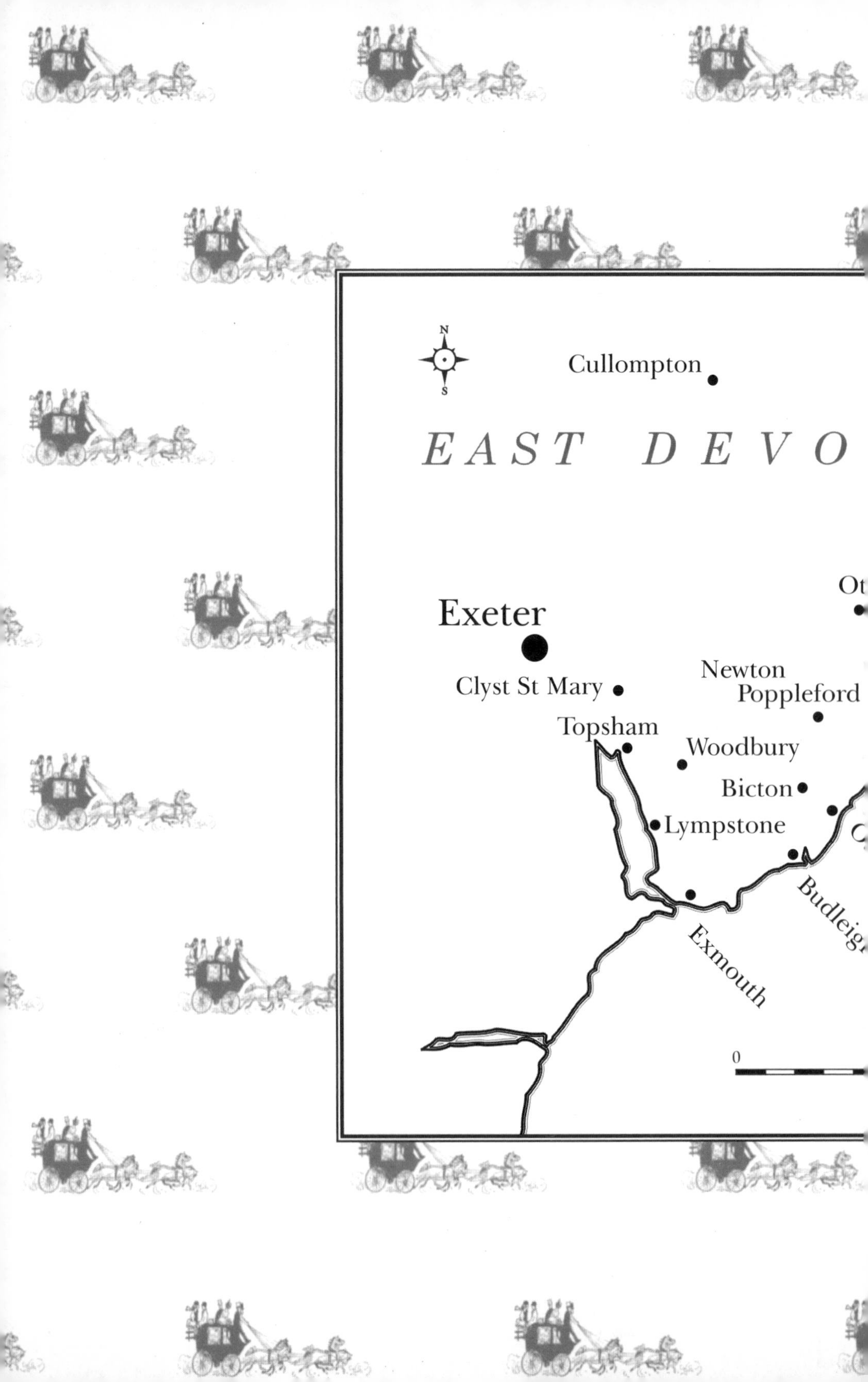
N
S
Cullompton
EAST DEVO
Ot
Exeter
Newton
Poppleford
Clyst St Mary
Topsham
Woodbury
Bicton
Lympstone
Budleig
Exmouth
0